KU-774-901

THE MODERN WORLD
A SURVEY OF HISTORICAL FORCES

Volume V : INDIA

THE MODERN WORLD
A SURVEY OF HISTORICAL FORCES

Edited by The Right Hon. H. A. L. FISHER, M.P.

The aim of the volumes in this series is to provide
a balanced survey, with such historical illustrations
as are necessary, of the tendencies and forces,
political, economic, intellectual, which are moulding
the lives of contemporary states. This volume is
the fifth of the series.

Already published:

IRELAND   by Stephen Gwynn

" *We know of no more searching study* . . . *it is
illuminating because it is without passion and does, on
the whole, manage to hold even justice.*"—MANCHESTER
GUARDIAN.

" *Mr. Gwynn does it admirably* . . . *real distinction.*"
—OBSERVER.

GERMANY   by G. P. Gooch

" *A very valuable and very remarkable book.*"—
TIMES.

" *What devoted study upon every line of thought.
What a tolerant and balanced judgment.*"—H. W.
Nevinson in the WEEKLY WESTMINSTER.

NORWAY   by G. Gathorne Hardy

" *Liberal, well-reasoned and humane, full of
learning gaily borne* . . . *its every chapter leaves the
reader more indebted.*"—TIMES.

RUSSIA   by N. Makeev and V. O'Hara

" *The best work—perhaps the only work—of its
kind.*"—MANCHESTER GUARDIAN.

In preparation :

TURKEY	by Arnold Toynbee
IRAQ	by Gertrude Bell
CHILE	by Agustin Edwards
ENGLAND	by the Very Rev. W. R. Inge, D.D.
ARGENTINA	by Professor C. H. Haring
AMERICA	by John Huston Finley, LL.D.
FRANCE	by Sisley Huddleston

INDIA

By SIR VALENTINE CHIROL

Author of " Indian Unrest " (1910), " India Old and New " (1921), etc.
Member of the Royal Commission on the Indian Public Services (1912-15).

WITH AN INTRODUCTION BY
THE RIGHT HON. H. A. L. FISHER, M.P.

And hear ye the beat
Of the ages' feet
  In strides of thousands of years ;
A muffled note
That low doth float
  On history's breath to list'ning ears.

E. Lloyd Pease.

LONDON : ERNEST BENN LIMITED
8 BOUVERIE STREET, E.C.4
1926

First Impression, January, 1926.
Second Impression, March, 1926.
Third Impression, April, 1926.

954.03
783

MADE AND PRINTED IN GREAT BRITAIN

By Thomas De La Rue & Co., Ltd., London

19.

INTRODUCTION

To the student of Indian society and politics, Sir Valentine Chirol needs no introduction. His great knowledge of the country, his affectionate appreciation of the finer sides of Indian life and character, his wide grasp of public affairs, have been evidenced in a series of weighty publications. He now gives to us the matured fruit of his long devotion to Indian enquiries. In this masterly survey all the factors essential to the comprehension of modern India are made to stand out in their true perspective. Sir Valentine Chirol has had the courage to deal with living men and burning issues, but of these he writes, not as one anxious to claim a party victory, but as the friend of India, offering the tribute of a dispassionate judgment and of a wide and well-balanced experience drawn alike from ancient and modern times.

H. A. L. Fisher.

21st November, 1925.

CONTENTS

INDIA

CHAPTER I

A BIRD'S-EYE VIEW OF INDIA

INDIA as a nation of the modern world is still in the making. For all that is modern in India—to the very name "India"—is of foreign and relatively recent importation, and all that has its roots in the soil of India is almost immeasurably ancient.

Nature herself fashioned India as a huge crucible into which at the dawn of history was poured from the high table-lands of Asia a great overflow of peoples still seeking their place in the sun. From their fusion with earlier and yet more primitive populations already in possession have proceeded Indian forms of social and religious life as enduring as they are unique. Egyptian and Minoan and Hittite and Babylonian civilizations are more ancient, but they are memories of a dead past which to-day merely provide fascinating subjects of archæological research. The Aryan peoples, who may be regarded as the first foreign conquerors of India, laid the foundations of Indian civilization long before Rome or Athens was born and longer still before the rest of Europe emerged from savagery, and unlike any of the ancient civilizations of the world, excepting possibly the Chinese, it has remained a living civilization. The religious and social system we call Hinduism which still governs the life of more than two-thirds of the population is peculiar to India. There is nothing even analogous to it elsewhere. Within it there has been only one great movement of spiritual dissidence, and for a brief moment the Emperor Asoka's apostolic zeal enthroned Buddhism as a state church, but when he and his Empire passed away, it was gradually re-absorbed into Hinduism

1

and disappeared across the Himalayas into the Far
East. Warring kingdoms and dynasties rose and
fell in obscure confusion, but for more than two
millenniums Hinduism was the one abiding force that
steered India through all the many vicissitudes of
her history until Islam was borne in on the crest
of successive waves of invasion from Central Asia.
Even then a large majority of her peoples was never
coerced or won over to acceptance of her conquerors'
creed, and though there was henceforth a Mohammedan as well as a Hindu India, Hinduism never
lost its vitality under Mohammedan domination and
is no less vital to-day after a century-and-a-half of
British rule.

Whilst Europe was groping her way through the
Dark Ages, India was to her little more than a
mysterious name, telling of fabulous wealth and
wonders of which rare and precious samples only
reached the markets of Europe by long overland
routes, slow and precarious. A new era was ushered
in for the whole world when, even those routes
being steadily closed by the rising tide of Ottoman
power, the seafaring nations of the West were
driven to explore the ocean for new highways to the
East and the far-flung shores of India were thrown
open to Western adventure. Throughout the
XVIth and XVIIth centuries, only the ocean fringe
of the Indian continent was touched, whilst the
Western nations fought amongst themselves for the
new markets of the Orient. Not until the strange
accidents of world history conspired with the disintegration of the Mohammedan ruling power in the
XVIIIth century to establish British dominion over
India were two races and two civilizations which
had grown up almost as far as the poles asunder for
the first time brought into intimate contact with
each other. Upon an ancient India steeped in
religious beliefs and social traditions already some

3,000 years old before the first English venturer trod
Indian soil, British rule has superimposed another
India created by the Western rule of law, by Western
education and by Western standards of efficiency;
but it has not yet welded them together.

British rule in India has no parallel in the world's
history. Just glance at the map. Several thousands
of miles away from the British islands, and largely
under a tropical sun, India stands out as a great
southern projection, roughly lozenge-shaped, from
the main continent of Asia. Divided from it by
rugged mountain ranges which culminate at the
northern apex in the Himalayan Roof of the World,
the Indian sub-continent tapers down between two
enclosing seas to Cape Comorin at the southern apex,
barely eight degrees north of the equator—a country
of vast distances, measuring nearly 2,000 miles from
north to south and about 1,800 miles from west to
east (excluding Burma*) with an area equal to that
of the whole of Europe less Russia, and with a huge
population numbering close upon 320,000,000 souls,
or nearly one-fifth of the whole population of
the globe, split up into a multitude of peoples
differing more widely from one another in racial
features and complexion, in language and even to a
great extent in religion than do all the peoples of
Europe, and most of them in different stages of
development, but all steeped in the same-atmosphere,
partly peculiar to India, partly common to the whole
of what we call the East as opposed to the West—
the atmosphere which has produced their different
types of civilization. To borrow John Morley's
eloquent phrase: "we can see in that vast congeries
of peoples we call India a slow march in uneven

* Burma has been excluded altogether from the purview of
this volume, as it has no racial or social or religious affinity to
the rest of India, with which it was incorporated during the last
century for reasons mainly of administrative convenience.

stages through all the centuries,"—primitive if not
aboriginal tribes driven in prehistoric ages into dense
jungles and mountain recesses where they still
subsist chiefly on the fruits of the forest and of the
untilled soil and the birds and beasts that fall to
their bows and arrows ; the immense mass of the
population spread densely over great alluvial plains
of unrivalled fertility, and more sparsely where
cultivation is less easy, living on the land just
as countless generations have done before them,
labouring with stolid patience on the ancestral soil
to wrest from the terrific forces of nature which they
have deified the harvests sometimes bountiful and
sometimes cruelly exiguous upon which they depend
for an existence seldom secure against starvation ;
ignorant but not unintelligent, and with few needs
or interests outside the narrow range of their own
and their neighbours' fields, but liable, nevertheless,
to be swept by sudden gusts of religious emotion or
superstitious fear ; here and there the picturesque
remnants of a feudal age, in the background a vision
of weather-beaten rock-castles, half palace and half
fortress, overhanging small sleepy towns in which
the clock has stood still for centuries, and in the
foreground the living figures of hereditary chieftains
and princely Maharajahs who have retained something of the jewelled wealth and barbaric magnificence of the mediæval East ; and everywhere, in
the most archaic surroundings and in the most
modern, in the humblest little shrines and in the
endless vista of railway platforms needed to discharge
at Puri the half-million pilgrims that throng from
far and near to the great Jagannath festivals, in the
most strangely different shapes, in the marble cupolas
and soaring minarets of the Moghul cities of Northern
India and in the mysterious twilight of the huge
Hindu temples of Southern India, always and everywhere, the visible and living manifestations of the

power, the most ancient and all-pervading in the land.

Look at India from another point of view and the contrasts are just as great. Her peoples speak no less than 222 distinct languages and countless different dialects. They have never possessed a common tongue, though some of the principal languages such as Hindu, Bengali, Mahratti, Telugu and Tamil are each spoken by tens of millions. The majority belong to the family known to philologists as the Indo-Aryan family ; a large Dravidian minority derives from pre-Aryan sources, and a much smaller minority are of Tibeto-Chinese origin. The variety of languages is greater than that of races, though these again have their own lines of cleavage, their own peculiar features and characteristics. Along the arid North-West Frontier the Beluch and Pathan tribes show marked Semitic affinities. On the Indian slopes of the Himalayas, and down into the humid Bengal delta of the Ganges, the Mongolian type predominates or is still strongly marked. It is on the great plateaus of Upper India that the Aryan type most widely, but by no means exclusively, prevails, sometimes with finely-cut features and a complexion that might belong to Southern Europe, whilst the Dravidian peoples of Central and Southern India are flat-nosed with dark brown skins often verging on black. The combination of race and religion gives some of the largest groups, such as the 50 million Bengalees and the 20 million Mahrattas, a strong claim to be called nations, whilst others numerically much less important, like the Rajputs and the Sikhs, derive equally good title-deeds from the part they have played in Indian history. Religious lines of cleavage cut athwart all these dividing lines. Mohammedans are relatively few in Southern and Central India, and are massed chiefly in the north, and they to-day preponderate in the

Punjab, once the Aryavartha or cradle of Hinduism. But Hinduism with the peculiar atmosphere it creates pervades and envelops the whole of India. There are a few ancient Christian communities in the south of India driven out of their Mesopotamian homelands by Mohammedan oppression long before European penetration began, just as the fire-worshipping Parsees of Bombay took refuge there at a much later date from Persia. Only in quite recent times have mass conversions, chiefly from the depressed castes of Hinduism, helped to bring the total Christian population of India up to near five millions. Fewer still in numbers are Sikhs and Jains, the former one of the most martial of Indian peoples, the latter a peculiar community of little over a million that has survived and led its own gentle innocuous life ever since the days of Buddha, with whose doctrines those of its founder have some kinship. Of the primitive tribes on the fringe of Hinduism or still beyond its pale there are many unclassified millions whose worship, if any, is paid to nature in such rude forms as best appeal to their untutored instincts. Only 13 per cent of the total population of India—and of these barely 2 per cent are women—come up to the elementary standards of literacy set up for Census purposes, and only 160 males and 18 females out of every 10,000 are styled " literate in English." But India has nevertheless at all times produced some of the finest and most subtle intellects of which the human race is capable, and great men of action as well as profound thinkers. Her genius for architecture has given equally splendid expression, both sacred and profane, to such opposite conceptions as those of Hinduism and Islam. Her arts and crafts possess the distinction as well as the restraint of long-descended traditions. Of her literature Max Müller has written that " . . . if I were to ask myself from what literature we, here in Europe, we who have been nurtured almost exclusively on the thought of Greeks and Romans, and of one Semitic race, the Jewish, may draw that corrective which is most wanted in order to make our inner life more perfect, more comprehensive, more universal, in fact, more truly human—a life not for this life only but a transfigured and eternal life—I should point to India." Yet nowhere have lofty ideals of self-renunciation been translated into such strange and sometimes revolting practices. Reverenced by the masses everywhere and tolerated at any rate by all, but strangely repulsive to Western eyes, there are to-day some four million ascetic mendicants who may be seen squatting at temple doors or outside the mansions of the great or lined up in serried ranks on the banks of some sacred river, or wandering in small groups from shrine to shrine all over India—often quite or almost naked, their faces and their bodies smeared all over with ashes and adorned with the emblems of their favourite deities, some of them worn to skeletons, or with withered arms uplifted, or finger nails ingrowing into their hands, from squatting everlastingly on their mats in the same posture of lifeless immobility which is supposed to kill desire. Impostors there may be and doubtless are amongst them with whom mendicancy is a lucrative profession, but their imposture would not pay if the superstitious worship of the masses, and of the women more especially, did not reflect an unalterable faith in the wonder-working powers of the godhead which has entered into possession of them.

Yet the whole of this Asian sub-continent, all this motley array of peoples are ruled to-day from a small island on the distant fringe of Western Europe, by a mere handful of Englishmen, less than 3,000 altogether in the higher branches of the administration, and, behind them, as the one visible sign of material force, rarely called in aid by the civil power, a British garrison of 70,000 men, as essential for the preservation of peace on the turbulent North-West Frontier as for the ultimate safeguarding of law and order throughout India. The British-born who are resident in India, excluding the British troops, are only 116,000, or not much over three per *mille* of the vast native population of whom millions and millions scarcely ever see an Englishman. And British power is paramount. Its symbol, as in England, is the British Crown, and the British Sovereign bears the title of Emperor of India. His representative is the Viceroy who as Governor-General in Council is head of the Central or Supreme Government of India responsible through the Secretary of State in London to the British Parliament. But British rule itself has drawn a fresh line of cleavage across India—one which we are apt to forget when we talk in general terms about India, as if under the British Crown at least she might be regarded as a politically-homogeneous whole. That is not so. British sovereignty though paramount over the whole Indian Empire assumes two separate and distinct shapes and fulfils two separate and distinct functions in that larger part, which is specifically termed British India under direct British administration, and in that smaller but still considerable part which consists of the Native States with their own hereditary rulers and their own administrative autonomy under the overlordship only of the British Sovereign. The distinction is important, for it is only for British India that Parliament can formally legislate. British India comprises, it is true, two-thirds of the area and three-quarters of the population of the Indian Empire, and it includes an even greater proportion of the progressive elements and of the wealth and enterprise needed for the building up of an Indian nation. But British India is not all India, and the Native States are a separate factor of which the existence and significance are often overlooked. Only in British India has the whole framework of government and administration been hitherto British, and it is within that framework that in British India provincial governments have grown up subordinate now to the Central Government, but charged with the government and administration of provinces in most cases much larger and more populous than the whole of England.

But British rule has done much more than bring the rule of law into India through direct administration in British India and through the indirect influence it exercises in the Native States. It is to British and largely to Government initiative or support that India owes the mechanical equipment of a modern state—roads and railways, telegraphs and telephones, electric power and wireless stations, canals and harbours, and in fact almost all important works—as well as the immense development of her commerce and industry and finance. The principal cities of the new India have grown up under British rule and it is from the West that they have borrowed all their chief features, not all equally acceptable to the Indian, but all very familiar to the Englishman's eye—spacious government and municipal buildings, law courts and universities, schools and hospitals, banks and club-houses, churches and racecourses, attractive residential as well as business quarters, and also many congested slums, especially in those over which a hanging cloud of smoke, belched forth from long lines of factory chimneys, reveals the rapid inroads of modern industrialism.

No less striking have been the results of British rule on the intellectual and political life of India. With Western education British rule has made English a *lingua franca* for all India and has trained up a new and rapidly-increasing class of Indians, not a few of them highly gifted, capable of mastering not only the language of the ruling race, but the literature and, though more rarely, the science of the West, and qualified to compete with Englishmen in almost all the higher activities of modern life, in the public services, on the Bench and at the Bar, in the liberal professions, in school and university teaching, in literature and in the press, and, if only more recently, in commerce and industry and finance.

It is this new class of Indians who have assumed the political leadership of India, and it is they who to-day dominate new representative assemblies designed to acclimatize in an Indian atmosphere parliamentary institutions and progressive forms of government presumed to be capable of future adjustment to the newest conceptions of democracy born into the world with the great war.

Of this new class of Indians and of these new Indian assemblies the Western paternity needs no demonstration. Only in the womb of British rule could they have been conceived and brought to birth. Yet with bitter irony it is from them that has now proceeded not merely a widespread and vehement reaction against British rule, but an emphatic repudiation of the Western civilization of which British rule has been the bearer. This is perhaps even more a psychological than a political phenomenon, but in either case we need to know the causes; and these must be sought in the action and reaction of old forces reaching deep down into the innermost life of India, not less than in the impact upon her of new forces imported from the outer world during a century-and-a-half of British dominion.

CHAPTER II

THE BEDROCK OF HINDUISM

THE religious beliefs and social customs that mould and govern the lives of the vast majority of the peoples of India are to an extent almost inconceivable to the Western mind the same to-day as they were two thousand years ago. What Western nation could in these times have acclaimed as its leader and credited with inspired wisdom a saint who preached self-renunciation and a return not merely to the spiritual but to the material conditions of life which prevailed in bygone ages ? Yet a great part of India, even of the India that has learnt to talk the language of the West, thrilled but yesterday to Gandhi's message of revolt and, if his prestige as a political leader has waned because he failed to accomplish the miracle of *Swaraj* within the brief term he too rashly promised, the disciples to whom he surrendered his mantle still fervently profess his gospel though they may have modified his forms of expression and methods of action. To them as to him British rule and Western civilization are anathema, though their ideas of strategy differ from his and are, maybe, less crude. They sit in serried ranks in the Western-made assemblies which he would have had them shun, but they still wear his homespun livery, and their appeal, though couched in more philosophic terms, is still to the " soul-force " which India can only develop by a return to the fundamental principles of her ancient civilization purged of the dross of an alien civilization imported by alien rulers.

No apology seems therefore to be needed for dwelling at the outset on the essential and abiding features of a social and religious system from which the soul-force of India has proceeded throughout the ages and still in a large measure proceeds to-day.

It is the system we call Hinduism, in which 230 out
of the 320 millions of the population of India live
and move and have their being, and the atmosphere
it has created since it was born during the first great
Aryan migration into the northern plains of India
has in a greater or lesser degree permeated all the
minorities whom we find to-day outside its pale.
Gandhi's cry was " Back to the Vedas "—back to
the prehistoric India depicted in the wonderful
collection of religious hymns which contain for every
Hindu the quintessence or the embryo of all
knowledge human and divine.   But for our purposes
we need not attempt to pursue Hinduism back to
its fountain head in the Vedas or through the many
stages of religious and philosophic evolution which
it underwent before India began to emerge about the
VIth century B.C. from the twilight of legendary
history and oral traditions.   As a religious system
it has always remained singularly fluid.   Unlike the
other great religions of the world it was never
identified with the personal inspiration of any single
great teacher or prophet.   It never had a Moses or
a Christ, a Confucius or a Mohammed.   It was
never encumbered with dogmas.   It never required
the acceptance of any definite creed or the worship
of any one or more particular deities.   It can
embrace every form of popular worship that appeals
to the masses and it has opened wide the portals of
its crowded Pantheon to the innumerable gods and
goddesses of the more primitive Dravidian populations gradually drawn within its fold.   It humours
such rude superstitions as the worship of peculiarly
weird stones and rocks and trees, or of serpents and
tigers and other terrifying creatures that require
to be propitiated.   It deifies the forces of nature in
the great gods, such as Vishnu the Preserver, and
Shiva the Destroyer, and in their consorts, such as
Lakhshmi and above all the great goddess Kali, the

consort of Shiva. It ensures the popularity of the
god Ganesh by giving him the head and trunk of an
elephant and of the god Hanuman by endowing him
with the face of a monkey. It promotes saints and
heroes to the rank of deities, and in the incarnations,
or avatars, which the gods may assume in order to
reappear in new shapes for the edification of mankind,
it provides, to borrow Sir Alfred Lyall's simile, " a
Jacob's ladder between heaven and earth. The
men are seen ascending until they become gods; they
descend again as embodiments of the divinities."
Fresh myths grow up around them, and their worship
takes every form which an imaginative and emotional
people can conceive, from the coat of red paint with
which the humble peasant smears the feet of some
local idol to the complicated ritual of splendid
temples shrouded in perpetual twilight, or the
orgiastic rites of Left-handed Tantricism. But if
there is much that to our eyes is hideous and even
obscene in certain forms of Hindu cult, there is in
others a great wealth of poetic beauty and human
tenderness of feeling. Nor does Hinduism set any
limits to the range of philosophic speculation. It
lends itself to the most divergent schools of thought,
sometimes verging on pure theism and sometimes
drifting into absolute atheism, but more often re-
solving themselves into universal pantheism. In all
ages many of the finest Indian minds have been
absorbed in the pursuit of some nobler solution of
the problem of existence and some more rational
satisfaction for the spiritual needs of humanity than
a gross idol-worship admittedly only fit for the
ignorant masses. The human intellect has indeed
seldom soared higher or displayed deeper meta-
physical subtlety than in the great systems of
philosophy in which many conservative Hindus still
seek a peaceful refuge from the restlessness and
materialism of the modern world, and it is from them

also that others of a less contemplative type are to-day drawing their chief inspiration for a definite movement of insurgence against the civilization of the West by which they dread to see the whole thought-structure of Hinduism undermined and laid low.

Entrenched against the West behind its philosophies as well as its superstitions, Hinduism has its most formidable stronghold in the social system which it has evolved with caste as its corner-stone. The Sanskrit word *Varna* means both caste and colour, and it may well be that in remote ages caste was little more than a colour-bar erected by the Aryan newcomers who were then a small minority in India to protect their own race from being swamped by the earlier races already in possession of the country, whilst their superior organization and their higher civilization were reducing them to subjection. The colour of their skins was relatively fair, whereas that of the primitive population of India exhibited much darker shades of brown, approaching even to black. In this respect the Aryans might be termed the first white conquerors of India, and in building up a new social structure, and basing it on caste, which was colour, they may well have been prompted by the same considerations as the Western nations of to-day who, in their oversea possessions, erect a colour-bar between the whites and the coloured races, black, brown or yellow, in order to maintain their prestige and preserve the purity of their stock, as well as in some cases to protect their economic interests, in the midst of indigenous populations vastly superior to them in numbers, but on a much lower plane of civilization. To-day the tables have after long ages been turned and it is the Indians who complain bitterly of the colour-bar enforced against them by the ruling white race in some of our oversea colonies and dominions ; but those who know their own history should ask themselves whether their forbears were not the first to create a precedent which the white man is only too ready to follow all over the world to-day.

The caste system as we still see it in India was only slowly evolved during the long period of transition from the tribal life of the early Aryans, mostly pastoral and agricultural, to more complex forms of society in populous towns and cities and in more or less highly-organized and centralized states. The Brahman who had been from Vedic times, as the appointed servant of the gods, the only lawful expounder of the scriptures, the maker of the laws to be deduced from them, and the ordained dispenser of divine favour through prayer and sacrifice, continued to mould Hindu beliefs, and it is not surprising that in building up a unique social structure on the basis of caste, he should have been able to secure for himself a position of unchallenged supremacy at its very pinnacle. He invested it with the highest sanctions of religion. The popular belief in India is still that the four great castes or divisions of Hindu society proceeded respectively at the creation of mankind from the head and the shoulders and the thighs and the feet of the creative Brahma. These four castes were the Brahman or priestly caste, the Kshatrya or warrior caste, the Vaishya caste or traders and tillers of the soil, and, far beneath these three, who were known as the Twice-Born and alone entitled to wear the Sacred Thread, the fourth or Sudra caste, a servile caste born into the world to serve the Twice-Born castes and above all the Brahmans. In the greatest of all Hindu law-books, the *Laws of Manu*, reduced to writing at some unknown date between the IIIrd century B.C. and the IInd century A.D., but deriving in any case from a far earlier body of unwritten customs law, the supremacy of the Brahman is fully established: "When a Brahman springs to light he is born above the world, the chief of all creatures, assigned to guard the treasury of duties, religious and civil. Whatever exists in the world is all, in effect though not in form, the wealth of the Brahman, since the Brahman is entitled to it all by his primogeniture and eminence of birth." Every offence committed by a Brahman involves a relatively slight penalty. However heinous a crime he may commit, he cannot be punished with death, for to kill a Brahman is the most heinous crime of all. For every offence on the other hand committed against him the direst penalties are enacted. As Sir William Jones observes in the preface to the translation which he was the first to make a little more than a century ago of these extraordinarily full and detailed ordinances, they represent a system of combined despotism and priestcraft, both indeed limited by law but skilfully conspiring to provide mutual support with mutual checks. However childish or sometimes barbarous the penal enactments laid down by Manu may seem to us, and however dangerously lax his moral injunctions occasionally are, they have as a whole an austere majesty and a spiritual elevation which explain the hold they have retained on Hindu society. Even to-day, side by side with English judges, there are Brahman judges sitting in the High Courts who still cling to the *Laws of Manu* in their private life, though from the Bench they administer our own very different laws, and often with profound learning and a strict sense of justice.

Already in the times of which the *Laws of Manu* have preserved for us a singularly trustworthy picture, the caste system had become the basis of the social order as it still is under the Hindu dispensation all over India to-day. It grew more and more complex as Hinduism drew the non-Aryan

The Bedrock of Hinduism

peoples of India into its expanding fold. The four
great castes into which Hinduism had begun by
dividing the peoples of India retained their importance as useful common denominators for the multitude of caste and sub-caste fractions evolved by
a sort of fissiparous process, with always some new
lines of cleavage between them, but all within the
old framework ; until in our own days the Census
of 1901, which for the first time included a careful
attempt to classify them, enumerated over 2,300.
Of the principal types into which these 2,300 castes
may be roughly sorted out and of the processes by
which they have been evolved, Sir Herbert Risley
gave in his Census Report a very full and lucid
description.

The functional or occupational type is the most
numerous. The Brahmans are on the topmost rung
of the ladder, though only relatively few of them are
engaged in religious functions and curiously enough
those who serve the temples are not held in high
repute. Then immediately below them the other
two twice-born castes of which the constituent
elements have been gradually changed and enlarged,
and below them again in a descending scale a host
of castes ranking as Sudras, whose avocations
entitled them to be regarded as " clean " castes, and
far lower still, another host whose functions make
them " unclean." These " unclean " castes, grouped
together sometimes under the comprehensive
designation of *panchnamas*, are barely on the fringe
of Hinduism and some quite beyond the pale.

Another type appears in the sectarian caste,
originating generally in religious sects which once
sought to emancipate themselves from the thraldom
of caste and began by proclaiming that all men
were equal, or at least all men who adopted their
views, but were driven ultimately by the extraordinary social pressure of the Hindu system to

repudiate such false doctrines and crave readmission as a new caste. Other castes of a mixed type have been formed in order to regularize the position of groups originally proceeding from marriages forbidden or discountenanced by Hindu law or by caste rules, but after a time for various reasons more or less fully condoned. Of the castes which can claim to represent an almost national type, the Mahrattas are the most numerous, but they too recognize many different castes within their caste. Some castes are formed by the migration of members of an old caste from one part of India to another. These castes try to preserve at first the customs which they bring with them from their former homes. Then after a time only the memory of their original habitat remains in a geographical name which is supplemented in due course by distinctive affixes as they in turn split up into further castes or sub-castes. Analogous to these is the tribal type which without migrating to another new part of the country has simply modified its primitive customs and manner of life in the direction of orthodox Hinduism, within whose pale it seeks to gain admittance or preferment, whilst preserving its tribal name and peculiar traditions.

An Indian judge has summed up in a few words some of the worst mischief done by the infinite subdivision of caste—"physically by narrowing the circle of choice in marriage, intellectually by cramping the energies, and morally by destroying mutual confidence and habits of co-operation." But a far more glaring evil is the condition of some fifty millions left far away at the foot of the social ladder, or just struggling for a place on the lowest rung. These constitute what are now generally described as the "depressed classes," somewhat loosely counted amongst the Hindus, though they are outside the recognized caste system and all

Hindus who are within it regard and treat them as
" untouchable." To come into physical contact
with them, or within reach of the shadow that their
bodies may project, or even in some cases within such
proximity as an elaborate table of distances forbids,
involves a spiritual defilement which can only be
purged by ceremonial ablutions or other religious
rites. The Nampudri Brahmans, amongst whom
matriarchy, *i.e.*, the very ancient custom of tracing
descent through the female line, still prevails, may
even still be heard on the Malabar coast warning
the " untouchables " by a curious bellowing sound
to clear out of the road at their approach. These
low-caste or no-caste people are restricted to menial
occupations of the lowest and most unclean kind.
They are strictly segregated from the rest of the
community. They can only dwell within their own
quarter. They can only deal in particular bazaars.
They are not allowed to draw water from any wells
but those assigned to them. These are not conditions which existed thousands or even hundreds
of years ago. They exist to-day all over India,
though in Central and Southern India more than
elsewhere. They are a blot on Hinduism and the
civilization which it has produced, and hard indeed
to reconcile with the political aspirations of educated
Indians who excuse or justify such a system, and
yet contend that India is ripe for the most democratic
institutions. It rests with the Indians themselves to
remove that reproach, for it impinges on the domain
of religion and is held therefore to lie beyond the
range of Government action. There have been
many Indian reformers courageous enough to
condemn it, but orthodox Hinduism opposes to any
real reform the *vis inertiæ* of long-descended tradition.
It is to Gandhi's credit that though he has not
attacked the main features of the caste system,
he has loudly denounced " untouchability " on the

highest grounds of social justice and morality. He
and other apostles of a return to the Vedic age
might even claim that in the Vedas themselves
there is as little warrant for the whole caste system,
as it exists to-day, as for " untouchability " alone.

The evils of the caste system do not however lie
only in the barriers erected between the different
castes. Equally harmful are many of the laws
which govern life within the caste. Of all the
customs which, in most of the higher castes at
least, have acquired the force of law, those that
regulate marriage are the most immutable, for upon
marriage depends the continuity of the Hindu family
essential to the salvation of the living and the dead
in past and future generations. One of them is
endogamy, or marrying in, which forbids members
of a caste to marry anyone outside that particular
caste, and the other is exogamy, or marrying out,
which forbids them to marry within their own
particular sept of the caste, usually supposed to
descend from a common ancestor, or associated with
a particular locality. Still more peculiar and
demoralizing is hypergamy, or marrying up, which
forbids a woman of a particular group to marry a
man of a group equal to or inferior to her own,
though of the same caste in the more comprehensive
acceptance of the term, and compels her to marry
into a superior group. Bridegrooms in the upper
groups thus become the object of vigorous competition and instead of the price paid according to the
more primitive usage for the bride, it is the
bridegroom for whom a price, and often a very heavy
price, has to be paid. Hypergamy, which chiefly
obtains amongst the higher castes, seems however
to be falling into disrepute and may be expected to
die out. But even in recent times, it not infrequently
happened that the poorer caste men who knew
they could never afford to buy husbands for their

daughters were driven to resort to infanticide, whilst
the Kulin Brahmans of Bengal carried the exploitation of their hierarchical status to such lengths that
it was no uncommon thing for them to have scores
of wives at the same time who all provided handsome
dowries and were visited in turn by the coveted
husband.   It was hypergamy also which on economic
even more than religious grounds sustained the
practice of *Sati*, or the self-immolation of widows
on their husband's funeral pyre, until it was
prohibited by law in 1827, and it has helped in
conjunction with other causes to maintain the
prohibition of the re-marriage of widows which is
still widely enforced.

Apart from the *jus connubii* which, though it may
vary in different castes, constitutes the most stringent of all caste laws, all have their own peculiar
customs prescribing with whom they may eat and
entertain ordinary intercourse, how they must
clothe themselves, what religious rites they must
perform, and finally the manner in which both their
bodies and their property must be disposed of
after death.   All have their own governing council
of caste elders who enforce observance of these
customs and visit breaches of them with penalties
of which the most extreme is excommunication from
the caste ; for it means that no one will eat or smoke
with the offender or visit his house or marry his
daughter, and even the caste barber and washerman,
some of whose duties have a religious implication,
will refuse to come near him.   As an illustration of
the much greater elasticity of Hinduism as a religion
than as a social system it may be noted that each
caste often has its special gods and goddesses and
its special forms of worship.   Each may even have
its own special Brahmans to watch over its caste
laws and perform the necessary religious ceremonies
and sacrifices—for value received.   The lower castes

may only find Brahmans of doubtful reputation and even of doubtful authenticity to minister to them, but even these help to maintain Brahmanical supremacy throughout the caste system. For just as a Brahman is born a Brahman—*nascitur non fit*—he never ceases to be a Brahman in this life, whatever his demerits may be, though for dire breaches of his own caste laws he may be outcasted and cut off from all the privileges of caste fellowship.

It must not, however, be thought that caste is associated with anything that corresponds to our own ideas of social position. A Brahman may pursue many quite humble avocations so long as they are not specifically prohibited by the ancient laws of Hinduism — motor-driving for instance was for obvious reasons not prohibited, and therefore many Brahmans have become chauffeurs—and he will nevertheless be able to claim and will secure from all orthodox Hindus of lower castes, though from a worldly point of view much higher in rank, authority and wealth, those particular forms of respect to which his more exalted caste entitles him. A high Government official who is not a high-caste Hindu may on occasion be seen to-day as he passes in to be received in audience by the Viceroy, stooping down to worship the bare feet of a Brahman *chuprassi* in the viceregal livery on duty at the door of Viceregal Lodge. For the liveried menial's *Karma* makes him in the peculiar hierarchy of Hinduism the undisputed superior of the otherwise more favoured visitor.

The Hindu caste system is bound up with the cardinal doctrine of the migration of the soul through an infinite cycle of births and deaths and re-births, under the iron law of *Karma* which determines the lot of every Hindu according to the sum of his actions not merely in his present lifetime but in all his former lives. It determines the caste into which

he has been actually born and will equally determine
the caste into which after his death he will be re-born.
All that he can do in this life is to contribute to the
fulfilment of the law of righteousness which is
Dharma, and righteousness consists in nothing so
much as in maintaining inviolate the social order
established in Hinduism.   Right conduct resolves
itself therefore into carrying out as faithfully as
possible the laws and traditions of his own caste
from which he cannot in this life emerge, so as to
deserve re-birth, at any rate into no lower caste,
and possibly into a higher one.   One need not
wonder that some of the greatest Hindu thinkers
have been driven to seek for suffering humanity
some way of escape at any cost from this endless
chain of existences, and that Buddha and the Yoghi
schools of Hindu philosophy have taught that release
from the intolerable wheel of fate has to be sought
in complete withdrawal from the world and the
practice of intense austerities in order to kill all
desires which are the mainsprings of human action ;
and action means life and life means bondage to the
wheel.   As the only possible form of salvation, they
looked, some to the self-annihilation of the individual
soul, some to its absorption by complete surrender
into an unknowable divine being that is itself
actionless.

Some of the gravest economic as well as social
problems with which India is confronted to-day
are due to the grip which the belief in the migration
of the soul according to its *Karma* has on Hindu
family life.   Whilst the Hindu is taught that his
future life will be irrevocably determined by his
Karma, he is also taught, rather illogically, that it
depends no less upon the regular performance of
the same funeral ceremonies and other ancestral
rites by his male descendants after his death as he
is required to perform for his ancestors during his

own life. Hence the immense importance for every
Hindu of leaving a son or a son's son to carry out
those duties when he is gone, and the gradual
lowering of woman in Hindu society, since her one
supreme function is to bear a son to her husband
for that purpose. Early marriages and even infant
marriages, often consummated before physical
maturity, are justified as a religious duty lest the
Hindu should die without leaving a male child to
carry on the essential family rites. To these early
marriages, combined with a complete ignorance of
both maternity and infant hygiene, is due the appalling infant mortality amongst Hindu babies. For
similar reasons the unfortunate Hindu wife who has
failed to bear a son is liable on that score alone to
be superseded by another, and is regarded and
treated as a failure. Worse still is the lot of a
sonless widow. Her head is shaved ; she can no
longer wear the jewels which, however paltry, are
the most cherished possessions of every Hindu
woman ; she has to put on the dishonoured widow's
garb ; she is doomed to perpetual widowhood.
And the justification of all this is that such is her
Karma, the merited retribution for transgressions in
some earlier existence. The *Baghavatghita*, the
finest book of the *Mahabharata*, universally popular
and now one of the favourite classics of *Swaraj*
explicitly teaches that to be born a woman is an evil
Karma due to sins in former lives. To be a sonless
wife is a worse *Karma*, but the worst of all is to be
a sonless widow. Even if she is an infant widow
and has been denied the physical possibility of
bearing a son that denial is part of her *Karma* and
involves the same penalties of sonless widowhood
as if her husband had lived to consummate the
marriage. There is no more pathetic sight than
that of a small mite of a girl, perhaps not more than
seven or eight years old, dressed in the despised

livery of perpetual widowhood and doomed to the contumelious treatment which her *Karma* is held to have earned for her.

Yet Indians are capable of very deep affection, and the family relations in one of those Hindu houses where two or three and even four generations live together beneath the same roof or within the same compound, under the paternal authority of the head of the family, are often singularly happy and beautiful, and there is perhaps nothing to pity in the women's lot save their rigorous seclusion, in which they themselves, however, glory as the pledge of a blameless and honoured life. The very contrast between the proud position and great domestic influence of a wife to whom sons and sons' sons have been born to fulfil the ancestral rites, and that of a barren wife or sonless widow illustrates the full force of the law of *Karma* in its worst aspects. To us, at least, it can only represent a cruel perversion of the Hindu's fine conception of the continuity of the family as one unbroken chain, sanctified by common worship, which stretches back to remote ancestors and forward to all the future generations. The conservation at any cost of that sacred continuity is part of the same *Dharma* which binds the Hindu to perfect his *Karma* by the assiduous fulfilment of his duties within and towards the caste into which he has been born. For the same Brahmanical authority presides over the Hindu family and over the Hindu caste system and gives to both the incomparable tenacity and organic rigidity to which Hinduism owes its enduring power as the paramount social as well as religious force in India.

The broad tolerance of British rule has always sought to avert any open conflict with Hinduism in its social as well as in its religious aspects, and the Government of India has shown even greater diffidence during the last four or five decades than during the first half of the last century in promoting legislation which might offend Hindu susceptibilities. Englishmen have trusted to the larger influence of Western ideals and of increasing contact with the West to modify the worst features of a social system so incongruous with the national aspirations of which many distinguished Hindus are the most eloquent exponents. Some Europeans believe that the caste system already shows signs of disintegration. But have they not attached exaggerated importance to the non-essential things that leap to the eye ? In such matters as crossing the seas, travelling in crowded trains, partaking of food cooked in unorthodox fashion and in company with others than their lawful caste fellows, caste laws have no doubt been relaxed, or at least the processes of " purification " for those who break them have been made easier. As a result of the introduction of so much of the modern machinery of life into India the caste system has had to yield to the exigencies of closer and unavoidable contact not only between Indians and Europeans but between Indians of different castes. But on the vitality of the caste organization as a whole, and in all matters that are essential, and especially in the matter of marriage, hardly any impression has yet been made; though chiefly under economic pressure infant marriages are somewhat less frequent and there is a tendency towards later marriages for both sexes: but on the other hand movements started for removing or diminishing the disabilities of widowhood have made little headway. As for "untouchability," Gandhi himself was threatened with excommunication by an influential conference of Hindu orthodoxy after a moving speech in which he denounced it before the Indian National Congress.

Of the tenacious grip of caste on the whole social

order and of the power still wielded by the Brahmans
who have informed and sustained it through the
ages, can there be a more vivid illustration than
the dramatic incident which occurred only a few
years ago when Lord Ronaldshay was Governor
of Bengal, a province that prides itself on being
in the van of Indian progress ?   In 1917 it was
persistently rumoured in Calcutta that the *ghee,* or
clarified butter, an indispensable article in all Hindu
dietary and even in religious ceremonies, was being
grossly adulterated with animal fat and other impure
substances equally abominated by the Hindu.
Some members of the wealthy trading caste of
Marwaris were suspected, an inquiry was held
and the analysis of *ghee* sold in the Calcutta markets
disclosed very widespread and gross adulteration.
There was great excitement amongst all classes, but
amongst the Brahmans above all there was consternation and wrath.   They had been betrayed into
the use of *ghee* rendered by adulteration " impure "
for sacrificial and ritual purposes, and, however
inadvertently, they had committed a dire offence
against the gods which must jeopardize their own
Karma.   So to wash it away they assembled in their
thousands on the river bank to go through the bathing
ceremonies of purification.   It was one of those
spectacular demonstrations by which the Brahmans
have always known how to stir the imagination of
the masses.   Yet Calcutta is a city in which English
residents would be apt to assert that Hinduism has
ceased to have any vital power.   Political Calcutta
was at that time in the throes of a violent agitation
for more democratic forms of government.   It was
at once hushed before the grave menace of adulterated
ghee to the religion enshrined just outside the city
in the great and sinister temple of Kali, the most
popular of all its shrines.   The daily abuse of
Government dropped out of the vernacular press to

make room for the much more burning question. An influential and representative deputation of Hindus waited upon the Governor to press for immediate action. A Bill was immediately drafted and passed through all its stages at a single sitting of the Bengal Legislative Assembly three days later. But infinitely more effective was the exercise by the Hindu castes immediately concerned of the powers which, as they stated, the caste *Panchayats*, or Councils, have possessed from times immemorial, under the unwritten laws of the country, for dealing with offences against society and religion. A Committee consisting of three different *Panchayats* belonging to three different castes, one of them the Brahmans, was constituted and dealt with the principal charges, inflicting heavy fines, up to a lakh of rupees, and long terms of caste excommunication on the chief offenders. This process was accepted as satisfactory, the ceremonies of purification were brought to a close and the Brahmans returned to their homes with all the prestige of their exalted caste strikingly vindicated and enhanced.

These facts are set forth by Lord Ronaldshay himself in the *Bird's-Eye View of India*, the first of an illuminating Indian trilogy published by him on his return to England. The moral to be drawn may best be quoted in his own words :

" Amid the surroundings of a great Western city of the twentieth century was enacted a scene culled from the drama of Indian life two thousand years or more ago. In this incongruous setting was performed an elaborate ritual reaching far back into Vedic times. The admittedly efficient administrative machinery imported from the West fell into the background of men's minds. It might be called in to assist in guarding against similar trouble in the future, but it was powerless to deal with the situation which had actually arisen. It

" Everything bore the signs of disintegration and decay " and national life seemed to be extinct, before the bursting of the storm that was about to descend upon India from Central Asia.

If India as she had been shaped by Hinduism during more than two thousand years of *Swaraj*, collapsed under that storm it was not that the influence of Hinduism had been circumscribed or intermittent. It was the one great force that preserved the framework of society through endless political vicissitudes. It produced a general uniformity of beliefs and customs amongst the innumerable peoples of a great continent, shut off from the rest of the world but having their own different languages and racial characteristics. It pursued its long evolution as a religious and social system seldom if ever disturbed by the rise and fall of dynasties and the clash of arms. The fall of the Gupta Empire did not arrest the great Brahmanical revival which had been one of its most signal features. It was then on the contrary that Hinduism gave one of the most remarkable proofs of its religious flexibility by its readiness to make great concessions to the forms of worship practised by the Dravidian populations of the south, where new states were emerging out of the political chaos of India, in order to embrace them within its fold, and to extend its social fabric by the inclusion of tribe after tribe for whom Brahmans were even willing to invent purely mythical claims to Aryan ancestry. It was then that the more sensuous and exuberant imagination of the south reacted powerfully not only upon the forms of Hindu worship, but upon the whole religious thought of Hinduism which had been born in the colder north. Popular idol-worship resolved itself into two main sects, often overlapping—those who placed the great god Shiva on a supreme pinnacle, and those who made Vishnu, or, as his incarnation,

Krishna, the principal object of their devotions. It was in the south and in the IXth century during that dark period of Hindu *Swaraj* upon which the patriotism of Indian Nationalists looks back with grief and shame, that Shankara was born and founded a new school of pure Vedantism which gave the fullest and most uncompromising expression to the doctrine of Maya or illusion. The universe, he taught, and all that it seems to man to be is unreal, and salvation lies in overcoming the great illusion of existence by merging the individual soul in the absolute which is alone real but actionless. Shankara preached in the north as well as in the south and has left his impress upon Hindu thought down to the present day. If India lost her independence to the invading hordes of Islam it was not from any decay in the vitality of Hinduism. As a social force it was constantly extending and hardening the caste system. As a religious force it was exalting the fervour of temple worship by surrounding it with increasingly gorgeous ceremonials in magnificent temples such as India had never seen before. As a spiritual force it was launching forth into new fields of bold philosophic speculation. Nor was it that the peoples of India were so unmartial that they could not have been organized to repel the foreign invaders. Except for the pacifist influence of Buddhism which had not endured, there had been nothing in their history to show that they were unwarlike. Never had the warrior caste produced more splendid fighters than the Rajputs who made the last great stand against the Mohammedans. The whole history of India, so far as we can follow it on the solid ground of fact as well as in her poetry and literature, sacred and profane, during the two millenniums and more when, save during Asoka's reign, Brahmanism was almost invariably the power behind the throne, is a well-nigh unbroken history

of war and violence. The rare periods when a
semblance of national unity prevailed were due to
a few forceful rulers and dynasties that rose by the
sword and perished by the sword.

Hinduism could not build up a nation because the
one vital structure which it did build up was the
negation of everything that constitutes a nation.
It confined the people within a multitude of separate
pens and taught them that individual salvation
through an endless cycle of existences was bound up
with the strict observance of the religious and social
forms established within each pen. To quote the
conclusion at which Mr. Narindra Nath Law, a
distinguished Hindu writer, arrives in his scholarly
book *Aspects of Ancient Indian Polity*, " the multiplication of castes and sub-castes, each more or less
stereotyped . . . proved, as it does at present, a
source of weakness to the body politic, each caste
and sub-caste being a fresh centre with its own
particular interests of various kinds, with its own
strong likes and dislikes and with its rigid wall that
hinders all real and practical identification of its
own self with that of other castes and with the
wider self of the body politic." Or, if one prefers
to follow Hindu writers who, perhaps anxious to
slur over the influence of caste, lay the chief stress
on the decay of the village community—itself,
however, bound up with caste—one of the most
brilliant of them, Dr. R. Mookerji, emphasizes the
fact that " ancient India presents the rare and
remarkable phenomenon of state and society co-
existing apart from, and in some degree of independence of, each other as distinct and separate units
or entities, as independent centres of life and
activity." The fundamental laws which governed
Hindu society as a whole were personal laws bound
up with caste, which took no account of the territorial
limits of the many states into which India was from

time to time politically split up. The allegiance rendered to the rulers of those states by their Hindu subjects was secondary to the loyalty each owed to his caste, since his caste was his *Karma*, determining much more than his present life, namely, all his lives still to come. There could never grow up between states, each made up of an infinity of separate and to a great extent independent and even conflicting units, any real sense of paramount national solidarity, and because Hinduism failed to create an Indian nation, the peoples of India were helpless to resist the first great onslaught of foreign invaders professing a very different creed, which at least taught Mohammedans of every race and class and condition that they were all equal and one in the great brotherhood of Islam.

CHAPTER III

MOHAMMEDAN DOMINATION

NEXT to Hinduism, Islam is the greatest force
that shaped the history of India before the advent
of the British, and it is still a great force to-day.
In its religious and social outlook it is alien to
India and was imported by a succession of Mohammedan invasions from Central Asia which began twelve
centuries ago. The spirit of a militant and sternly
monotheistic creed, which is in so far democratic
that it recognizes the equality of all who recite its
simple profession of faith in Allah and his Prophet,
was and still is repugnant to that of Hinduism, and
their antagonism is not lessened by the memories of
several centuries of Mohammedan domination which
the Hindus still dread, and the Mohammedans
perhaps still hope, to see some day revived. But
Islam has not wholly resisted the subtle influence
of an Indian atmosphere. India's Mohammedans
number over 70 millions, or more than a fifth of
the whole population. Only a small proportion can
even pretend to trace their ancestry back to any of
the Central Asian conquerors, and the immensely
larger proportion descend from Hindu converts and
have more or less consciously preserved some of their
Hindu traditions and customs. In spite of the very
deep lines of cleavage between Mohammedans and
Hindus their common antipathy to the spirit of
the West tends to draw them fitfully together as
was seen during the great Mutiny, and has been
seen again much more recently when the lure of
Swaraj brought them at least temporarily into line.
The forces of mutual attraction and repulsion that
racial affinities and religious and social antagonism
exert upon them are factors that still have an
important and direct bearing on the present condition of India.

There is no need to hark back to the first incursions of the Arab followers of the Prophet within less than a century after his death, as they came across the sea from Mesopotamia and never penetrated beyond the lower valley of the Indus : nor to dwell on the earliest irruptions through the northern passes during the XIth and XIIth centuries of the Central Asian hordes, who gave the Hindu peoples of Upper India a taste of Mohammedan ruthlessness in the sack of Somnath, one of their holiest and most famous shrines. These were little more than plundering expeditions, but on an increasingly large scale, which whetted the greed of tribe after tribe. The Turks of Ghazni had to make room for the Afghans of Ghor, and these in turn were ousted by a dynasty of Slave Kings whose founder, Kutb-ud-Din, for the first time established in 1206 the seat of Mohammedan power at Delhi, where his Kutb-Minar, the loftiest of all minarets, still towers above the great mosque into which he built the ruins of Hindu temples, proudly naming it "The Power of Islam." Other dynasties supplanted the Slave Kings and like them produced great warriors and splendid architects who were often at the same time monsters of depravity and cruelty. They or their lieutenants carried fire and plunder further and further into the heart of India, reaching even as far south as Madura, before, at the end of the XIVth century, Timur the Lame swept down with his Moghuls like a whirlwind from the North and smote Hindus and Mohammedans with equal fury. He disappeared as suddenly, but when he went back to Samarkand he left Delhi a charnel-house. Its power as an Imperial city was broken for more than a century. Then Baber, a great-grandson of Timur, in turn invaded India in 1525, not like his terrible ancestor merely to kill and destroy, but to found the Moghul Empire which was to be for more than two centuries the paramount power in India. Its fortunes were not however established until his grandson, Akbar, not yet quite 15 years of age, won in 1556 the decisive battle of Panipat on the plains of Delhi, where the destinies of India have been so often fought out.

It is with Akbar that the history of Mohammedan domination begins to have a close bearing upon modern India. For he was the first and only Mohammedan ruler of India who systematically attempted to weld her many peoples into an Indian nation by other means than force. The Moghuls like ourselves were aliens in the land, and though in the course of four centuries their alien faith had already won at the point of the sword a firm foothold in India, Mohammedan rule had never found any enduring centre of stability. The Moghuls were, however, Asiatics, and though they came of a stock ethnically further removed than our own from the Aryans who built up Indian civilization, the larger kinship of Asia gradually promoted a racial fusion between the conquerors and the peoples of India towards which the Indians and their white rulers of to-day have never moved. Akbar may have been a dreamer of impossible dreams, but they were the dreams of a genius. What he dreamt of was nothing less than one great unified empire of Hindustan of which he was to be the spiritual as well as the temporal ruler. An Eastern autocrat and bent on bringing the whole of India under his sway, he used force where force was necessary, whether to subdue the Mohammedan Sultans of Middle India or to secure the submission of the proud Rajput clans, but he knew also when to employ the more subtle methods of diplomacy and conciliation. He not only contracted matrimonial alliances for himself and for his family with the blue-blooded Hindu houses of Rajputana, when once they had acknowledged

both of his master's financial genius and of the country's prosperity under his rule, a magnificent increase in expenditure which was four times as great as under his predecessors. The Moghul Court reached the high-water mark of spendthrift splendour under Jehanghir and Shah Jehan but their grip of Empire was weakening. Treachery had become a habit of the reigning house which every Emperor practised and suffered from in turn. Jehanghir rebelled against his father, Akbar, and Shah Jehan against his father, Jehanghir, and Aurangzeb deposed and imprisoned his father, Shah Jehan, and removed his brothers by fraud and violence in order to seize the throne. He was cast in a sterner mould and he extended the Empire by finally subduing the still independent Mohammedan kingdoms of Middle India. But, when he died in 1707, its mighty fabric already showed deep fissures. His fanaticism roused the dormant forces of Hinduism, and he spent the last 14 years of his reign, during which he never once revisited his capital, in fruitless endeavours to stamp out the Mahratta rebellion in the Western Deccan to which Shivaji had already given the double impress of a national uprising against the foreign domination of the Moghuls and of a religious revolt of Hinduism against Islam.

Nothing in the history of India, except perhaps the slow and relentless re-absorption of Buddhism into Hinduism during the twelve centuries before the first Mohammedan invasions, is more eloquent of the enduring power of Hindu civilization than the passive resistance it offered to Islam during successive centuries of Mohammedan domination. Whilst Hindu states, rarely capable of any organized effort in the field, were one after another brought under subjection to Mohammedan rule over almost the whole of India, except the remotest south, Hinduism as a social and religious system not only held its own against Islam but continued to pursue its peculiar course of evolution, sometimes influenced by the spiritual aspects of Islam, but never disturbed by its triumphant assertion of material force. The Mohammedans were already spreading terror in the north of India when Ramanuja, the great Vishnuite teacher of Southern India in the XIIth century, introduced into the worship of the gods a new element of personal devotion and love which was the antithesis of the Vedantic conception of an unknowable and actionless divine being. His successor, Ramanada, carried the greater humanity of his teaching into Northern India itself, and, impressed with the austerity of Mohammedan doctrine and worship, tried to purge Hinduism of its grosser forms of idolatry, and, moved perhaps by the Islamic doctrine of the brotherhood of all True Believers, ignored in worship and in doctrine the traditional distinction between the castes admitted within and those kept beyond the pale of orthodox Hinduism. His successor, Kabir, still more directly influenced by Mohammedanism, definitely broke with caste and with idolatry whilst retaining the outward marks of Vishnuism. Before the coming of the Moghuls Nanak who taught the unity of God and condemned the servitude of caste was the founder of religious Sikhism in the Punjab, and not until two centuries later did Mohammedan persecutions under Aurangzeb and his successors drive the Sikhs into creating the military organization which they used to carve a powerful Sikh state out of the ruins of the Moghul Empire. Chaitanya, a contemporary of Nanak, imported a new spirit into Hinduism by carrying the doctrine of personal devotion and adoration into a mystic cult of Krishna, though the god's amorous exploits displaced in the popular mind the spiritual attributes upon which Chaitanya concentrated his ecstatic worship. In the hey-day of Mohammedan domination Tulsi Das flourished as the Hindu poet who has made the deepest and most lasting impression upon his fellow-countrymen. His popular version of the Ramayana is still recited in thousands of Hindu villages whose simple folk never fail to be deeply moved by the dramatic representations of its familiar story on festival days. It lends a new meaning to the ancient epic, and, perhaps under the influence of the early Nestorian churches in India, has almost a ring of Christianity in its praise of the incarnate Rama born to overthrow evil and returning to heaven after a life of glorious deeds to answer the prayers of suffering humanity and rescue it from its misery by his own divine grace and compassion. Nowhere did Tulsi Das's teachings find a greater echo than amongst the Mahrattas whose chief poet, Tukram, drew his people into a unity of Hindu religious fervour which Shivaji knew how to blend with an appeal to national Mahratta sentiment in the first great movement of Hindu revolt against the alien Mohammedan rulers—a movement of which the undying memories were effectively revived in the Deccan against British rule in quite recent times by a Brahman who was in the direct line of spiritual descent from Shivaji's teachers and advisers.

Under Mohammedan domination caste never relaxed its hold on Hindu society, but on the contrary extended and multiplied its outworks as a protection against Islamic penetration. Tentative movements for the emancipation of Hinduism from Brahmanical ascendancy may be traced in part to contact with Islam, but they ebbed and died away before the end of Mohammedan rule. Hinduism survived the Moghul Empire as it had survived all the earlier and often more barbarous phases of Mohammedan domination. Islam had left much of Southern India almost untouched, and there even more than elsewhere Hinduism remained firmly entrenched behind the unyielding walls of ancient orthodoxy. Mohammedan society itself caught the contagion of caste, of which there are still numerous and very visible traces even amongst the more compact Mohammedan population of Northern India. One of the worst effects on the other hand of the Mohammedan conquest on the Hindus, and especially on the higher castes, was to lower the position of Hindu women whose close seclusion within the walls of the *zenana* dates back to the Mohammedan invasions, whether in the first instance from fear of the conquerors' unbridled licentiousness and violence or whether in servile imitation of the domestic institutions of India's new masters.

Mohammedan domination had not, however, reached its apogee in the Moghul Empire when an entirely new influence swept across the seas into India from the far distant shores of Western Europe. On May 20, 1498, Vasco da Gama cast anchor off the city of Calicut on the Malabar coast after nearly a year's arduous voyage from Lisbon round the Cape of Good Hope. For the first time since Alexander the Great, men of European stock stood on Indian soil ready to do battle. The spirit which inspired Portuguese enterprise is reflected in the instructions given two years later to the commander of another Portuguese expedition. He was " to begin with preaching, and, if that failed, to proceed to the sharp determination of the sword." The Portuguese, however, though as ready to use the sword for the propagation of their faith as any of the Mohammedan conquerors, were not above trading also, and after the great Albuquerque had firmly established their power at Goa and up the Western coast of India to the Persian Gulf, Portugal held for a century the monopoly of Indian trade as the only European power with any foothold in

India. But the significance of these incursions from beyond the " black water " was lost upon the rulers of a divided India, whether Mohammedan or Hindu. The Portuguese never penetrated far beyond the coast, and when they were at the height of their power in the middle of the XVIth century, Southern India was absorbed in the long struggle between the Mohammedan Sultans of Middle India and the great Hindu kingdom of Vijayanagar, the last one to make a prolonged stand against the inrush of Islamic conquest. When the Portuguese star had waned and the Dutch and British engaged in their century-long struggle for the trade of the Indies, they too confined it mainly to the seas and to a few districts close to the sea, and the Moghul Emperors were too far away to take much note of them. They had come down from the inland plateaus of Central Asia and established their seat of Empire in the plains of Upper India equally distant from the Arabian Sea and from the Bay of Bengal. They were never a sea-power nor did they know the meaning of the term. Akbar's long reign which closely coincided with that of Queen Elizabeth was nearing its end when the first Merchant Venturers of London armed with the charter she granted to them established a few precarious traders' settlements on the coast, and his son Jehanghir was on the throne when Sir Thomas Roe's embassy proceeded to the Moghul Court as a suppliant for Imperial favour. The British East India Company was still in its infancy and the Moghuls took little interest at first even in the trade which brought the Infidels to India, except in so far as it introduced them to curious exotic wares which amused their curiosity or ministered to their inordinate love of luxury. Yet it was these outlandish traders whose enterprise was already fashioning, though still quite unconsciously, the instrument which a few generations later salvaged the wreckage of the Moghul Empire when it fell to pieces in the hands of Akbar's degenerate successors.

If the methods sometimes employed by the East India Company during its gradual transformation from a great trading corporation into the paramount ruling power in India may sometimes lend themselves to criticism, it can legitimately claim to have rescued India, and to have been the one power that could rescue her, from the chaos into which she was once more relapsing with the passing of Mohammedan domination. The present-day reaction against British rule has nevertheless driven many Indians to ignore the conditions which prevailed in their country during that chapter of her history, and some Indian writers even profess to believe that India still enjoyed a wonderful measure of prosperity and freedom before the British rushed in with their lust of dominion to rob her of her independence and grind her down for their own selfish purposes of political and economic exploitation. It is fortunately a period concerning which we have much more and abundant and trustworthy information from both native and European sources than we have as to the earlier " golden age" of Hindu *Swaraj*, of which Hindu writers are wont to extol the still greater glories, and we can draw at least a rough comparison between the India of to-day and the India of the Moghuls, not only in their last stage of moribund decay, but in the most brilliant phase of Moham-medan domination when the Moghul Empire was at its apogee.

Aurangzeb, the last of the three great successors of Akbar, was laid to his rest in 1707, before the East India Company had even begun to be a political power in India, and, whatever were the general conditions, whether of prosperity or misery, which then prevailed there, they were such as the Moghul

Empire had created during the century-and-a-half of its greatest splendour.

The tillers of the soil then as now formed the vast majority of the population, and bore a heavy burden of taxation. Then as now their poverty was very great. Their dwellings, generally of sun-dried mud where there is a relatively cold season, and of coco-nut matting and bamboo where the heat is constantly tropical, were probably not more miserable than they are now. As to their food, it was of the same character. When the harvests were good, the cost of the foodstuffs on which they chiefly live may have been lower, but mainly because the local markets were then glutted owing to the absence of adequate means of transportation to more remote and profitable markets. They probably therefore had a little more to eat on those occasions, as there was no sale for any surplus food which they could not consume. But neither could they put anything by, even if they were inclined to save, which the Indian peasant seldom is. They seem to have had less to spend on their clothes, and woollen garments and blankets appear to have been unknown, whilst any sort of footgear was much rarer than now. Their religious festivals and family ceremonies were then as now a perpetual drain on their scanty resources, and pilgrimages were as popular but must have cost more and taken up more time and certainly been more arduous when, beyond the great strategic highways built for the Imperial armies, there were only a few unmetalled roads and a very small number of bridges, and no organized medical assistance even on the very low plane of medical science at that period. Slavery was a permanent and recognized institution. Foreign slaves imported from Africa and Western Asia were luxuries for the rich, and the majority of Indian slaves, whose status was hereditary under both

Mohammedan and Hindu law, were either born as such or had been captured in lawless raids on helpless villages, or seized as children and sold by the tax-gatherer when their parents could not satisfy his demands, whilst in times of famine they were simply abandoned and left to starve.   When once, on the other hand, a slave had passed into the hands of a permanent master, there is nothing to show that he was badly treated, and the position of a domestic slave was doubtless not substantially different from that of the hired servant or family retainer.

What was the general impression made on the few foreigners who lived or travelled in the country ? None is more trustworthy than the Frenchman, Bernier, who travelled widely and reported exhaustively to Colbert when Louis XIV's great Minister included India in his vast schemes of colonial expansion for France.   This is what he writes just at the end of Shah Jehan's reign when the farming-out of land revenue to which Akbar for a time put a stop had become once more the common if not universal practice : " The ground is seldom tilled otherwise than by compulsion. . . . As no person is found willing and able to repair the ditches and canals for conveyance of water . . . the whole country is badly cultivated and a large part rendered unproductive from want of irrigation." The officials and revenue contractors, who were themselves at the mercy of those in authority over them, held that the state of the land was no concern of theirs and that their business was to " draw from the soil all the money we can, though the peasant should starve or abscond." To-day, at least, when once the *ryot* has paid his appointed share of taxation, of which he is always able to ascertain the exact amount, he has no fear of extortionate demands from tax-farmers or greedy officials in so far as the Englishman in authority can protect him from the relatively

petty greed of subordinate officers and red-coated
menials of his own race.

But the most searching test of all is to compare
the famine records of the Moghul days with those
of our own time. Some reckless critics of the British
raj write as if there had been no famines in India
before British rule. So long as large areas exist in
India as they have always existed and continue to
exist, in which the sowing and the harvesting depend
entirely on the sufficiency of an annual but uncertain
rainfall determined by natural forces beyond all
human control, famines must from time to time
recur of varying intensity and extent. What was,
however, the aggregate of human suffering from
famines under the Moghul rulers then and the
British rulers of India to-day ? It was in the hey-
day of the Moghul Empire that occurred the terrible
famine of 1630–1 which devastated the Deccan
and Gujarat and extended right across India. The
Dutchman, Van Twist, describes all its horrors.

"Men deserted their wives and children. Women
sold themselves as slaves. Some families took
poison and so died together ; others threw themselves into rivers. Mothers and their children went
to the river-bank and drowned themselves hand in
hand so that the rivers flowed full of corpses. Some
eat carrion flesh. Others cut up the corpses of men
and drew out the entrails to fill their own bellies ;
yes, men lying in the street, not yet dead, were cut
up by others, and men fed on living men, so that
even in the streets, and still more on road journeys,
men ran great danger of being murdered and eaten.
. . . This famine lasted throughout the year, and
pestilence and fever followed, so that scarcely a
healthy man could be found. The dead lay
scattered in the streets. Corpses lay for days in
the houses, because men could not be paid to
carry them out. Wood could not be had for

pyres, and unburnt corpses were buried or thrown into the river. May Almighty God protect all Christian lands from such terrible calamities."

We have some more detailed evidence of the general economic effects of the famine in the correspondence of the English factories, notably Surat : "The artisans were abandoning their habitations in multitudes and perishing in the fields. Gold was falling in price because the poor were selling while the rich could not buy ; the yield of indigo in Gujarat was about one-twentieth of the normal, and nothing but old refuse was available in the market ; cotton and yarn were doubled in price ; the roads were unsafe owing to bands of desperate robbers, and even messengers ran risk of being murdered."

The authorities did little or nothing to help. It took several years for nature to restore normal conditions. Aurangzeb, appointed Viceroy of the Western provinces in 1633, was for some time unable to collect enough revenue even to defray local expenditure. In 1645–6 there was an intense famine on the Coromandel coast, and " the people give themselves for slaves to any man that will but feed them," whilst reports from the Madras district state that " all the painters (of Indian muslins) and weavers are dead." In 1647 it was the turn of Rajputana which " either by mortality or by peoples' flight became wholly depopulate." In 1660 famine raged in Sind " the living being hardly able to bury the dead." In 1718 there was famine in Gujarat and children were sold for one or two rupees each. From 1729 to 1733 there was severe scarcity in Southern India. In 1739, in the wake of the invasion of Nadir Shah, famine completed in Northern India the ruin wrought by the Persian armies. Another very severe famine occurred in 1747, not only throughout Gujarat but in a large part of the Deccan, when according to the Padshahee

4

Diwan " not a drop of rain fell nor did a blade of grass grow." The people died in numbers and left their homes to wander from jungle to jungle. This list does not include many other seasons of great scarcity and distress and may be closed with the appalling Bengal famine of 1769–70 which carried away one-third of the population a couple of years before Warren Hastings came out to consolidate the new authority of the East India Company.

There have been terrible famines since then and some of the most terrible within the last thirty years. But the difference is that before British rule the famine-stricken populations were usually left to shift entirely for themselves. To-day there are few if any deaths from actual starvation in the towns and large cities where owing to modern facilities of communication a state of actual famine has ceased to be even conceivable, and with the development of roads and railways few country districts are beyond the reach of some supplies from other parts. The problem to-day is not so much to feed the famine-stricken areas as to provide work for them, and an elaborate organization has been created to deal with it from the moment when the first signs of serious scarcity are reported. Under a carefully-elaborated famine-code relief works are at once taken in hand to give employment to the peasantry so long as no useful work can possibly be done on the parched land, and they are extended in proportion to the magnitude of the calamity, the effects of which are afterwards mitigated by large reductions of taxation or by its entire remission for definite periods.

Were the townspeople better off ? The small artisans and craftsmen, let alone the lower labouring classes were, as we have seen, almost as liable to be decimated by famine as the country-folk. But they could in normal times look for some

protection against oppression to their own guilds
and their caste organizations. The best off were
those attached to the household of persons of rank
or to temples or mosques. They lived from hand to
mouth, but they at least did not tempt the greed
of their social betters as did the middle classes, and
especially those of them who were seen to be more
prosperous, such as traders, shopkeepers and professional men, if the scribes and lawyers and medicine
men of those days can be properly so termed.
Safety lay for them in living inconspicuous lives
even if they were sufficiently successful to afford
themselves greater ease. For to launch out into
any open expenditure meant courting heavier
exactions from their rulers. A very few, chiefly
in the European settlements on the coast and
through foreign trade, amassed great wealth and
wielded great financial power. We hear of one
Virgi Vora as a famous capitalist credited with a
fortune of 80 lakhs of rupees. The East India
Company had to put up with his monopoly of
important markets ; but, though he lived at Surat
where the British had a factory he had to reckon
with the native authorities, and in 1638 he was
seized and thrown into prison. We are left to guess
at the methods by which he propitiated the Moghul
Court when he was summoned to answer the charges
brought against him, but in the end, as was to be
expected of a millionaire, he secured the removal of
the Governor who had arrested him, and he doubtless
saw to it that his further career should not be
seriously hampered.

Of the upper classes, almost exclusively high
State officials, military and civil, whether in the
capital or in the provinces, a very different tale has
to be told. " For," as Pelsart says in a quotation
given by Mr. Moreland in his admirable studies
of the economic conditions in India under the

Moghuls, " the pen which has described bitter poverty . . . wet with daily dew of tears must entirely change its style and tell that in the palaces of these lands dwells all the wealth there is, wealth that glitters indeed, but is borrowed, wrung from the sweat of the poor." Even that wealth was precarious, for they enjoyed it only subject to the favour of their Imperial master. There are ample records of the luxury and magnificence of the Moghul Court. Costly supplies were obtained from great distances. Crowds of menials were maintained for domestic service and for purposes of sport and amusement. When the Emperor was in the field the Imperial camp alone employed between two and three thousand servants. According to the account of the Imperial household in the Ain-i Akbari, it included 5,000 ladies attended and watched by a legion of servants and female guards and eunuchs. The great noblemen emulated the extravagance of the Court. One of them, we are told, employed 500 torch-bearers, and another required 1,000 dishes for his own table. Fashionable poets and musicians and artists and doctors, many of them foreigners, lived on their exalted patrons from whom they received official rank and stipends in cash or endowments in land. Another drain on the Imperial revenue were large grants and assignments made to Mohammedan religious institutions and to the swarms of religious mendicants and ascetics. Even the great Hindu temples also had, under Akbar at least, their share of Imperial benefactions and often accumulated vast wealth which made them tempting objects of plunder under Aurangzeb. Corruption amongst all official classes was rampant and was doubtless held to be justified by the insecurity of public service. The lists of imports in the ledgers of foreign merchants illustrate the futile and often childish extravagances on which the wealthy wasted their substance. Indians of all classes have always spent upon ornaments and jewellery of every kind sums which seem to us to be entirely out of proportion to their income, often, no doubt, because they are a portable form of wealth easy to carry about or to conceal. Never was there a greater profusion of them and especially of precious stones than at the Moghul Court. India's mysterious power to draw in and absorb huge quantities of gold has been noted from ancient times, and one of the principal charges brought in early days against the East India Company by its opponents in England was that the export of bullion by which it was chiefly able to finance the trade of its Indian factories was bleeding England white. Akbar's Court not only consumed large amounts of gold for sumptuary display, but he himself hoarded it to the value of over £40,000,000 which lay idle and yielded nothing to the country, though it was paid for in Indian produce by the sweat of the toiling peasantry. Yet the splendour and extravagance of the Moghul Court and of other Mohammedan Courts were not altogether new in the history of India, and were equalled and even perhaps exceeded at the Hindu Court of Vijayanagar, the last of the great Hindu kingdoms of the south to fall before the sword of Islam.

The drain of military expenditure was on a corresponding scale and far exceeded anything in modern times. The Emperor disposed of all appointments and as the Moghuls were of foreign origin and his Empire was based on conquest it is not surprising to find that a large number were held by foreigners. Much is made nowadays of Akbar's impartiality in the employment of Hindus as well as Mohammedans in the service of the State, but in the course of 40 years he appointed only 21 Hindus altogether to the higher commands. The military career was always the most important, but it remained a precarious one as appointments and promotions and also dismissal depended upon the caprice of the sovereign who was also heir to all his officers. Though they might and sometimes did amass great fortunes they could not when they died pass them on to their sons. Even when they received large jaghirs, or grants of land, that were nominally permanent, their tenure was never really safe, and they preferred to remain at Court as absentee landlords, exploiting their estates to maintain their rank by great and costly establishments and purchasing continued favour by constant attendance on their master.

The fabulous wealth accumulated at the Moghul Court and by the nobles who enjoyed its favour yielded no economic return to the country at large. Most of it evaporated in sheer waste or was consumed in the upkeep of huge armies for wars of conquest and, worse still, for civil wars sometimes between father and son, sometimes between rival heirs to the Empire. Even the famous monuments which still bear witness to the artistic greatness of the Moghul days serve also to illustrate the amazing contrast between the splendour and the havoc of Moghul rule. The Taj Mahal is peerless, but it cost 917 lakhs to build—far more in those days than the £46,000,000 which would be the equivalent in present-day currencies. At Akbar's command a whole city of sandstone and marble palaces sprang up in a few months at Fattipur Sikri as a new royal residence within only a few miles of Agra, then the capital, and was entirely abandoned after barely fifteen years. The Punjab canals afford one of the few instances of works of real public utility, upon which, as a rule, little money was spent except when strategic considerations or the convenience of the Court required the construction of new high roads.

Encouragement was given to the fine arts which attracted the interest or ministered to the entertainment of the upper classes amongst whom medicine, with which astrology was intimately connected, also had generous patrons. The Moghuls prided themselves on their literary taste and some of the Court poets and chroniclers have won enduring celebrity. But there was no organized system of education outside the Mosque schools in which the Koran was learnt by rote. The administration of justice was based on Mohammedan sacred law, tempered under Akbar by the frequent exercise of Imperial clemency and under his successors more often by the usual methods of corruption. Of individual freedom or of justice in the modern sense, there was none. To borrow a metaphor still current throughout the East, the big fish ate up the little ones.

If such was the condition of India when the Moghul Empire was at its apogee and there was a strong central government and a highly organized system of administration of which some of the main features have been preserved down to the present day, it is needless to expatiate on the lot of the Indian peoples during the great Anarchy when the Moghul Empire fell to pieces and Tippu's armies and Afghan invaders and Mahratta soldiers of fortune and roving bands of Pindari marauders spread terror over the country, until British power intervened as the *deus ex machina* that could alone evolve order out of chaos.

CHAPTER IV

THE GOVERNING PRINCIPLES OF BRITISH RULE

In a work concerned chiefly with the results of British rule as we see them to-day in India, there is no room for the wonderful story of its rise except in so far as it illustrates the fundamental principles which have governed British policy.

For more than a century after Queen Elizabeth had granted it a charter for the trade of the Indies, the British East India Company was engaged in a perpetual fight for life. The power of the Portuguese, who had been the first to discover the ocean route to India, had already waned, but the Dutch were making a strong bid for the monopoly of the Eastern trade when the British joined in the struggle, which was waged mainly on the high seas and barely slackened even when peace occasionally prevailed in Europe. Cromwell almost alone among the British rulers of that period recognized in the Indian trade a great national interest and upheld it firmly in his foreign policy. The Company passed through many vicissitudes at home, sometimes exciting the greed of ministers by its financial prosperity, sometimes itself in such acute distress that it had to sue for help from them, and assailed in turn by Court intrigues which favoured high-placed " interlopers " and by popular prejudice which vented upon it the whole fury of the economic quarrels of the time. In language that often sounds singularly modern, its critics alternately denounced its operations as an intolerable drain upon the minted wealth of England, or as an unfair competition with home industries, or as an oppressive restraint on free trade. The Company's existence was more than once in jeopardy, and it was only by a final compromise with its chief rivals at home that it obtained a new and enduring lease of life as the United East India Company under an Act of Parliament which received the Royal Assent from Queen Anne in 1708, the year after the death of the Emperor Aurangzeb marked the beginning of the end of the great Moghul Empire.

In India by that time the English had outlasted both the Portuguese, who of their great possessions have retained little more than Goa, and the Dutch who, though originally far more substantially supported from home than the East India Company, had to withdraw ultimately to the East Indian Archipelago which they still possess. The English came merely as traders and had for a long time no other ambition than to remain as traders and nothing more. Their policy, already foreshadowing that of a later period in a vastly expanded field, was to cultivate friendly relations with the indigenous rulers and especially with the great Moghul on whose favour depended the safety of their small settlements or " factories " precariously scattered on or near the immense line of coast ; at Surat in Western India, at Madras on the Coromandel coast and up the Hoogly river in the Bay of Bengal. Nothing was further from their intentions than to become entangled in the internal affairs of the country or in warlike enterprises. They ran their settlements on rough-and-ready lines of self-government in accordance with the traditions they brought out with them, and encouraged Indians to trade with them by remaining on good terms with their immediate neighbours and making easy regulations for the natives who in increasing numbers flocked into the British settlements to seek under their shelter closer opportunities of trade or permanent refuge from the misrule and insecurity of indigenous government. Sir Josiah Child, whose influence in the councils of the Company during the latter part of the XVIIth century was for many years

paramount, laid it down as an instruction to all its
agents on the spot " that we would have you to be
always most kind and indulgent to the inhabitants
that observe our laws, and protect them in the same
uninterrupted liberty of the several religions in
which they were born and bred as you do those
of our own Church and nation." Every British
" factory " was to be a British stronghold against
outside aggression, but at the same time a patriarchal
state in miniature, affording tolerance and security
to the Indians residing under its protection and
a shining example to those outside the limits of its
jurisdiction. It would be too much to say that
those admirable ideals were always translated into
practice, but they tallied with the material interests
of the Company, and its directors at home seldom
failed to impress upon their agents in India that
trade could only be damaged and perhaps ruined
by political and especially by military adventures.

With the gift of Bombay to the British Crown as
part of the dowry brought by Catherine of Braganza
to Charles II and its transfer to the East India
Company in 1668, the latter for the first time
acquired full rights of rulership on Indian soil. But
its headquarters in Western India remained at Surat
in Moghul territory, and it paid rent to the representatives of the Moghul Emperor for its settlements
on the Hoogly, and for Madras as well when
Aurangzeb made himself for a short time master of
Southern India. The Company's hands were forced
when the Moghul Empire began to disintegrate on
the death of Aurangzeb in 1707, and the aggressive
action of the French East India Company directly
involved India in the long struggle between France
and England for naval and colonial supremacy,
which began under Louis XIV and lasted till
Trafalgar. In the XVIIIth century that duel was
as fiercely fought out in the Indian Ocean and on the

Indian continent as in the Atlantic and in North America. The Company's policy of non-interference in the internal affairs of India was dictated by an intelligent appreciation of the interests of trade, and it adhered to it so long as trade could be carried on under reasonable conditions of security. Those conditions ceased to exist when France attempted to drive the Company lock, stock and barrel out of India, and the decay of the Moghul Empire led to violent and widespread upheavals which threatened the Company with slower but equally certain ruin. India was relapsing into one of those periods of internal strife and anarchy which throughout her history have always followed the collapse of any great controlling power capable for a time of holding the internal elements of discord in check, and the Company with its immense interests in jeopardy could see no other alternative but to take an active part in grave events to which it could no longer safely remain indifferent. It began to seek alliances amongst the rival Indian factions, and to raise forces which would make its alliance worth having. Fortunately for the Company the new departure was forced upon it only after it had been reconstituted on a more solid basis at home, and when it could rely with increasing confidence upon substantial support from the Mother country. The East India trade had grown to be recognized at home as a national asset which England could not afford to lose. At the critical moment British fleets and British troops were sent out to stiffen the Company's local forces, raised after the example set by the French under Dupleix and even further back by the early Portuguese conquerors, and to co-operate with the native armies of its Indian Allies. Then, even more than now, the fighting value of Indian troops depended largely upon a British co-efficient. The fate of India was settled as between

England and France by British naval power, but on the Indian continent by the battle of Plassey in 1757, and more decisively still by the battle of Buxar in 1764. In both those battles only ten per cent of the Company's army were British soldiers, but they were its backbone.

The beginning of British dominion has been commonly held to date from Plassey. It was there that British military supremacy was established by the signal fighting superiority of the British soldier and the co-ordination of British and native troops, which was to develop into the present system, *i.e.*, a regular Indian Army with a portion of the British Army always stationed in India behind it. But towards paramount political power the first great stride was only made after Buxar, when, in the distracted state of the Moghul Empire, the Emperor Shah Alam was driven to take refuge with the East India Company, and agreed to purchase its protection by surrendering to it the Diwanee, or financial administration, of the wealthy Gangetic provinces of Bengal, Behar and Orissa and of the northern Circars. Clive, fully conscious of the magnitude of the task devolved on to the Company, advised the immediate assumption by the Crown of full and direct rights of government over all British possessions in India, and did so admittedly because he held a mere trading corporation to be ill-fitted to discharge such immense responsibilities. That advice was not to be followed until just a century later, but the British people realized that Clive had had good reasons for giving it when from the newly-acquired Diwanee provinces there came the wretched story that constantly repeats itself in history whenever power is divorced from responsibility. The British servants of the Company had always been traders first and foremost, and free to trade partly for their own benefit as well as for the

Company's. They found themselves all at once invested with almost absolute power, but without any definite duties or responsibilities except the collection of revenue. With none of the traditions and experience of administration on a large scale behind them, the temptation to misuse their unlimited opportunities was overwhelming. Ready to their hand were all the old agencies of native government of the worst type, versed in its time-honoured methods of oppression and corruption, and the new masters asked no questions so long as the Company's exchequer and their own pockets were abundantly filled. Ugly reports filtered home, and whilst the magnitude of the financial transactions between the Company and British Ministers aroused the politicians' suspicions, the vast fortunes which many of the Company's servants brought back from India to spend in ostentatious luxury or in the purchase of rotten boroughs set people talking and gradually alarmed the public conscience.

The horizon of the British people was broadening. Englishmen had attained much sooner than their Continental neighbours to a general conception of personal rights and civic freedom as the basis of national life, and they had with some measure of success imposed the rule of law, which associates responsibility with power, upon their own rulers after a long struggle of which the Commonwealth and the Revolution of 1688 were great episodes still relatively recent. With the growth of British possessions beyond the seas they came to realize that the rule of law applied equally, if in a different form, to the distant dominions brought under their sway. The motives which prompted English colonial enterprise in its earlier days had not materially differed from those which prompted our chief European competitors. We and they had all been driven to explore remote continents and untravelled seas in quest of wealth. Some had looked for it chiefly in the conquest of vast territories which they drained of all their natural riches in silver and gold, and whose inhabitants they ruthlessly exploited. We had chiefly sought it, and especially in India, in the development of trade, and, by the middle of the XVIIIth century when the protection of our trade in the peculiar circumstances of India had led Englishmen to assume far-reaching rights of government, we were learning almost instinctively that, even in dealing with remote and alien peoples, power could not be dissociated from responsibility, and that the rights which we claimed in virtue of our higher civilization involved also duties to be discharged.

It was in this spirit that by Lord North's Regulating Act of 1773 the British Parliament for the first time interfered directly in the system of administration hastily set up by the East India Company in its sudden transition from a mere trading corporation to almost absolute rulership. But North's Act was a warning to the Company to put its house in order rather than an attempt to establish any direct and permanent control over it. This was not done until eleven years later under Pitt's Government of India Act when the lessons of responsibility had been driven home by the loss of our North American Colonies, albeit the problems of American colonial government had differed very widely from those with which the rise of British dominion was confronting us in India. Whilst George III's obstinacy and the short-sighted policy of British Ministers had cost us the great position which our armies and fleets had won for us from France in North America, the genius of Warren Hastings had redressed the balance for us in India where Dupleix's dreams of a French Empire had been shattered and the Moghul Empire itself was falling to pieces. Hastings had done more than that.

Clive had initiated important reforms before he left
India, and Hastings when he succeeded him carried
them very much further. In the spirit of Lord
North's Regulating Act, he put the Company's
house in order. Far-sighted and an indefatigable
worker, he laid the foundations of the system of
judicial and civil administration which, whilst
retaining as far as possible the old indigenous framework, enforced new standards of integrity and
efficiency that have been maintained in the Indian
Public Services to the present day. But in his
dealings with native rulers he had laid himself
open at times to the attacks of many formidable
enemies, and when he returned to England he was
indicted before the House of Lords on a long series
of charges of " high crimes and misdemeanours,"
of which he only cleared himself after the terrible
ordeal of a seven years' trial, borne with great
fortitude and dignity. The attacks directed against
him were largely but not exclusively inspired by
personal animosity and political partisanship. It
was his misfortune that he was made to suffer as
a scapegoat for a shameful, though a relatively
short, period of gross misrule which he had himself
done wonders to amend. Public opinion, if misdirected and undiscriminating, was moved on the
whole by a healthy determination to strike once for
all at an arbitrary and irresponsible system which on
the very threshold of a new era had allowed the
gravest abuses to stain the British name and the
Company's honourable record in India. Only later
on was it realized that the Government of India
Act of 1784, already passed into law four years
before Hastings' trial began, had in fact been a
solemn consecration of reforms which he had himself
inaugurated. It contained careful and drastic
provisions for the prevention and punishment of
corruption and oppression amongst the Company's

servants and it guarded against the recurrence of abuses which Hastings had already put down. It did not go to the full length of Clive's advice that the Crown should at once assume direct responsibility for the government of its Indian possessions, but it brought the Crown for the first time into close relationship with them. For it transferred from the Company to the Crown the right to appoint the Governor-General and immensely strengthened his position; whilst the Company was placed under effective restraints in London by the creation of a Board of Control, of which the President was ultimately to develop into the Secretary of State for India, over the Courts of Directors and Proprietors.

In Pitt's Act the British Parliament assumed the responsibility for the welfare and advancement of the people of India which is still reserved to it under the Act of 1919. The guiding principle which it introduced is not however specifically stated in the terms of that Act; but Burke had already enunciated it the year before in his great speech on Fox's abortive Bill when he declared that " all political power which is set over men . . . ought to be in some way or other exercised ultimately for their benefit," and that the rights and privileges derived therefrom " are all in the strictest sense a trust." " It is," he went on to say, " of the very essence of a trust to be rendered accountable. . . . To whom then would I make the East India Company accountable? Why, to Parliament, to be sure; to Parliament which alone is capable of comprehending the magnitude of its object and its abuse; and alone capable of effective legislative remedy." (Burke's Speech, December 1, 1773.) Fox's Bill fell through for reasons of purely domestic policy, and Pitt's Bill which passed through both Houses of Parliament in 1784 placed the Government of India under their unquestionable control as a great British trust to be exercised in accordance with the principle for the first time publicly laid down by Burke as the " magna charta " of India, and in the spirit, as his words clearly implied, of the Magna Charta which the British people had learnt long ago to cherish as the bulwark of their rights. It set before the world the principle of trusteeship as the governing rule in the relations between stronger and more advanced nations and the weaker and more backward over whom they assume authority. From that principle, the British people, in spite of many human shortcomings in its interpretation and application, have never deliberately departed in India, and they have endeavoured to apply it, though sometimes less thoroughly, in their other Asiatic and African possessions. All civilized nations have now learnt to pay homage to it and it stands enshrined to-day in Article 22 of the Covenant of the League of Nations.

One important limitation must, however, be noted. The principle of trusteeship can only be fully applied to that part of India which is under direct British administration, and in the subsequent expansion of British dominion a distinction arose which neither Pitt nor the British Parliament could foresee when the great Act of 1784 was framed. A policy of further expansion was not then contemplated either by the British Government or the East India Company. There were in fact special provisions in Pitt's Act to prevent the Governor-General from engaging in operations or entering into engagements which might lead to such expansion. But no statutory prescription could arrest the disturbing activities of lawless forces outside British India. They could only be suppressed by the extension of full British authority. In order to avoid as far as possible any additions to the areas under the Company's direct government and administration, resort was had to a system of alliances with the neighbouring "country states," by which it was hoped to surround British territory with a ring-fence of friendly states without having to assume any responsibility for their internal administration. But such a policy, though it looked well at a distance and was only reluctantly abandoned in London, proved unworkable, as the alliances themselves tended to involve the paramount Power in the quarrels of its allies with their more unruly neighbours, and there were still powerful forces ready to challenge British ascendancy rather than abandon ambitions which could only be fulfilled by war. One need only mention the Hindu Mahrattas in Western India and the Mohammedan Tippu Saheb in Mysore. There was no escape from the conclusion that peace and order would only prevail when the whole or very nearly the whole of India had been brought to accept the supremacy of the British power. But if this was not to involve a wholesale extension of direct British rule by force of arms, the only way was to preserve the administrative autonomy of all the Native States that were already in alliance with the British power or were ready to enter into similar or even closer relations with it. This policy was for the first time carried out systematically about a century ago in the series of treaties between the Government of India and the Rajput States who saw their only defence against Mahratta aggression in seeking British protection. The earlier treaties of alliance with Native States—as, for instance, the Treaty of 1800 with the Nizam of Hyderabad, who had already cut himself loose from the moribund Moghul Empire—had, at least, implied equality between the contracting parties, and the Indian Princes who signed them were treated as independent rulers. Under the new system which postulated the definite overlordship of the Supreme

Government, the rulers of the Native States were confirmed in their hereditary rights and, to a greater or lesser extent, in their administrative autonomy ; but they had in return to surrender some of the attributes of sovereignty, such as the conduct of independent foreign relations and the maintenance of armed forces at their own discretion, and to acknowledge definite obligations towards the British sovereign power, amongst others that of conforming their methods of rulership to such standards of humanity and decency as even conservative Indian opinion required. Treaties on similar lines were in turn concluded with the principal Mahratta and Sikh chiefs who thus escaped extinction when the power of the Mahratta and of the Sikh confederacy was successively broken. The alliances to which the Native States thereby subscribed were no longer alliances between equal powers, but subordinate alliances of which the implications tended at one time to stretch beyond the provisions formally embodied in them. The stern application by Lord Dalhousie of the doctrine of lapse by which Native States escheated to the Supreme Government on the death of a ruler without natural heirs, and his annexation of the kingdom of Oudh, though he justified it on the very strong ground that " the British Government would be guilty in the sight of God and man if it were any longer to aid in sustaining by its countenance an administration fraught with suffering to millions," created much alarm amongst the rulers of other Native States and were contributory causes of the Mutiny. But confidence was restored when, in her famous Proclamation of 1858, Queen Victoria, on assuming for the Crown full and direct responsibility for the government and administration of India, solemnly confirmed all the treaties contracted with Native States under Company rule.

The effect of this policy has been to divide up India into two parts in which the power as well as the responsibility of the Supreme Government differs very widely. There is British India, properly so-called, under direct British administration, and there are the Native States of India under the direct administration of their rulers. The relations between the Native States and the Supreme Government are officially conducted through the Indian Foreign Office, a department of which the Viceroy reserves entire charge for himself. On important matters he corresponds direct with the principal rulers, and, so long as the Supreme Government really represents the British Crown, his authority suffices to secure the adjustment of all the minor differences which may arise from time to time between British India and the authorities of a Native State. In matters in which All-India interests are concerned, such as railways and posts and telegraphs and customs, the special interests of the Native States are as far as possible taken into consideration, but they must yield when necessary to the larger interests of India as a whole. Whilst respecting whatever measure of autonomy has been assured to each Native State by Treaties and agreements, the Government of India exercises through its Agents and Residents some supervision over their methods of administration, but only steps in with remonstrances, and ultimately with sterner measures, if misrule assumes dangerous or intolerable proportions. So long as the ruling princes and chiefs loyally discharge their Treaty obligations they enjoy an official status of recognized dignity graduated in due proportion to their importance, and in late years increasing weight has been given to their opinions and wishes individually and collectively in the councils of Government both in India and at home. They had their own representatives in the Imperial War Councils held in London during the War, and at the Paris Peace Conference, and since then at the annual meeting of the League of Nations of which India is an original member. Further recognition has been given to the peculiar position they occupy by the creation of a Chamber of Princes, in order to bring the Native States into corporate association, however loose, with the Government of India, and to enable their rulers to take counsel together on matters affecting their common interests. But the Native States remain outside the constitutional charter granted by Parliament to British India under the Act of 1919, as it is only for that part of India which is under direct British administration that Parliament can thus legislate.

The merest glance at the map of India suffices to see how large a place on it is occupied by the Native States and in what different proportions they are scattered about as a result of the various historical circumstances to which they owe their preservation. They cover in the aggregate more than a third of the total area of India and their population only falls a little short of a quarter of the total population. There are about 700 of them altogether, counting the very smallest, but not more than 20 or 30 are of major importance. Hyderabad claims the position of the premier Native State in virtue of its size and population and its ancient ties of friendship with the British in the XVIIIth century, and a few others, *e.g.*, Travancore and Mysore in the extreme south and Gwalior and Baroda and Indore in Central India, might in many respects rank with, or little below, some of the minor states of Europe. Distributed somewhat irregularly over the whole peninsula they display as many varieties of creeds and castes and languages and customs as the provinces of British India, and they also are in many different stages of social and political evolution. Except in a few cases where some little approach has been made to the representative

institutions introduced into British India, their
rulers are autocrats of the old Oriental type, some
of them of another race and creed than their subjects.
The Nizam of Hyderabad is a Mohammedan, the
vast majority of his subjects are Hindus. The
Maharajah of Kashmir is a very orthodox Hindu,
whilst his subjects are mostly Mohammedans. The
rulers of Gwalior, Baroda and Indore are Mahrattas,
but few of their subjects are of that race. The whole
level of administration is generally lower and less
efficient in the Native States, and, except in Baroda,
education, and especially Western education, is less
advanced. None of them, except perhaps Kashmir,
can cut itself off from the stream of modern life
but there are very few if any in which it runs nearly
as freely as in British India.

In the preservation of the Native States with the
very large measure of internal autonomy which
most of them enjoy, the British rulers of India have
demonstrated their desire to maintain wherever
they could the forms of government to which their
peoples had been accustomed and grown attached.
But from the administrative point of view it has
often proved embarrassing, and it must inevitably
tend to produce grave political difficulties, of which
there has been already a foretaste within the last
few years, if British India develops on democratic
lines whilst Native States remain as mediæval as
some of them still are. Interpreting in the generous
spirit generated for a time by the Great War the trust
assumed as far back as 1784, the British Parliament
enacted in 1919 a great measure of Indian reforms.
But they operate only in British India. They are
inoperative in the Native States. Such are the
invisible walls that divide the two.

In these two distinct parts of the Indian
Empire, the principle of trusteeship laid down by
Parliament 140 years ago cannot be applied

in the same degree. In British India, which we administer, success and failure are of our own making. But in the Native States, which are not under our direct administration, British authority can only make itself indirectly felt. In the latter, our Treaty obligations have made us trustees for the rights of the hereditary rulers whom British rule found and left in possession. That trust, though the consequences could not be foreseen when the Treaties from which it still derives were concluded with the Native States for another purpose altogether, the British rulers of India can claim to have on the whole honourably discharged, and, indirectly at least, to the benefit of the peoples of the Native States themselves. But no one acquainted with the conditions that exist in most of the Native States can wish for an extension of the system, and only in very rare cases are there the requisite materials for its extension. If at the present day they are not already anachronisms which are bound to disappear, should India ever become a really united nation, they are survivals from a bygone phase of Indian history, and survivals may be preserved but cannot be created.

CHAPTER V

THE FLOWING TIDE OF WESTERN INFLUENCE

OF all the forces that under British rule have helped to mould the India of to-day the greatest is unquestionably Western education, and its introduction into India has been our greatest endeavour to give effect to the principle of British trusteeship for the moral as well as the material advancement of India. For when or how has a ruling race ever shown greater faith in its own civilization than by seeking to raise on to its higher plane the peoples of a remote dependency brought under subjection to it, as the pioneers of Western education in India for the most part firmly believed, by the working of the superior Power that shapes the destinies of mankind ? What other issue has been approached by Englishmen in India with a deeper sense of responsibility ? They all worked towards the same goal, though from different angles of vision. Clive, Warren Hastings, Cornwallis, successively faced with the huge task of building up a reformed administration for the vast territories which were rapidly passing under the East India Company's control, looked chiefly to the better training of young Indians for administrative work. The great missionaries who played a leading part in the educational movement, the Serampore trio, Carey, Marshman and Ward, and the dour Scotsman, Alexander Duff, whose influence was, perhaps, greatest of all, saw in the introduction of Western education an unparalleled opportunity of extending the Kingdom of Christ. A more secular school put its trust in the broad cultural enlightenment that would proceed from Western learning. As to whether English or the languages of India, and if the latter, which of them, would be the best vehicle for its diffusion, a fierce controversy raged for many years before

Macaulay's vigorous Minute of February 2, 1835, irrevocably closed it in favour of English. Even then, however, few of the "Western" school contemplated such neglect of the vernacular as subsequently occurred, with the disastrous result that higher education has remained top-heavy because it has always lacked the solid foundation provided by a broad system of popular education.

That there is a spiritual side to the ancient civilization of India and that it was grossly under-rated by some of the pioneers of Western education, there is no need to deny; but it is equally undeniable that it was then at a singularly low ebb. It was to the West that some of the most spiritually-minded Hindus of that period first turned for a new inspiration when a small band of enlightened Hindus, some of them Brahmans, opened on their own initiative a Hindu College for Western learning in Calcutta, where agnosticism carried the reaction against all the restraints of their ancient faith to dangerous lengths before it came under Duff's evangelizing influence.   It was Hindus who thronged the first English school opened by Duff himself in Calcutta in 1830, and Duff had no more ardent supporter in the campaign for English education than the great Hindu, Rajah Ram Mohun Roy, who, as far back as 1780, had ventured to launch a vigorous attack on "the idolatrous system of Hinduism," and was profoundly imbued with the spirit of Christianity though there is no definite evidence that he ever embraced its doctrines.   Others, including Brahmans, publicly professed the Christian faith, and many more who did not were none the less sincere converts to Western learning.   From the latter were born the great movements of social and religious reform which were carried on the tide of Western education to all the chief centres of intellectual life in India before the first half of the century was over.

They for the most part originated in Bengal where Western influences were at first strongest. They still survive there most conspicuously in the Brahmo Samaj, a theistic church of which the members repudiate idolatry and generally speaking caste as well as infant marriage, and condemn the perpetual widowhood to which Hindu widows and even virgin widows are doomed. Ram Mohun Roy was its founder, but he had a scarcely less distinguished successor in Keshab Chundra Sen, who carried on his work into the latter part of the XIXth century. Like them, their followers were reluctant to cut themselves entirely adrift from Hinduism, but they were not less deeply impressed with the ethics of Christianity to which they did not hesitate to attribute the acknowledged superiority of Western civilization. The Brahmo Samaj has passed through many vicissitudes and its numbers, always small, have tended to shrink during the last few decades, but its influence spread from Bengal into every other part of India where Western education struck its strongest roots.

Not less close than in Calcutta was the co-operation between the great British administrators in other provinces and those who were engaged in the actual work of education. Lord William Bentinck, who was Governor-General from 1830 to 1835, took the lead in the capital of the premier Presidency. But there were others who shared and even anticipated his views. Two Minutes written in the same year, 1824, by Sir Thomas Munro, Governor of Madras, and Mountstuart Elphinstone, Governor of Bombay, are landmarks on the road of Western education as an essential part of England's mission in India. Munro had already two years previously instituted an inquiry into the whole subject of education, and initiated a movement which took shape, but not till a good many years later, in the General Assembly's

School, subsequently the famous Madras Christian College under the Rev. John Anderson, the pioneer of educational work in the South of India, though it was then and indeed still is a stronghold of orthodox Hinduism. In Western India where the Prirthana Samaj was founded on somewhat different lines from the Brahmo Samaj but, like it, under the auspices of many high-caste Hindus seeking enlightenment from the West, it was Elphinstone who gave an even more vigorous impulse to higher education by starting at Poona, as soon as the Mahratta power was broken, the college which has grown into the Deccan College, whilst in Bombay another college bearing his name remains the finest tribute which he would have desired to his memory.

Some Englishmen to-day contend that the introduction of Western education was a crucial blunder to which alone we owe the growth of Indian unrest and Indian Nationalism and the *Swaraj* movement and every other manifestation of Indian discontent. They are men of little faith, and not by such was British rule built up in India. But it may be conceded that many of the warmest advocates, the British pioneers of Western education, did not and could not foresee all the fruits that it would yield. Some of them indulged in hopes that went very far beyond the mark, and none more than Macaulay himself who predicted that within a few generations there would be nothing to distinguish a Western-educated Indian from an Englishman except his dusky complexion. But none also was more willing to look the consequences in the face should Western education train up an Indian nation capable of ruling itself. If that was a contingency with which we have to reckon, he, for one, could contemplate it without dismay, for then England's mission in India would be gloriously consummated, and she would hand back to the people of India the control of her destinies with legitimate pride in an unparalleled achievement. The case, of course, presented itself merely hypothetically to Macaulay and his contemporaries and in a shape quite dissimilar to that which it now threatens to assume. But it might perhaps have presented itself very differently to-day if their successors had always lived up to the fine spirit in which a great generation of Englishmen approached the task that lay before England in India. Whatever was the particular work on which they were engaged, whether judicial or land revenue or social reforms, they displayed the same single-minded zeal for the betterment of the Indian people and the same painstaking anxiety to understand their ancient customs and preserve all that was best in them because they were convinced that, as Munro wrote just a hundred years ago when Governor of Madras, it was England's mission to train the Indians to govern and protect themselves.

Equally characteristic of that period was the response of Indians to the confidence displayed towards them. Duff, like many of the best missionaries of the present day, saw in medical work amongst Indians the surest means of breaking down the barriers of ignorance and prejudice, and the Medical College at Calcutta, now one of the largest in the world, of which he witnessed the opening in 1835, is a lasting monument to his labours in that field. When he found the orthodox Hindu pundits of Benares prepared to declare it lawful for Brahman students of medicine to handle and dissect corpses for anatomical purposes without losing caste, there seemed to be reasonable grounds for hoping that Western education would gradually sweep away all other caste prejudices, and that the influence of the great Brahmanical caste which had moulded popular beliefs and customs from times immemorial might yet be enlisted on the side of Western progress.

Just as encouraging was the support steadily given by many influential Hindus to Lord William Bentinck's courageous action in decreeing the abolition of *Sati*, though the self-immolation of widows was a practice hallowed by ancient traditions, if not actually enjoined upon Hindus as a religious duty, and still so widespread that no less than 700 widows had been burnt alive in one year and in the one province of Bengal. There was scarcely even a murmur but rather a general sense of relief when Thuggism was stamped out, though its murderous rites were placed under the special patronage of the great goddess, Kali.

Throughout the first half of the XIXth century Englishmen and Indians lived in many ways much further apart than they do now, but their relations were free from many of the complications that have resulted from modern conditions of life and the growth of racial feeling on both sides. The relations between a ruling and a subject-race must always be difficult especially when, as in the case of India, there is so much else to divide them besides the nature of their political relationship. But not until more than a hundred years after British rule had been established, and then not primarily against Indians, did the white man set up the colour of men's skins as the great dividing-line between the peoples of the earth. The colour-feeling is very largely a modern growth and the French and most of the nations of Southern Europe are still on the whole free from it. It is strongest amongst the English-speaking peoples of the Old World and the New. It has grown upon Englishmen with the expansion of an Empire in which the coloured races preponderate over the white race in the proportion of seven to one, and nowhere is it quite so strong as in those parts of our oversea Empire in which the climate allows Englishmen to settle and make permanent homes for themselves, and at the same time to acquire land and create great industrial interests, of which the development largely depends upon the cheap labour of a coloured population.

For climatic, besides other reasons, India is never likely to have any large permanent white population, and until late in the XIXth century there were very few signs of any such colour-feeling amongst the English in India or of any deep racial antagonism to the white man, as such, on the part of the Indians. Even mixed marriages from which several well-known families have sprung, and other unions more irregular and temporary, were much less infrequent than they are now. To that period dates back a large proportion of the existing community of mixed descent, which was for a long time called Eurasian, but is now officially designated as Anglo-Indian, though with many other strains of European blood besides English. It numbers only 113,000, and, whilst not a few have striven hard and successfully to live up to the best standards of the European ancestry on which they rather pathetically pride themselves, its position as a community grows increasingly painful and precarious, for, like the proverbial poor relations, it gets little sympathy from the white race to whose coat-tails it makes desperate efforts to cling, and none at all from the Indians who resent its claims to any sort of racial superiority far more than they do those of the pure-blooded Englishman.

British rule, in its beginning, had this in its favour to ease relations with the subject race, that, unlike, for instance, Mohammedan domination, it had not been imposed on India by brutal wars of invasion and sheer lust of conquest. It had sometimes been promoted by methods which we should have to reprobate to-day, but on the whole it had been established quite as much with Indian consent, and often at Indian solicitation, as by British arms; and in almost every war waged for its consolidation and extension the British had had as many Indians fighting on their side as against them. Nor had the British, when they became the masters of India, behaved as conquerors usually behaved in Asia. They respected the customs of the people, tried to understand their needs and gave the humblest folk a new sense of security from arbitrary oppression and a new conception of justice as a boon that was to be neither bought nor sold. They reassured the well-to-do classes by recognizing established rights of property and especially those of the great native landlords, though they erred sometimes through ignorance, as when Cornwallis made the permanent land settlement of Bengal. The still greater ignorance displayed by Macaulay's scathing gibes, not only at Hindu mythology but at all Oriental literature, must have deeply wounded many grave and reverend pundits; but they could find abundant compensation in the sympathy and understanding of the much larger company of Englishmen, often great administrators or missionaries, who threw themselves heart and soul into the study of Indian languages and ancient learning. It was Englishmen in India, Sir William Jones, the first translator of *The Laws of Manu* as well as of *Sakuntala*, the finest of Indian dramas; Colebrook, who continued his work and wrote the first *Sanskrit Grammar*; Charles Wilkins, who translated the *Baghavatghita*; Carey, who was the first English teacher of Sanskrit at the College of Fort William, though the Bengalee vernacular was, perhaps, nearer his heart; H. H. Wilson, who published the first *Sanskrit Grammar*; Tod, the immortal author of the *Annals of Rajasthan*—it was these and many others who blazed the trail for Max Müller and Monier Williams and Roth and Sassen and Burnouf and the great host of European scholars who have revealed to India herself scarcely less than to the Western world the majesty and wealth of the Sanskrit language and its kinship with the whole group of European languages now designated as Indo-European, and the historical as well as literary value of the great body of Hindu literature which is the key to India's civilization.

Dislike and distrust of Western education were not always easy to overcome, but there often grew up between Indian pupils and European teachers a relationship of respect and affection not unlike that which bound the *chela* to his *guru* under the old Hindu dispensation. The Englishman who went out to India in those earlier days to play his part in ruling the country, usually showed the qualities rather than the defects of a class that, whatever its human weaknesses, had been brought up to believe that *noblesse oblige* ; and he sought to act up to that maxim by comporting himself as a Christian and a gentleman towards people of a race less fortunately situated than his own, though very different habits of life discouraged any intimate social intercourse. It was by this type of Englishman that the up-country Indian who, as he seldom if ever travelled and therefore never knew any other, chiefly judged the ruling race. The number of Englishmen in India was very small. Only in the big cities, mostly on or near the coast, did the Indian often rub shoulders with the British merchant as he had learnt to do for a good many generations past when the British settlement was merely a trading settlement.

In England the periodical inquiries held by Parliament into the state of India before every renewal of the Company's Charter kept alive the national sense of responsibility which has found expression in the Act of 1784. When the Charter was renewed in 1833, Parliament laid it down emphatically that "no native of the said Indian territories shall by reason only of his religion, place of birth, descent, colour, or any of them be disabled from holding any place, office or employment under the Company"; for the Committee of Enquiry had reported that "such exclusion is not warranted on the score of their own incapacity or the want of application or trustworthiness," and had strongly recommended their employment to the largest possible extent in Indian administrative work. The number of young Indians trained in the new system of Western education was still small, but many of them showed that as far as brains were concerned they were quite capable of competing with any European stock; and the best at once passed into Government employment, and, if still employed only in a subordinate capacity, they could count upon the same encouragement from their British superiors as they had received in the new schools and colleges from Western teachers, who still looked upon their work as a vocation rather than a profession, and could still keep in personal touch with their pupils. The future was yet to show what formidable reactionary forces were already working beneath the surface of India's submissive acceptance of British rule. But just before the Mutiny a great scheme had been worked out for the reorganization of the educational system and its extension to the humbler classes, whom it had not yet touched; and it had begun to receive execution when Lord Dalhousie, the last and greatest of the Governors-General to complete his period of office under the East India Company, left India in 1856. The storm cloud on the Indian horizon was then "no bigger than a man's hand." The exhaustive dispatch in which he reviewed the work done in India in every branch of the administration under his indefatigable impulse was a record not only of splendid achievement in the past, but

of splendid hope in the future. None was more
keenly alive than that indomitable Scotsman, constantly racked but never conquered by illness, to
the deep moral responsibilities of British rule.
Hence his faith in education as the greatest agency
for furthering the advancement of India, and if he
took special pride in having introduced into India
the two great discoveries which were revolutionizing
the Western world, railways and telegraphs, it was
because, besides their economic value, he saw in them
powerful instruments of education. The promise
which he was able to make of further facilities for
the higher education of Indians and of Universities
to be shortly created in each of the three Presidency
cities seemed to be the crowning consummation of
a great period in which men of the intellectual and
moral elevation of Bentinck and Munro and Elphinstone and Thomason and Dalhousie himself humbly
but firmly believed that in trying to found " British
greatness on Indian happiness," and in seeking to
associate in the accomplishment of that task the
intellectual élite of India, trained in the new Western
schools, they were carrying out a lofty mission
entrusted by Providence to the British people.

A fine Puritan spirit was strong, too, in the
Lawrences, in John Nicholson, in Herbert Edwardes,
and in many other of the stout fighters who put
down the Mutiny, which was the first great revolt
of the old India against the modern West ; though
only dimly discerned at the time beneath the surface
of a fierce military uprising for which the blunder
of the greased cartridges seemed to afford an
adequate explanation. It was confined within a
relatively small area, and in the end completely
crushed, but only after a stubborn struggle in which
the savage excesses committed by the mutineers
and the stern repression exercised by the British
left bitter memories behind them on both sides.

The whole atmosphere of mutual confidence and goodwill which had been growing up between the two races for half a century had been rudely disturbed, though the effect was not at once apparent.

The transfer of India to the Crown was followed by a long period of internal tranquility and material progress. The disappearance of the old East India Company produced no radical change in the machinery or methods of government. The Indian's reliance on the Englishman's integrity and sense of justice was unshaken. The Collector or principal executive officer, in charge sometimes of several millions of simple tillers of the soil, remained the pivot of the administration, and his devotion to their welfare, never more conspicuous than in times of acute distress from famine and pestilence, continued to earn for him the affectionate nickname of *Ma-bap*, or " father and mother " of his people. But the increasing complexity of Indian administration and the specialization of work in separate departments to meet the growing needs of Indian development led by degrees to excessive centralization in the Provincial and Central Government Secretariats, and these developed the usual tendency of all powerful bureaucracies to believe in their own infallibility and to regard departmental efficiency as the sole test of good government. The first signs of change manifested themselves in the relations between this growing bureaucracy and the Western-educated Indians, a class that was more than any other the direct offspring of British rule. The demand for Western education was greater than ever, but its fine edge was growing blunt and it was tending to lose in quality what it gained in quantity or output. It was ceasing also to produce as ready and general an acceptance of Western tutelage as in the early days. No race has been so successful as the British in ruling primitive and backward peoples who do not aspire to equality, but are content, as children are, to be treated in the spirit of kindliness and fair play which most Englishmen possess. But the Englishman is apt to grow impatient when those whom his tutelage has raised begin to chafe under it and to demand emancipation from his leading-strings. It was something of this change of temper that went on in India when from the schools and colleges which we had ourselves set up there emerged a new class of Indians who ventured not only to criticize the Englishmen who ruled them, but to declare that they could now perfectly well rule themselves. As a first step they agitated for a larger and more influential share in the administration. In Queen Victoria's generous Proclamation of 1858 when she assumed " the Government of the territories in India hitherto administered in trust for us by the ' Honourable East India Company'" she reiterated the assurance that had been given by Parliament in 1833, and pledged her Royal word that "as far as may be" her subjects " of whatever creed or race " would be freely and impartially admitted to offices in the service of the Crown. But the years continued to pass without bringing Indians the increased share of public appointments to which in their opinion their educational qualifications now fully entitled them. Disappointment had already become acute when under Lord Lytton's Viceroyalty the first Royal visit paid to India by the then Prince of Wales (afterwards King Edward VII) in 1876, which produced great demonstrations of Indian loyalty, and in the following year the assumption by Queen Victoria of the title of Empress of India, in 1877, as a definite symbol of India's great position in the British Empire were followed, not, as the educated classes expected, by progressive measures for giving

them a larger share in the government and administration of their country; but by repressive enactments for dealing with "seditious" utterances in the
Press and on the platform, often merely re-echoing
the fierce Parliamentary attacks at home on Disraeli's
Indian policy and Afghan wars. That there was
some excuse for that sense of disappointment may
be gathered from Lord Lytton's own quite cynical
confession in a document, which was certainly not
intended to receive publicity in India. Referring
to the claims and expectations based by Indians on
the pledges given in the Queen's Proclamation,
Lord Lytton wrote :

"We all know that these claims and expectations never can or will be fulfilled. We have to
choose between prohibiting them and cheating
them, and we have chosen the least straightforward
course. . . . Since I am writing confidentially,
I do not hesitate to say that both the Government
of England and of India appear to me up to the
present moment unable to answer satisfactorily
the charge of having taken every means in their
power of breaking to the heart the words of
promise they had uttered to the ear."

But when Lord Lytton resigned, after the defeat
of Lord Beaconsfield's administration in 1879, he
was succeeded by Lord Ripon, whose sympathy for
Indian aspirations was unconcealed. He was the
nominee of a Liberal Government in England, and
Indian hopes revived, but only to be dashed
again during the heated controversies over the
Ilbert Bill, when the fierce and almost mutinous opposition of the great majority of Englishmen in
India, whether belonging to the official or the non-
official classes, defeated a Liberal Viceroy who had
behind him a Liberal British Cabinet backed by a
large Liberal majority in the British Parliament,
and compelled him to whittle down almost past

recognition a legislative measure which, though not of first-class importance in itself, was intended to remove certain racial inequalities of judicial procedure. It overshadowed all other questions, for it raised the racial issue as a matter of principle on a point on which Indian feeling was most sensitive, as it was connected with the administration of justice, and it was treated on both sides, and not least on the British side, in such a passionately racial spirit as had never been displayed in India before, except during the short spasm of the Mutiny. It was a writing on the wall.

Not only Western education but vastly increased facilities of travel and much more frequent opportunities of intercourse were affecting the general attitude of Indians towards Englishmen even before that disastrous incident which was deeply resented not only by the younger, but the older generation of educated Indians. Amongst the latter were many of good position who, through frequent visits to England, had acquired a Western outlook and a fairly intimate knowledge of British political institutions, which had no counterpart in India under a form of government, paternal, possibly, but essentially autocratic. When in England they were often welcomed with great cordiality and on a footing of complete social equality, especially in Liberal political circles, and felt all the more keenly the frigidity and aloofness of the British official world when they returned to India. Even there, however, they still had some English friends—a few in the Civil Service —who understood their feelings and sympathized with their aspirations; and, in consultation with them, they proceeded to carry out a scheme of which the first conception dated back to Lord Lytton's Viceroyalty, for the mustering of a representative body of Indians from all parts of India for the discussion of Indian affairs, who might gradually assume the position of an informal Parliament and gain recognition as a weighty if not absolutely authoritative exponent of educated opinion. Western education had removed one great practical difficulty, as, for the first time in Indian history, there were Indians from every province who had in the English language a common medium for the exchange of thoughts which none of their own vernaculars could have afforded them, as these are rarely understood outside the particular region where they are commonly spoken. To their English education they owed, too, a new conception of Indian nationhood, greatly quickened by European nationalism, of which the British people themselves had welcomed the triumph in the unification of a new Kingdom of Italy and of a new German Empire.

It was a remarkable gathering of Indians who, styling themselves the Indian National Congress, met for the first time in Bombay in the last days of 1885. There was amongst them no trace of hostility to the British connection nor any animosity towards the Government of India as by law established, though they were resolved to press by all lawful means for the larger participation in its councils and in its Public Services of which the repeated promise had so long eluded fulfilment. One has only to recall the names of the most prominent Indians associated with the movement and the language they used to describe its spirit. Many of them had studied in England or had resided there for some years, and had returned to India with a profound admiration for British institutions and British character. They were drawn mostly from the cities and had little connection with the great landed interests or with the agricultural masses, and they were mostly Hindus with a sprinkling of Parsees, because it was Hindus and Parsees who had been most eager from the very first to avail themselves of the opportunities

of Western education; whilst the Mohammedans
had held aloof from it, and the pride of a once ruling
race made them reluctant to be dragged in the wake
of a movement in which Hindus were taking the
lead. Amongst the Hindus there were men who had
absorbed the best of Western civilization, and held
prominent positions in the State, like Mr. Justice
Ranade and Mr. Justice Telang, both Brahmans
by caste, but both convinced advocates of social
reforms by which alone the practices of Hinduism
could be raised to a higher plane that would justify
India's claim to emancipation from British tutelage.
The Parsees are a small community—little over
100,000 to-day—who play in Indian life a part
quite disproportionate to their numbers. Of Persian
origin, but driven out by the Mohammedan rulers
of Persia because they clung to their ancient
Zoroastrian faith, they have long been settled in
Bombay. Intelligent and active and with a remarkable aptitude for trade and finance they have pros-
pered exceedingly under British rule. Their religion
keeps them apart from other Indians as well as
Europeans, but their status is officially that of all
other natives of India, and though their higher
standards of education, and especially female education, and very often their great wealth and the
Western habits of life which they have been quick
to learn draw them towards the Europeans, many
of them, and some of the ablest, have joined hands
with the rest of the Indian educated classes in
upholding the claims of a common Indian nationhood. At the opening of the Congress their most
eminent representative was Dadabhai Naoroji who
sat for a time as Liberal member at Westminster—
the " black man " of one of old Lord Salisbury's
most unfortunate jibes. Other Parsees of note
were A. P. Malabari, the most tender-hearted of
Indian idealists, who devoted his life to the cause of

Indian womanhood; and Pherozeshah Mehta, an acute lawyer called to the Bar in England and afterwards a very militant figure in the public life of his native city of Bombay. The chair was taken by a widely respected Bengalee barrister, W. C Bonnerji, who was supported by a few warm English wellwishers. Of these none were more helpful than A. O. Hume, a retired member of the Civil Service, and Sir William Wedderburn, M.P., who had been Secretary to the Government of Bombay. It had even been originally suggested that Lord Reay, the Governor of Bombay, a statesman of liberal ideas known to be in complete sympathy with the movement, should be asked to preside ; but when the matter was laid before the Viceroy, Lord Dufferin pointed out that it was undesirable for the head of a province to identify himself so closely with what should be essentially a popular movement. In Mr. Bonnerji's Presidential Address there was not however a single expression to which Lord Reay would have demurred. It was a much shorter and more simple address than it afterwards became the fashion for Presidents of the Congress to deliver. The number of the delegates was very small— barely 100—though they came from almost every part of India, and Mr. Bonnerji was guilty of less exaggeration than many Englishmen thought at the time when he stated that " never had so important and comprehensive an assemblage occurred within historical times on the soil of India." His meaning was made clearer at the second session, held in the following year in Calcutta, when Mr. Naoroji, the veteran Parsee, was in the chair.

" I ask," he said, " whether in the most glorious days of Hindu rule, in the days of Rajahs like the great Vikram, you could imagine the possibility of a meeting of this kind, whether even Hindus of all different provinces of the Kingdom could have collected and spoken as one nation. Coming down to the later Empire of our friends the Mohammedans, who probably ruled over a larger territory at one time than any Hindu monarch, would it have been—even in the days of Akbar himself—possible for a meeting like this to assemble composed of all classes and communities, all speaking one language and all having uniform and high aspirations of their own. . . . It is under the civilizing rule of the Queen and the people of England that we meet here together, hindered by none, and are freely allowed to speak our minds without the least fear and without the least hesitation. Such a thing is possible under British rule and under British rule only. Then I put the question plainly : Is this Congress a nursery for sedition and rebellion against the British Government ; or is it another stone in the foundation of the stability of that government ? There could be but one answer, and that you have already given, because we are thoroughly sensible of the numberless blessings conferred upon us, of which the very existence of this Congress is a proof in a nutshell. Were it not for these blessings of British rule I could not have come here to-day, as I have done, without the least hesitation and without the least fear that my children might be robbed and killed in my absence ; nor could you have come from every corner of the land, having performed, within a few days, journeys which in former days would have occupied months. These simple facts bring home to all of us at once some of the great and numberless blessings which British rule has conferred upon us. But there remain even greater blessings for which we have to be grateful. It is to British rule that we owe the education we possess ; the people of England were sincere in

the declaration made more than half a century
ago that India was a sacred charge entrusted to
their care by Providence, and that they were
bound to administer it for the good of India, to
the glory of their own name, and the satisfaction
of God."

This profession of faith is worth quoting in full
when—*quantum mutatus ab illo*—the Congress has
long since forgotten it, and now openly repudiates
it. Would it have gone the way it has if the majority
of Englishmen in India had not failed to see in such
a movement the natural outcome of the contact
established between India and the West by half a
century of English education and increasing facilities
of intercourse ? Greater insight was shown by the
two distinguished British statesmen who then
successively held the Viceroyalty, and were prepared
at least to watch the new movement with not un-
sympathetic tolerance. Lord Dufferin, with his
wider experience at Ottawa of the different but
equally genuine loyalty of British and French
Canadians, was ready to bestow an unofficial blessing
upon it. Lord Lansdowne, whilst passing orders
against any participation in its proceedings by
active members of the Public Services on the general
grounds which led Government to restrain them
from all political activities, described it as a perfectly
legitimate movement " representing in India what
in Europe would be called the more advanced
Liberal Party as distinguished from the great body
of Conservative opinion that exists side by side
with it." But this was an attitude of philosophic
detachment from which the rank and file of Englishmen were far removed, who regarded the Congress
either as a small matter unworthy of official notice,
or as a pernicious symptom of unruly independence.
Neither the Viceroys who greeted the birth of the
Indian National Congress with measured benevolence

nor the majority of Englishmen in India who
watched it, some with contempt, and some with
hostile suspicion and alarm, nor even the older
generation of Western-educated Indians who stood
sponsors to it with a robust faith still in British rule
and Western civilization realized that it was fated to
mark the close of a period in which the flowing tide
of Western influence had on the whole swept forward
all along the line, and the beginning of another and
very different period—a period of stubborn and
often violent reaction against every form of Western
influence.

CHAPTER VI

THE FIRST WAVE OF ANTI-WESTERN REACTION

THE spiritual torpor in which the old faiths of India were plunged during the Great Anarchy of the XVIIIth century continued all through the first half and well into the second half of the XIXth century. Indian Mohammedans were still stunned by the downfall of the Moghul Empire which brought their domination to an inglorious close. Hinduism retained its enduring *vis inertiæ*. But it produced not a single prominent champion of orthodoxy to challenge the new schools of thought which had promoted or been promoted by the introduction of Western education. Scarcely a serious protest had been uttered even when Lord William Bentinck had declared that in abolishing *Sati* his " first and primary object " was " the benefit of the Hindus," as if he, an alien and a Christian, could know better what was for " the benefit of the Hindus " than generations of Brahmans who had blessed the self-immolation of widows on their husband's funeral pyre. The modernizing spirit of the Brahmo Samaj and Prirthana Samaj spread far beyond the relatively small congregations that attended their particular forms of worship. There was no class that could be called intellectual to dispute the leadership of the Western intellectuals who prided themselves on thinking and even on dreaming only in English and who went almost as far as Macaulay in preferring a single shelf of English books to the whole ancient literature of their own country. Nothing inspired more general confidence than Government's anxiety to preserve as much as possible of Hindu and Mohammedan personal law in the administration of justice and of ancient rights and customs in the revision of the land revenue. The Mutiny indeed revealed the *ignes cineri suppositos doloso* of great reactionary forces which British rule failed to curb. But there was no deep spiritual movement behind it, though the fatal blunder of using for the greasing of army cartridges the fat of cows sacred above all animals to Hindus, and of pigs abhorrent to the religious prejudices of the Mohammedans fired the train. The annexation of the Mohammedan Kingdom of Oudh, however much it could be justified by its intolerable misrule, alarmed kindred Mohammedan interests, and Mohammedans rose at Delhi as well as at Lucknow to the cry of *Din ! Din !* Our religion ! Our religion ! But on the surface the Mutiny seemed to be mainly a military rising, and in so far as it was political, Mohammedan rather than Hindu, though it was the Hindus who supplied the brains, and the most sinister figure of all was Nana Sahib, the son and heir of the ex-Peshwa and the heir, too, of all the traditions of Brahmanical supremacy in the Mahratta Deccan. Not till 50 years later did one of the fiery apostles of modern revolutionary methods produce a passionate history of the Mutiny as " the War of National Independence" in which he claimed with perhaps more reason than had been ever realized at the time the chief " glory " of it for Hinduism and, being a special worshipper of Vishnu, for the " great god, Hari Dev."

The Mutiny, like a tropical storm, devastating but short-lived, passed away and seemed to leave few traces behind it. The deeper waters of Hinduism still lay dormant. They had last been moved when the gentle soul of Tulsi Das breathed over them in the XVIIth century. They were to be stirred once more by a much fiercer spirit when Swami Dayananda Saraswata founded the Arya Samaj in 1875. He had already spent 30 years of his adult life wandering about India in search of a new sign in the heavens, sometimes as a Sanyasi with a begging bowl in his hand and the emblem of Shiva painted on his forehead, sometimes at the feet of Keshab Chudran Sen and the Bengalee reformers, always seeking and never finding the teacher whom his restless soul could accept. For he used to say of himself : " I am born to command and not to obey." The confused body of doctrines which he finally evolved was inspired by a passionate desire to rouse Hinduism out of its sloth. His frontal attack was directed against Christianity and Islam, but his plea for the return of Hinduism to the pristine purity of the Vedic age, when the Aryan stock was itself still pure, foreshadowed Gandhi's religious slogan of " Back to the Vedas," and the political slogan of one school of Nationalists : " India for the Aryans." Whilst he imported into Hinduism a new spirit of aggressive militancy against everything foreign to India, he was still, however, to this extent under the influence of the Western ideas which stirred the Hindu reformers of the first half of the XIXth century that he denounced idolatry, and, without altogether repudiating caste, threatened to break down one of its great barriers by demanding that the study of the Vedas hitherto reserved to the " twice-born " should be thrown open to all Hindus without distinction of caste as the key, which none had the right to monopolize, to all spiritual truths as well as to all modern science. He only lived for a few years after he had founded the Arya Samaj and transferred its headquarters to Lahore, but it struck vigorous root in the Punjab and, moving with the times, it has made itself by its educational work and its strong spirit of nationalism one of the living forces in modern India.

Another vital, if more histrionic, figure in the Hindu reaction against the West was Swami Vivekananda, a high-caste Bengalee, born in 1862. He graduated from a Mission College in Calcutta where he received a Western education, but became an ardent disciple of a saintly, if somewhat heterodox, Hindu ascetic, Ramakrishna, who, unlike Dayananda, believed from time to time in a Divine revelation from Jesus and Mohammed as well as in the living grace of the Great Mother, Kali. For Hinduism, as it was for Christianity in one of its early phases, asceticism is the pathfinder to spiritual enlightenment, and after Ramakrishna's death Vivekananda retired into the Himalayas and lived there for six years as a Sanyasi absorbed in contemplation and penance. Then he returned to deliver his message all over India. It was a strange message full of extraordinary contradictions. All religions were true and good, but Hinduism was the oldest and noblest of all and every particle of it must be held sacred. God was impersonal, unknowable and non-moral, and as He permeated the whole universe the human soul, too, was both divine and non-moral, and no human being could consequently sin. Idolatry was a healthy and spiritual form of worship, whereas Western civilization was grossly materialistic, though to defend his religion and civilization every Hindu was justified in making use of Western methods and Western education, and should even become if need be an eater of beef in order to build up a virile race that would render India immune against the poison of the West. Vivekananda was the first to introduce into the Hindu revival a missionary spirit hitherto foreign to Hindu traditions. His opportunity came with the holding of the " Parliament of Religions " in 1893, at Chicago, where his handsome presence in Oriental robes, orange and gold, his complete mastery of the English language and his impressive voice and delivery lent to his fervent if unhistoric vindication of Hinduism, an emotional intensity which swept his unaccustomed audience off its feet, and made Americans hail him with astonished admiration as the inspired prophet of a wonderful creed and of an ancient civilization which had nothing to learn from Western missionaries or Western rulers. He made fewer converts during his less sensational visit to England, but amongst them was one gifted young Englishwoman best known under the name borne by her in India, Sister Nivedita, when she went out as his disciple and cast a powerful spell over the renascence of Hinduism by pouring forth her mystic love for the religion and the people of her adoption in a stream of poetic enthusiasm. Vivekananda, who attended with less success another Congress of Religions held in Paris in 1900, died relatively young in 1902. Some of the monasteries which he founded in India are still tenanted by his disciples, but the orthodox looked askance at many of his doctrines; and his fame has survived chiefly as the first Hindu whose personality won demonstrative recognition abroad for India's ancient civilization and for her new-born claim to nationhood.

These first manifestations of spiritual reaction against Western influence still had this in common with the earlier Hindu reform movements which drew their inspiration from the West, that they, too, admitted the need for some rejuvenation of Hinduism, and their antagonism to British rule was more often implicit than openly avowed. They assumed an entirely different aspect when Hindu orthodoxy found a great leader prepared to vindicate and uphold the whole Brahmanical position as the one real bulwark of Hinduism and the only sure foundation of an Indian nationhood capable of overthrowing the political as well as the spiritual domination of the West. Such a leader arose in the Deccan where out of the first great revolt of Hinduism against Mohammedan domination had emerged the formidable Mahratta power from which the advent of the British alone snatched the inheritance of the moribund Moghul Empire. Poona had been until early

7

in the XIXth century the stronghold of the religious and secular supremacy of Brahmanism, and Bal Gangadhar Tilak was a Poona Brahman of the Chitpawan caste who claim descent from a stock specially favoured by the gods. No other caste has, perhaps, produced in our time so many men of commanding ability and force of character, whether prepared to tread the new paths of Western progress or determined to stand fast in the ancient ways of orthodoxy. To the latter school belonged Tilak, the most striking personality in the India of our times, except, perhaps, Gandhi, whose essential gentleness and humility he lacked, whilst he possessed on the other hand far greater gifts of intellect and far more political acumen. With a stubborn and arrogant faith in his religion and his race, he was a born leader of men and a ruthless fighter; though he fought not with the sword, but, as became his caste which ranks higher than the warriors', with his pen and his tongue. He spoke and wrote English well, and of his own rugged Mahratta language he was an incomparable master. When he first appeared on the scene the progressive school represented in Western India by the Prirthana Samaj had got a strong foothold even in Poona under the leadership of Western-educated Hindus like Ranade and Chandavakar and Bhandarkar who held strongly that if the National Congress which they had just helped to found was to win for India her political advancement on the lines of Western self-government, Hinduism must begin by emancipating itself from the thraldom of antiquated customs and beliefs which were themselves a perpetual challenge to Western ideals of human freedom. Such men were in Tilak's eyes the mere satellites and slaves of British rule and had to be crushed before any successful assault could be made on British rule itself. With an eloquence as full of religious imagery as that of any

Roundhead, Tilak thundered against them in the Press and on the platform, and his followers bore them down by sheer weight of numbers and intimidation.

He could then stand forth as the undisputed leader of extreme orthodoxy, and his next campaign was waged against Lord Lansdowne's Age of Consent Bill of 1890, for raising the age at which a husband could lawfully enforce upon his infant-wife the consummation of their marriage. The arguments in favour of the Bill were reinforced by a fatal tragedy which had recently occurred in Bombay as the result of violence exercised by the husband on a mere child married to him in accordance with Hindu custom. Tilak deplored the case, but only as the wrongful and exceptional abuse of the religious law which made it the first duty of every Hindu to beget a son to carry on the ancestral rites from generation to generation for the fulfilment of his own and his forbears' *Karma*. The law itself, he maintained, was sacred and immutable, and he indignantly denounced an alien Government for venturing to draw down the wrath of the gods on a subject-people by changing so much as an iota of it. He struck there a chord to which all Hindus, whether Brahmans or of much lower castes, were certain to respond, and the agitation against the Bill travelled far beyond the confines of the Mahratta country. The Bill itself, nevertheless, passed into law with the full support of the more courageous reformers and the more timid approval of others. It was, however, a Pyrrhic victory, for the opposition had been so fierce that Government never again ventured to initiate legislation on any matters which might be deemed, however unreasonably, to impinge on the domain of Hindu religious and social custom.

Conscious of his growing power outside the Deccan, Tilak neglected no means of strengthening his hold

on his own people. To the prestige of his high caste
he added an intimate familiarity with the habits of
thought and speech of his Mahrattas, and he knew
how to play on their religious emotions when he
gave a new meaning to the cult of their favourite
god, the elephant-headed Ganesh or Ganpatti by
making his festivals the occasion of popular demonstrations in which he grafted a new hatred of British
rule on to the old hatred of Mohammedan domination, still kept burning fiercely in their folk-songs
and semi-religious plays. He used them especially
to revive the memory of the great Shivaji, the
glorious protector of the Brahman and of the sacred
Cow, who never laid his victorious sword aside until
he had freed Maharashtra from the alien yoke of the
accursed meat-eaters who, like the British, con-
taminated its hallowed soil with the blood of animals
ruthlessly spilt in their brutal slaughter-houses. Had
the Mahratta race so fallen from grace as to suffer
tamely the same oppression that Shivaji had taught
them to shake off ? How far Shivaji was guilty of
treacherous murder in killing his Mohammedan foe,
Afzul Khan, is perhaps a debatable point of history,
but, instead of disputing that it was murder, Tilak
praised the deed and justified it on religious grounds,
" as the Divine Krishna tells us in the *Baghavatghita*
that we may kill even our teachers and our kinsmen
and no blame attaches if we are not actuated by
selfish desires." This was at a great Shivaji celebration at Raighur over which Tilak himself presided to
commemorate the Mahratta chieftain's " coronation " after he had destroyed both Afzul Khan and
the whole of his Mohammedan army. Another
Brahman pointed the moral by declaring that
" every Hindu, every Mahratta must rejoice at the
spectacle, for we too are all striving to regain our lost
independence."

This was the first public glorification of political

murder under British rule.   Government, with its
usual tolerance, paid no serious attention to it, even
when Tilak was chosen shortly afterwards to be
a member of the Bombay Legislative Council ; but it
was to bear fruit.   Tilak was the first Indian to study
European politics for the lessons to be drawn for use
in India from Western methods of agitation.   His
" No rent " campaign, during a severe famine in 1896,
was borrowed from the Irish Land League, but
without much success.   A far more effective handle
was given to him in the measures taken by Government to deal with the first great outbreak of the
bubonic plague in our times in India.   In such
visitations the panic-stricken masses see, as they
did in Europe in the Dark Ages, a manifestation of
Divine wrath which has to be submissively endured
or appeased by prayers and incantations.   The
British authorities, taken unawares by the sudden-
ness and the violence of the epidemic, tried to stamp
it out by drastic measures, sometimes not very wise
or very wisely carried out, such as house-to-house
visitations and segregation camps, more terrifying to
the ignorant populace than the plague itself.   Tilak
denounced them as an oppressive invasion of the
Hindu home, outraging the sanctity of its domestic
shrines and the modesty of its sheltered women, and
stirred up a desperate temper of resentment and
resistance which was soon ripe for murder.   And
murder followed.   On June 27, 1897, the day of
Queen Victoria's Diamond Jubilee, Mr. Rand, a
member of the Indian Civil Service who was marked
down as President of the Poona Plague Committee,
was shot dead, together with Lieutenant Ayerst of
the Commissariat Department, on the way back
from an evening reception at Government House, by
Damodhar Chapekar, a young Chitpawan Brahman
whom Tilak's fiery denunciation of British oppression
had worked into a state of murderous frenzy.   No

direct connection was ever established between the murderer and Tilak. The former was hanged, and the latter, though prosecuted shortly afterwards for a seditious article and condemned to two years imprisonment, was released before the completion of his term. But murder had made its first appearance under British rule as a method of political agitation, and, though it was not to reappear for another ten years, the seed had been sown and ultimately yielded a terrible harvest.

Meanwhile the heavy set-back given to the Hindu social reformers had reacted profoundly on the Indian National Congress, for it owed its birth largely to them, and it was to have represented in the pursuit of political reforms a movement parallel to that of the National Social Conference in its own field of social reform. The latter, however, was somewhat ignominiously pushed into the background when it was found to be much easier to form a common front for a long-range attack upon Government than to wrestle at close-quarters with the insidious forces of a religious reaction. These and other anti-Western forces soon penetrated also into the Congress, but did not obtain complete control until much later. For many years the Congress mainly reflected the growing estrangement between the official world and the Western-educated classes who had been not unjustifiably embittered by the unfortunate recommendations of the Public Services Committee of 1887, which, by segregating Europeans and Indians into separate pens, very artificially created, tended to deepen the growing racial cleavage.

The Indian Councils Act of 1892 was a first approach to the admission of the elective principle in the representation of Indian unofficial opinion in the Viceroy's Legislative Council, but on such a minute scale and in such a roundabout way that it could not seriously weaken the Congress's claim to constitute the only independent body in which opposition to Government could find representative expression. It drew up for itself a very elastic constitution and had its provincial organizations all over the country. But it lacked the real power which brings with it a real sense of responsibility. It attracted an increasingly large and noisy following and the pace was frequently set by an irresponsible native Press which was apt to make up for its poverty of thought by sheer violence of language. It only met once a year in solemn conclave during a short session held in rotation in all the principal cities of India, and for a good many years the more moderate elements succeeded in preserving in its proceedings a tone not altogether unworthy of its claim to possess something of the authority of an Indian parliament, condemned, it is true, to play no other part than that of an impotent opposition to an autocratic government. It enjoyed complete freedom to criticize the policy of Government in all its various aspects and often, and with growing acrimony, the official actions of its agents. The Presidential address consisted generally of a lengthy catalogue of grievances, some real, some imaginary. Amongst them always figured prominently the heavy " home charges " and the large military expenditure with which the Indian exchequer was saddled. Insistent demands were put forward for the separation of judicial and executive functions, the granting to Indian officers of British and not merely of Indian Army commissions and, with more reasonableness, for the extension of primary as well as higher education. The irreconcilable elements pushed their way, however, more and more to the front, and not content to attack merely Government measures and servants, assailed the whole system of alien and autocratic rule as in itself intolerable. In 1899 the

Presidential address of Mr. R. C. Dutt, who had held a high position in the Civil Service and was a well-known student of Indian history, and, in the following year, that of Mr. N. G. Chandavarkar, afterwards a very distinguished Judge of the High Court of Bombay, still warmly acknowledged India's great debt to England and to Western education. But even they felt constrained to humour the predominant temper of hostility by striking a note of distrust as to the sincerity of British promises which other speakers translated into far stronger terms of scorn and hatred.

All opposition, even in the shape of criticism which it can treat as mere waste of breath, is distasteful to an autocracy and apt to be regarded even as pregnant with sedition, and the British officials in India honestly believed in an autocratic form of government, though they tried to make it as paternal as possible. They had persistently regarded the Congress movement from its very inception as either futile or dangerous. As the Congress was largely composed of lawyers and professors and other intellectuals who had little personal knowledge of the vast inarticulate India outside the great cities, there was a disposition in the highest official circles to see only a safety-valve, troublesome perhaps but not seriously harmful, in a political debating society which was content to make up for its lack of practical experience by unpractical displays of pompous or even truculent oratory. The plodding British civilian, conscious of the solid and unostentatious work that he was himself doing in some remote *mofussil* district, resented far more strongly being subjected to daily vilification in the local organs of the Congress party, and periodically lectured by a pack of talkers, as he regarded them, who wanted to substitute *Vakil raj*, i.e., the reign of lawyers, for the British *raj*. He was not only ill-fitted by training and temperament to enter into public controversies, but debarred from doing so by Service regulations, whilst Government, still unconscious of the importance of training and informing public opinion, especially in such a country as India, merely wrapped itself in a rarefied atmosphere of official secrecy and, systematically affecting to ignore the very existence of Congress, made no attempt to counteract its influence by any spadework of its own.

By the beginning of this century a new generation and a new temper very different from its founders' had invaded the Congress. The numbers that attended its annual session had swelled enormously. Crowds of delegates chosen rather haphazard under its loosely-drafted constitution flocked in to its annual session from all the provinces, each with its own separate organization and local conferences as a constant stimulus to political agitation. It still consisted mainly of Hindus, with a small but active leaven of Parsee " intellectuals " who dwelt with Dadabhai Naoroji, the " grand old man of India," in a dreamland of constitutional theories. The Mohammedan community as a whole continued to hold aloof from it, though a few Western-educated Mohammedans had joined it and sometimes even occupied the Presidential chair. It had not yet passed entirely under the control of extremist factions bent on the subversion of British rule and of every form of Western ascendancy. It conducted its proceedings in English. The majority still professed to borrow the methods and the arguments of Western democracy and to aim only at securing the application of Western principles of government in India, and the introduction of representative institutions on the British model. But whilst its programme was in this respect utterly foreign to the spirit of the Hindu social and religious system, it included many of the leaders of the reactionary school which Tilak had led for the first time into the open. That school was steadily gaining ground also, though purely as a fervent religious revival, amongst conservative Hindus whose loyalty to the British *raj* still remained unshaken. It took shape chiefly in the creation of new societies for the preservation of caste. Their promoters were often genuinely animated with the desire to improve spiritual and material conditions within each caste and to remove some of the existing abuses from the system; but they were at the same time strengthening the caste-structure of Hindu society which the Hindu reformers of a past generation had recognized as the greatest obstacle to the advancement of India. These movements, represented at first by separate associations, culminated in a " National Conference " held at Delhi in 1900 under the presidency of the Maharajah of Durbangha, a conservative and orthodox Hindu with great possessions, and universally respected, who walked barefooted and carrying a copy of the Vedas at the head of a vast procession numbering nearly 100,000 people. The Conference resulted in the creation of one large organization, with branches all over India, known as the Bharata Dharma Mahamandala, for the exaltation of the " Eternal Religion " and the defence of the orthodox system of Hinduism against the disintegrating influence of Western beliefs. The only concession made to the spirit of the age was that Hinduism was to be regarded not only as the " Eternal Religion " of India, but as the religion predestined from all time for the salvation of the whole world.

Government ignored these religious movements just as it ignored the Congress movement, though both disclosed, each in its own particular shape, the birth of a new spirit of revolt against Western ascendancy. Optimism was the keynote in the highest official quarters, and it was the optimism

not merely of self-confidence but of solid achievement. The internal peace of India had not been
seriously disturbed. Mere passing ebullitions, as
for instance in the Deccan, could be left to run their
course and melt away into a serene atmosphere of
almost universal tranquillity and loyalty, which the
Congress had so far been even more powerless to
disturb. If that irresponsible body was a nuisance,
it was after all a mere negligible quantity amidst
the scores of millions who were scarcely aware of
its existence. Even if it came to counting heads
amongst the Western-educated classes, its followers
were hardly as numerous as the legion of public
servants who, like the Indian Army, were more than
content to eat the salt of the *Serkar*. A troublesome
piece of grit would no doubt sometimes get into the
machinery of a huge administration, but it was
growing all the time more efficient and more powerful
and the wonderful progress made by India since the
Crown had superseded the old East India Company
was the admiration of the world.

Yet there was a warning note worth listening to
in the measured but insistent representations of
many Indians who still valued the British connection
and regarded it still as essential to the welfare and
safety of India. Of these none spoke with more
authority than G. K. Gokhale, a Poona Brahman
of the same sept as Tilak, but who, unlike him, had
sought to adapt the lessons of Western civilization
to the needs of India's moral and social advancement.
Higher education on Western lines had no more
convinced supporter though none pressed more
urgently for the extension of popular education as
the surest means for promoting the regeneration of
Hinduism as a social as well as religious system, if
India was to take her place amongst the progressive
nations of the world. The " Society of India," which
he founded a few years later, was based on ideals of

social service irrespective of creed or caste or race, by which alone the peoples of India would be able to justify their claim to a common nationhood. At the same time he held strongly that Indians were entitled to a larger share than they had hitherto been given in the government and administration of their country. Often a fearless critic of Government policy and one of the few whom Lord Curzon himself deemed worthy of serious attention as a skilled debater in his Legislative Council, Gokhale showed no less courage in telling many unpalatable truths to his more impatient fellow-countrymen. For it required no mean courage to acknowledge before a large Indian audience that the British officials in India "are a body of picked men ; that man for man they are better than ourselves ; they have a higher standard of duty, higher notions of patriotism, higher notions of loyalty to each other, higher notions of organized work and of discipline." But he refused either to have implicit faith in the monopoly of knowledge and power which they claimed to possess or to share the sentiment of despair which was already driving many Indians to seek for other and more forceful remedies than those of constitutional agitation, however slow and fruitless the latter might at times seem. Gokhale was perhaps the sanest and finest character that India has produced, blending accurate knowledge of Western history and Western thought with a profound understanding of the Indian mentality and of the ancient civilization that has moulded it. He too, however, was generally regarded as a mere disaffected agitator, only the more dangerous because of his admittedly greater ability.

Never did the prestige of the British *raj* seem greater, and never was the word more frequently used to describe its consciousness of intangible superiority than at the close of Queen Victoria's

majestic reign. Nor could it have a more splendid
apotheosis than the great Durbar in which Lord
Curzon celebrated in 1902 King Edward's accession to
the throne of Empire. Yet things were happening or
in the making which might well shake India's long
belief, always largely compounded of fatalism, in the
omniscience and omnipotence of the British *raj*.
Fear was taking possession of the masses. They
read the wrath of the gods into the exceptionally
severe and widespread famines in 1896 and again in
1899–1900, which placed an unprecedented and
excessive strain on the great organization provided
by the State for coping with them, and they read
it still more into the ravages of the bubonic plague
which had stubbornly defied all the efforts of
Government to arrest its devastating progress. No
such visitation had ever been known under British
rule, and it provoked amongst the masses the dark
distrust invariably quickened in such circumstances
by every form of superstition destroying their
faith in all human agencies, including Government,
usually in their eyes the highest, and in India the
most mysterious of all as it comes from so far away
and wears so foreign a garb. A sinister belief even
arose that Government had deliberately imported
the plague into India in order to thin out the
population. Apart from the widening estrangement
of the Western-educated intellectuals, the growth of
Indian trade and industry was creating new causes
of friction with the West, amongst other classes who
scented the unholy influence of London capitalists
in the fall of the exchange and the depreciation of
the rupee and, not quite so unreasonably, the
jealousy of Lancashire in the cotton duties which
handicapped the growing Indian industry. There
was some resentment, too, of the frequency with which
the Indian army was employed at the expense of
the Indian exchequer for co-operation in distant

military expeditions undertaken for Imperial rather than Indian purposes, though there was never any such feeling amongst the Indian troops themselves. Then, as they began to look further afield, Indians took to wondering whether the material resources of the Empire were as overwhelming as they had been taught to believe when they seemed to be strained for two-and-a-half years almost to the breaking point in order to bring two small Boer Republics in South Africa to their knees. Observant Indians had already noted with amazement, in 1895, the destruction of an Italian army in Abyssinia as a revelation that white troops in conflict with coloured races were not always invincible, and many of those Indians had secretly rejoiced. For was there not increasingly frequent evidence in their relations with the ruling race that they counted for little more than any other coloured people born into the world as the white man's inferiors and servants. What more convincing proof could they have than the treatment of Indians assimilated to the coloured natives in South Africa and in some other parts of the British Empire ?

Racial feeling had increased on both sides since the ill-starred Ilbert Bill. A much larger number of Indians travelled and went to England, mostly in order to complete their education. Some learnt to value the more highly the best aspects of our civilization. Some only became acquainted with its seamier sides. Those who were fortunate enough to be admitted into the intimacy of refined English homes or the *camaraderie* of collegiate life at Oxford and Cambridge often had their enthusiasms promptly chilled when they got back to India to find themselves treated with suspicion by their own people as denationalized, whilst the Englishman, accustomed to the Oriental deference of an older generation, resented the new ideas of social equality and national independence which the young Indian had imbibed in contact with the free life of European cities, and sometimes displayed with the aggressive self-sufficiency of his years. On the other hand, the increasing facilities of communication, the expansion of trade and commerce and the intro-duction of the mechanical and industrial appliances of modern life which required more technical knowledge than was yet to be found in India brought out a great many Europeans of a type almost unknown in earlier times in India—rougher and less educated—who knew nothing and cared very little about Indian susceptibilities, and when the climate, or perhaps merely the unfamiliar ways of the Indian worker, tried their tempers, were inclined to give muscular demonstrations of their racial superiority. Even amongst the better classes the opportunities of closer intercourse between Europeans and Indians did not always have happy results. The hyper-sensitiveness of the Indian and the Englishman's calm assumption of a superiority inherent to his race came into more frequent conflict. Unfortunate incidents occurred in which Indians of good position were subjected to personal indignities by Englishmen who ought to have known better and were some-times allowed to get off too lightly ; and the Indian newspapers retaliated by giving them, often in a highly-coloured form, a publicity never extended to the thousand-and-one instances of the Englishman's genuine kindliness, and, in times of stress, often wholly self-sacrificing devotion, towards Indians.

Englishmen and Indians can and do get on quite well when their professional occupations or business relations or, in some parts of India, a common love of sport, brings them together. But few Englishmen, even if they have the capacity, will take the trouble that Lord Ronaldshay did when Governor of Bengal, to establish with them the intellectual contact for which there is ample scope in the wide field of Indian art, music as well as painting, or in the more abstruse domain of Indian philosophic thought. More usually, as the Englishman feels himself precluded by the peculiarities of Indian domestic customs from venturing to manifest any curiosity concerning the Indian's home-life and family concerns, the dearth of common interests is a great bar to social relations of an intimate character between men of the two races. It became a still greater bar when, with the growing facilities of travel and the increasing amenities of European life in India, and the opening-up of "hill stations" in which refuge could be sought during the "hot weather" from the sultry cities and the sunscorched plains, a much larger number of Englishwomen came out to make a home for their husbands during their term of exile in India. Their racial prejudices are apt to be stronger than those of their men-folk. The terrible memory of all that Englishwomen suffered during the Mutiny is not unnaturally more often present to their minds. They have above all an intuitive perception of the Indian's customary views as to the relations between the two sexes outside the precincts of the *zenana* in which he is careful to keep his own women safely secluded. There have been many fine exceptions, and not a few Englishwomen have spent their lives in working for their Indian sisters and in endeavouring through them to draw the two races together. But, speaking generally, the influence of the Englishwoman in India had not lessened the minor occasions of racial friction when much graver ones supervened to swell the tide of reaction against Western ascendancy.

Those who sat in the seats of the mighty at Calcutta and Simla took no heed of all these *imponderabilia*. Pontifical utterances in the Legislative Councils and stereotyped official *communiqués* were the only antidotes they vouchsafed to provide against the virus of distrust and disaffection with which Indian public opinion was being inoculated by an uninformed and irresponsible native press that was growing and multiplying apace. Nor did they even take heed of the sudden thrill of exaltation that ran through the whole of India with the unbroken succession of Japanese victories by land and by sea over Russia, the formidable European power in whom England had for nearly a century recognized her one dangerous rival in Asia. Yet to many Indian minds it at once meant a complete change of all the old values and the birth of entirely new hopes. Where now, they asked themselves, was the vaunted superiority of the white man over the coloured man? Where was England's particular claim to "hold the gorgeous East in fee"? If the young Asiatic David could smite down the European Goliath, what might not 300,000,000 Indians dare to achieve?

CHAPTER VII

THE PARTITION OF BENGAL

ENGLISHMEN were slow to note the meaning which Indians read into the Japanese victories. From the British point of view the triumph of Japan was that of a friendly power with whom Great Britain had concluded only a few years before a close alliance which was in itself a signal departure from all the traditions of her foreign policy, unless under the stress of actual or imminent war. From the point of view of the Indian Government in particular it was doubly satisfactory in that it banished, at least for a very long time to come, the spectre of a Russian invasion of India, which had haunted British statesmen for over a century, and none more constantly than the then Viceroy, Lord Curzon. To that extent there were good grounds for Englishmen as well as Indians to welcome the discomfiture of Russia. But there were Indians to whom it meant even more than a mere humbling of a great European power by an Asiatic race. It meant also a mighty blow to the autocratic system in Russia, and to that system the Indian extremists never tired of likening a system of Indian Government concentrated in the hands of an all-powerful bureaucracy. British officialdom in India was denounced as the counterpart of the *chinovniks* who ruled and ruined Russia in the name of the Tsar, and to be fought if necessary with the same weapons which the Russian revolutionists were learning effectively to employ.

At that turning-point in the history of modern India when the axiom of the white man's supremacy even in the domain of material force had been seriously shaken if not shattered before her astonished eyes, Lord Curzon was accepting the doubtful boon of a renewal of his term of office as Viceroy. None has ever invested that office with more magnificence

than at the great Delhi Durbar of 1903 for the
celebration of King Edward VIIth's accession to
the Imperial throne of India.　None had been more
impressed with the greatness of India's past or done
more to preserve all the noble memories of it that
survive in her historical monuments.　None has left
a deeper and in many cases more admirable mark
on the chief departments of Indian administration.
None was a greater autocrat, but none set a finer
example of indefatigable industry and courage often
in the face of acute physical suffering.　With just,
perhaps, that excess of generosity which Lord Morley
sometimes displayed towards a great political opponent, he once said of Lord Curzon that there would
never be sent to India " a Viceroy his superior, if
indeed his equal in force of mind, in passionate and
devoted interest in all that concerns the well-being
of India, with an imagination fired by the grandeur
of the political problem that India presents."　But
India presents not only political but psychological
problems of the first magnitude, and with all his intellectual gifts, Lord Curzon, seldom, if ever, showed
himself possessed of the spiritual vision which is of
the essence of real statesmanship.　India he regarded
as the brightest gem in the British Crown of Empire,
but as a gem of an antique and somewhat barbaric
lustre which a modern setting could only spoil.　For
him England's mission in India was not as it had
been for Sir Thomas Munro, 80 years earlier, to train
the Indians to govern and to protect themselves.
Lord Curzon preferred to govern her himself, and
government for him meant the highest possible
standards of administrative efficiency required to
make her a great Imperial asset, and not least in
the sphere of international politics in which he was
himself an expert, having graduated in the latest
school of Victorian Imperialism.

It was on grounds of administrative efficiency that

he committed himself to the partition of such an unwieldy province as Bengal had become, without stopping to ask whether the remedy could be justified on any higher grounds of statesmanship. With a population of close on 80,000,000 Bengal had outgrown the capacity of a single governor. What simpler remedy than to divide it up into two provinces, each of them more homogeneous, as the new province of Eastern Bengal would comprise a large Mohammedan majority, whilst the Hindus would preserve a more overwhelming majority than before in the reduced province of Bengal, which was to retain its old designation ? Lord Curzon reckoned without the Bengalees and without Indian public opinion, which he held in slight esteem when it differed from his own. In no part of India, not even in the Mahratta Deccan had there grown up a stronger local patriotism than in Bengal, and, unlike that of the Mahrattas, it had been greatly fostered by the new conditions which British rule had created. The great majority were Hindus, and having never forgotten the days when they had been ground down under Mohammedan domination, they had learnt to repay their former masters with scorn when they left the Mohammedan minority far behind them in all the activities of modern life. Proud both of their language, spoken by nearly 50,000,000 people, and of their modern culture—for they had led the way in Western education—they called themselves a nation, and regarded Calcutta, then still the capital of the British Indian Empire, as the symbol of their primacy amongst the peoples of India. Lord Curzon had already deeply wounded that national sentiment by one of his measures of educational reform which they construed into a menace to the independence of the Calcutta University, the largest in India, and another treasured symbol of their primacy. Just as the great Bengalee thinkers of the beginning of

the XIXth century had been the pioneers of the early
social and religious reform movements in India, so,
at its close, the political leaders of Bengal had played
a conspicuous part in the Congress movement for
which Lord Curzon had even more intellectual
contempt than political aversion. Was it to pay
them out for that, as was whispered not amongst
Indians alone, that the Viceroy proposed to deal
such a blow at the province in which he himself
chiefly resided ? They were up in arms at once
and stuck, it must be confessed, at nothing to
spread amongst all classes an unreasoning terror of
what partition portended for all. There followed an
extraordinary explosion of popular feeling which
once more showed how easily the religious forces of
Hinduism can be mobilized to supplement the
modern political forces engendered by contact with
the West. Whilst the politicians appealed to London
for the sympathy and support of the British people,
and especially of the Liberal party, still in the cold
shade of opposition, against an act of autocratic
tyranny repugnant to the principles of modern
freedom and a cruel *diminutio capitis* inflicted upon
the principal seat of Western learning in India, it
was at the famous temple of Kali, in the Kalikat
suburb from which Calcutta derives its name, that
they mustered the masses and invested political agitation with all the sanctions of religion. There in the
presence of the great Black Mother, with two dead
bodies for ear-rings and a string of skulls for a
necklace, holding a sword in one of her four hands
and in another the head of a giant she has just
slain, a goddess as terrific as her consort, Shiva the
Destroyer, 50,000 people took a solemn oath to
boycott all British goods and carry out all other
measures of resistance which the leaders of the
Bengalee nation might enjoin, rather than tamely
submit to the outrage done to her by the accursed

foreigner in the sacrilegious mutilation of a province specially devoted to her cult. The boycott which was to enforce the substitution of *swadeshi* or Indian-made goods, and especially of Indian-made cotton cloth for those of British manufacture, failed as an economic weapon to bring the British people to their knees, but nothing could serve better as a war cry. Schoolboys and students were brigaded as national volunteers to enforce the boycott by picketing reluctant tradesmen's shops. An old folk-song, *Bande Materam*, "Hail to thee, my Mother!"— the Mother being interpreted at will to mean Kali, or Bengal, or, at a later stage, India—was resuscitated as the "Marseillaise" that was to carry young Bengal to the storming of the British Bastille. Surendranath Banerjee magnetized his people who acclaimed him the "uncrowned king of Bengal." From the Deccan, Tilak responded in the same key to the call of Bengal, where they were in fact merely borrowing the methods he had himself preached a few years before in Maharashtra. Neither to popular clamour nor to the representations of more responsible Indians like Gokhale, perhaps the ablest and certainly the most single-minded political leader of the time, did Lord Curzon yield an inch. So the fevered imagination of the Bengalees saw in his sudden resignation, announced the day after one of their demonstrative pilgrimages to the temple of Kali, a sure proof that the great goddess was fighting for them. All that had happened was that the Viceroy had been thrown over by the Home Government in the last phase of his protracted controversy with the Commander-in-Chief, Lord Kitchener, in regard to army administration. Even the better-informed Bengalees, who did not ascribe his departure from India to the wrath of the Mother, regarded it as a great triumph for the anti-partition agitation which they could now afford to damp down in view of the impending visit of the then Prince and Princess of Wales to India. When their arrival was soon followed by a change of Government in England, where a powerful Liberal Ministry, with John Morley at the India Office, seemed to promise an early reversal of Lord Curzon's policy, one of those sudden transformation-scenes took place which the emotional Indian temperament so readily enacts. The reverence due to Kingship, common in theory, at least until recently, to all Oriental peoples, is part of the ancient faith of Hinduism, and nowhere was it more strikingly exhibited than in Calcutta, where the Royal visitors were enthusiastically greeted by the very same crowds that had been only a few weeks previously crying to Kali for vengeance on the British oppressors of the Mother.

But after the Prince and Princess had departed, and Morley himself, whose sympathies were alienated by some of the reactionary features of the anti-partition agitation, refused to go back upon the policy which his predecessor at the India Office had sanctioned, the embers were quickly kindled into fresh flame. The Press grew more vitriolic, the popular demonstrations more tumultuous, the National Volunteers more unruly. The boycott of British goods was renewed and enjoined as a religious duty, students and schoolboys were encouraged to make bonfires of their foreign clothing and their English textbooks. These " beacons of freedom " glowed as freely on the hill-sides of Maharashtra as in the plains of Bengal. Tilak not only presided over the bonfires and bestowed on them the blessings of a Brahman, but in his old paper, the *Kesari*, he enforced the boycott with the most awful sanction that a Brahman could devise. He threatened with the curse of the gods in the shape of a barren marriage all young Hindu couples who should dare to use their British-made articles at their wedding festivities. The proceedings in the Indian National Congress were less lurid, but it loudly proclaimed the determination of the whole of India to stand shoulder-to-shoulder with Bengal and its " Grand Old Man," invoking a recent aphorism of Campbell-Bannerman, the British Prime Minister, that " good government could never be a substitute for government by the people themselves," intimated that henceforward India's demand must be *Swaraj*, which he defined as the same full measure of Self-Government that Great Britain and her Dominions enjoy.

The agitation increased in volume and in intensity. Nationalism in Maharashtra and Bengal had meant hitherto little more than Mahratta and Bengalee nationalism, each flowing in a separate stream. They were now both merged in a larger stream which spread over a great part of India, and Indian nationalism was fed by racial passion with visions of India as the protagonist, more formidable even than Japan, of all the coloured peoples of Asia in revolt against the white man's supremacy. Had not the voice of Kali been heard to clamour for the blood of " white goats," and was it not clearly the blood of the white oppressors of India for which the Black Mother was athirst ? Worked into a religious frenzy, young students and schoolboys—modelling themselves on the Russian Nihilists as closely as the Indian extremist papers declared British oppression in India to be modelled on Tsarist oppression—banded themselves into secret societies for the manufacture of bombs and the clandestine purchase of firearms. But the Russian Nihilists professed atheism, whereas the *Yugantar*, whose open incitements to violence gave it a circulation which no other Bengalee paper had ever reached, preached to the Indian Nihilists that they were " the Hindu incarnations of God, saving the good and destroying the wicked," and that " their minds must be excited and maddened by pictures of everlasting salvation, until all considerations of right or wrong were laid at the feet of the Goddess of Independence." The revolutionary press treated murder as a culture to be scientifically developed in a religious medium. With that culture the young generation was day by day inoculated who took part in the long campaign of " direct action "—another term borrowed from the Russian terrorists' vocabulary—of which the resounding prelude on April 30, 1908, was the bomb that killed Mrs. and Miss Kennedy at Muzzaferpur, instead of the Magistrate, Mr. Kingsford, for whom it was intended. Tilak, recalling the Poona murders in 1897, since which there had been " no act worth naming," hailed the advent of the bomb as an " amulet " with which India would work out her salvation. It ushered in a series of similar outrages of which the victims were not always British officials, but frequently Indians, whose one crime was that they were loyal servants of the British Government in India. Closely connected with the murder campaign, and to supply it with the necessary funds, was one of robbery with violence, carried on even in remote districts of Bengal by *bandralog* youths, *i.e.*, of the respectable classes, who revived the old lawless *dacoities* of pre-British times, plundering rich and poor alike, even helpless villagers, in order to fill the national war-chest.

Nor were the murders confined to Bengal. One of the most odious was the murder of Mr. Jackson, the collector of Nasyk, a city on the sacred Nerbudda river, famous for its Hindu shrines; and the Mahratta youth who perpetrated it, and was, like almost all his accomplices, a Chitpawan Brahman, confessed that he had never suffered injustice himself nor known who did, but he had read many instances of oppression in Tilak's *Kesari* and other newspapers of the same type, and learnt to believe that it was by the killing of Englishmen that " people can get justice." Before he was hanged he expressed his regret at having killed " a righteous man," and one, too, who was so deeply respected for his love of India and his Indian learning that he was affectionately nicknamed " Pundit " Jackson. Tilak had by that time been transported to Mandalay under a sentence of six years' imprisonment passed upon him by an Indian Judge for seditious articles " preaching violence and speaking of murders with approval," but he had been the first to create the atmosphere which breeds murderers. The contagion spread even amongst Indian students in London frequenting " India House," where they were indoctrinated by Shyamji Krishnavarama who had left India shortly after, but not, he declared, in connection with, the Poona murders, and edited a notorious paper called the *Indian Sociologist*, for some time actually published in England. Lectures were given there on the making of bombs, and Vinayak Savarkar, who smuggled out to India amongst other weapons the pistol and ammunition with which Jackson was shot dead, used to read out chapters from his history of the Mutiny, or, as he called it, " the war of Indian independence." On July 1, 1909, one of the young Indians associated with "India House" gained admittance to a great reception at the Imperial Institute and in its crowded rooms struck down Sir William Curzon Wyllie, an India Office official, who since his retirement from India had constantly devoted himself to the welfare of young Indians in England.

Moderate Indian opinion had at first been as reluctant as Government, both in England and in India, to acknowledge the gravity of the evil. Indians who could not bring themselves to condone murder cast the main responsibility on official obduracy to the legitimate aspirations of India, and the murderers

were euphemistically described as unfortunate
" turn-headed " youths, sometimes with an under-
current of admiration for them, especially in Bengal,
as heroes who had shown that the despised Bengalee
babu was capable of laying down his life for patriotic,
if misconceived, ideals. But Indian parents and
even Indian politicians, unless they actually belonged
to the revolutionary party, gradually woke up to
the danger of the poisonous gangrene which was
eating into the youth of India, and so austere a
Radical as Morley recognized the necessity of
strengthening the hands of the Indian executive for
the repression of crime and of revolutionary conspiracies by measures which were as repugnant to
him with his old recollections of coercion in Ireland
as to the majority of Indian politicians who have
since then so frequently agitated and not without
avail for their repeal. These measures fulfilled their
immediate purpose, but terrorism, though scotched
for a time, was not killed, and the havoc it wrought
amongst the youth of India for several years after the
explosion of the first murderous bomb at Muzzaferpur in 1908 is still part of the living history of India.

What was the intellectual apart from the political
genesis of that movement ? If some of the murderers
were obviously degenerates and moral perverts, and
many of them were the failures and, in their own
eyes, the victims of an educational system for
which they were totally unfitted, some were youths
of great promise, like Birendranath Gupta, who had
lived as a student in the Oxford Mission Hostel in
Calcutta and had borne there the highest character
for exemplary conduct and fine ideals. In some of
their secret societies the initiates bound themselves
solemnly to a life of self-denial, and, specially hard
for Indians, to celibacy. But the strangest and
most ominous feature of all was that most of them
had been brought up at schools and colleges at

which the educational system was Western, and many of them were excellent English scholars. Out of 186 persons convicted of political crimes, 68 were actually students and 50 were under 20 years of age. There were high-schools and colleges that had become forcing houses of conspiracy, where some of the teachers systematically trained up their pupils to believe in murder as the patriot's duty. But the oaths which all had to swear on initiation were administered in the name of Hindu gods and goddesses and most commonly of all in that of the Black Mother, Kali.

Was that to be the nemesis of Macaulay's gibes at Hindu mythology when he wrote his famous Minute in support of English education which would, he declared, within a few generations transform Indians into Englishmen so that only the colour of their skins would be left to differentiate them? What had happened that it should have been distorted to such strange uses as the cult of the bomb and the sacrifice of " white goats " to the dread goddess in the sacred name of freedom; though freedom was a concept that had little substantial meaning for the young Indian's mind until he found it writ large in his English textbooks? *Corruptio optimi pessima.* But it is not enough merely to take note of so grave a phenomenon. Nor can it be dismissed as a passing wave of insanity cast up by a powerful stream of reaction against the masterful impact of the West; for Indian terrorists who drew their inspiration twenty years ago from Russian Nihilists, can turn to-day to Russian Bolshevists not only for inspiration, but for secret assistance. May not a partial explanation be sought and found not only in the racial and religious and social clash of two widely different civilizations, but in the educational processes actually employed for pouring into the old Indian bottles the strong new wine of Western education?

CHAPTER VIII

THE TANGLE OF WESTERN EDUCATION

EFFICIENCY was the watchword of the administrative era ushered in by the transfer of India to the Crown after the Mutiny, and amongst the tasks inherited from the old East India Company none was more vital than that of guiding the youth of India on the path of Western education. But the one thing that era utterly failed to produce was any coherent educational system even in respect of the higher education on which the energies of Government were almost wholly concentrated. Such was the conclusion arrived at in 1919 by the only strong and independent Commission that ever sought assistance from Indian as well as British educational experience. Sir Michael Sadler's Commission was appointed in 1917 by Lord Chelmsford, who had taken great interest in educational problems at home before succeeding Lord Hardinge as Viceroy. It was appointed for the specific purpose of inquiring into the condition of the Calcutta University, which had long been notoriously unsatisfactory. But as that University had always been the chief centre of Western education in India and then numbered 26,000 students, *i.e.*, almost exactly as many as the students in all the British Universities put together, though they were drawn in Bengal from a population of which ninety per cent were still entirely illiterate, its condition could not be studied apart from Indian education in all its various aspects, and the Commission's monumental report, therefore, throws a flood of light upon its evolution during the whole of the critical period when the inflowing tide of Western influence reached its high-water mark and then ebbed and began to recede before the successive waves of reaction that poured in from the unplumbed depths of India's social and religious life.

The pioneers of Western education in the early part of the XIXth century entered upon the great experiment in a fine crusading spirit, trusting mainly to the future to control and guide the new forces which they were setting in motion, with a supreme confidence in the faith that was in them. The early results though confined almost entirely to the Hindus, as the Mohammedans continued for a long time to hold aloof from Western education, may well have seemed to justify that confidence. But just before the Mutiny, Parliament used the opportunity afforded by the impending renewal of the East India Company's Charter in 1853 to review the educational situation in the light of the experience available after two decades had elapsed since the grant of the last Charter in 1833 and the official introduction of Western education. An enormous amount of evidence was submitted to Committees of both Houses and none carried greater weight than that of witnesses who, like Alexander Duff, had actually stood sponsors, or like Sir Charles Trevelyan, Macaulay's brother-in-law, and J. C. Marshman, the son of John Carey's fellow-worker, were closely connected with the original sponsors for Western education in India. Parliamentary inquiry furnished the basis for Sir Charles Wood's great dispatch of 1854. The President of the Board of Control in London showed a new appreciation of the danger of building up a top-heavy structure of higher education without providing the necessary foundations of preparatory education. He was ready to take further steps to encourage higher education, but he laid the chief emphasis on elementary education, dropping at least by implication the old theory that education would filter down from the top. He impressed upon Government the duty of creating a properly articulated system of education leading up from the primary school to the Indian Universities, of which he promised the speedy creation; whilst, in accordance with the ideas that then prevailed at home, he contemplated the ultimate relaxation of Government control over educational agencies in favour of a larger policy which would enlist every form of independent local and private effort by grants in aid from Government. Nor was the need forgotten for extending education to the women of India in spite of the peculiar difficulties arising out of Indian social conditions. Sir Charles Wood could reasonably boast that he had propounded a really national system of education for India, if Indians, whether Hindus or Mohammedans or of other creeds, were prepared to take advantage of it. His dispatch was in fact to remain the nearest approach ever made to the coherent system of education for which the Sadler Commission still looked in vain three-quarters of a century later. Lord Dalhousie in full sympathy with it responded by setting up before he left India, two years later, some of the machinery required for the new policy by establishing special departments of public instruction; by extending vernacular education, which from the beginning had had warm supporters amongst the most zealous champions of English as the great vehicle of higher education; and by creating a training college for teachers of which, with the constant spread of education, the need had already become urgent. Female education had long engaged Dalhousie's deepest interest, and when he stated that " a far greater proportional impulse is given to the education and moral tone of the people than by the education of men," it was the result of a profound conviction that whatever the restraints imposed by Indian customs on the social emancipation of women, their influence within their homes is a factor of incalculable importance either in retarding or accelerating the diffusion of Western ideas.

Then came the thunderbolt of the Mutiny, and during the subsequent period of reconstruction Government shrank from the heavy expenditure required to carry out a more vital feature of the Wood dispatch, viz., the development of primary education, to which the Western-educated Indians were themselves, it must be admitted, still generally indifferent. The same thing happened twenty-five years later when a Commission appointed by Lord Ripon in 1882, on which the official element was predominant, set out to extend primary education, but ended by concentrating once more at its expense on secondary education within the narrow limits of its terms of reference. It was thus left to the Indian National Congress to include primary education amongst other items in its catalogue of Government sins of omission, but without perhaps much conviction until Gokhale imported into the subject his wide knowledge and enthusiasm. He fought many losing battles, but though one of his most powerful efforts failed to carry a resolution for free and compulsory primary education in the Imperial Council in 1910, its principles were practically accepted three years later by Government.

The one promise of the Wood dispatch that was promptly carried out after the Mutiny was the creation in 1858 of Universities in the three Presidency cities, Calcutta, Madras and Bombay, and the interest they at once excited overshadowed everything else. The University of London was taken as a model. Unlike the older British Universities it had no residential colleges and was not a teaching but an examining body that conferred degrees after the examination of candidates from a number of colleges affiliated to it, and prescribed the textbooks and standards of proficiency on which its examinations were based. This was the system transferred to India. With the help of the Sadler

Commission's Report the results can be most clearly followed in the history of the Calcutta University, and though they differed in degree rather than in kind in the other Indian Universities, they have been nowhere so unfortunate as at Calcutta, partly because of certain features peculiar to Bengal, and partly because owing to its size and association with the great city which was until 1912 the capital of India, it came to be regarded as the Premier University.

One of the features of the system which dominated the development of University education in India was the affiliation of particular colleges, which was abolished in London the very year after it had been copied at Calcutta. But even the drawbacks of affiliation, which were to become nowhere so prominent as at Calcutta, passed unnoticed at first, as the total number of colleges which were almost all Government or missionary institutions was small. Less harm would have been done had the power of granting or withholding affiliation implied for the University the power and duty of exercising supervision over the staff and equipment of the colleges, but no such power had been vested in the ruling bodies of the University, the Senate and the Syndicate. The Viceroy was, *ex officio*, Chancellor of the University, and a strong Educational Service was built up for administrative, inspecting and teaching purposes, through which Government proposed to exercise an effective control. It was at first from the Educational Service that the teachers were mainly recruited for the Government Colleges which, with some admirable missionary institutions, almost alone provided University teaching. But the policy of the University was framed by the Senate which was only brought indirectly under Government influence. An almost blind belief in the value of examinations as the one criterion of a sound education was setting

9

in at that time in England, and it was imported into India in an intensified form with the introduction of competitive examinations at home for the Indian Public Services. Education itself was conceived almost exclusively in terms of a literary education as the vast majority of the Indian Civil Service, the most powerful of all the public services, were themselves brought up on the humanities. Examinations, therefore, at once became the chief preoccupation of the new University Senate, to which distinguished administrators and public men were appointed as a matter of course, but far more rarely, and never as a matter of right, the men engaged in the actual work of teaching, who were constantly liable to be depressed under the burden of rules and regulations imposed upon them, with little opportunity, and no right, of consultation.

With examinations on hard and fast lines imposed from above as the sovereign test of the University education through which almost alone access could be obtained to constantly enlarging fields of employment, especially in the Public Services and at the Bar, under the new conditions of Indian life, instruction assumed a more and more mechanical character. In 1854 there had been only 129 students in Government colleges in Bengal, and an unknown but much smaller number in non-Government colleges. In 1882, within one generation, the numbers had grown to 2,394 in the former and 1,483 in the latter. The actual accommodation rapidly became wholly inadequate, class-rooms and lecture-rooms were terribly overcrowded; the personal contact between professors and students, always important, but absolutely essential when education had to be imparted through a foreign language and an equally foreign medium of thought, suffered, and, with rare exceptions, was gradually lost. The teachers were discouraged and the students led astray by a system which tended to make examinations the be-all and the end-all of education. Quality had to be subordinated to quantity. New colleges sprang up to which affiliation was almost automatically granted because the University was not organized or responsible for ascertaining whether they were adequately equipped, and when the Education Commission of 1882 was appointed in Lord Ripon's Viceroyalty, it never touched the one all-important question of the effect of the University system on the educational development of India, as the Universities were excluded from its purview. So highly officialized a Commission could not presume to challenge the paralysing parsimony of Government. It had to throw the main burden of extending primary education on to the Municipal Councils and District Boards which had just been created. That was a burden which they seldom cared to assume, as the only public demand was for higher education, and that part of its recommendations either remained ineffective or produced results which were as unforeseen as they turned out to be disastrous. With regard to secondary education, on the other hand, the Commission was driven to eke out such financial assistance as Government was willing to spare from other seemingly more urgent tasks by reducing the number of institutions controlled and supported or aided by the State and trusting to an appeal to private and local effort which was promised abundant encouragement but little or no material help.

Shortly afterwards on the recommendation of another official Commission, the Public Services Commission of 1886–7, the heart was taken out of the Indian members of the Educational Service by its reorganization on a basis of almost flagrant racial discrimination to their detriment. All the Public Services were divided into two branches denominated, sometimes quite illogically, Imperial and Provincial, the former a superior and the latter an inferior branch. Nowhere did this discrimination have such an unfortunate effect as in the Educational Service in which Englishmen and Indians had hitherto worked side by side, and more harmoniously perhaps than in other services because on a footing of greater equality. The Indians found themselves now relegated to an inferior pen, though their work might often be quite as responsible as that of the English members of the Service, and their influence, as teachers of the rising generation, was never of more vital importance then when Government colleges themselves were compelled to meet the growing pressure of numbers by increasing the proportion of Indians on their teaching staff without much regard for their capacity to impart what was still professedly an English education.

This was happening, too, just when the demand for Western education as an Open Sesame to lucrative employment was spreading far beyond the classes that had originally provided the bulk of Indian students. These had at first been mainly drawn from the higher castes that had once enjoyed a monopoly of Indian learning and had often inherited the fine intellectual gifts of their ancestry. They had come, at any rate for the most part, from the large cities, if not actually from families, that were to some extent in contact with Western ideas and habits of life. The new rush of students came from another class, the *bhadralok*, who, though of high caste by descent, consisted of small landholders and professional men in a small way and traders, not infrequently doing a little usury, living up-country or in the larger villages, on the fringe as it were of the purely agricultural community. The Mohammedans continued to stand in the ancient ways, but amongst the Hindu *bhadralok*, often as backward as the Mohammedans, many parents seized the new opportunities for starting their sons on the road to more dignified and remunerative careers than any to which they themselves had ever dreamt of aspiring. The sacrifices they were prepared to make were often pathetic, though sometimes the son's education was regarded as a financial investment which he would be expected to make good, and with heavy interest, as soon as his B.A. secured him the coveted appointment that was the one purpose of his education.

The enormous influx of boys of this class, for the most part quite unfitted for their new surroundings, dragged down a structure already dangerously top-heavy. In 20 years, from 1882 to 1902, the number of University students leapt up from 2,394 to 8,150 and less than one-fourth were in Government colleges. Considerably more than one-half were in unaided colleges often poorly staffed and equipped because they depended entirely upon the miserable fees which competition drove them constantly to lower in order to satisfy parents who could barely afford even the lowest, and who were far too ignorant to appraise the relation between cost and quality of education. Almost greater was the deterioration in the schools which fed the University. To meet this pressure from below which no one had the courage or perhaps the sense of responsibility to resist, the standards of instruction had to be gradually lowered and matriculation had to be made easier, until the first two years of the college course had to be usually devoted to the sort of work which should have been done in the last two years of the secondary school courses to bring the boys up to proper University standards.

What was the result ? Though they were pushed, often at too early a stage, to acquire some knowledge of English as the University courses were in English, they seldom learnt enough to be able to follow them with any understanding; and as they had not been taught their own vernacular, they were left without any language in which they could learn to think. They were thrown back on learning by heart, with the help of an often excellent memory, their textbooks and, above all, the note-books which the cleverer boys were ready to pass round, many of them just from good-nature and many also for value received in other ways. Some boys scrape through the whole of their course of studies without having seen a book except their textbooks and these circulating notebooks. Others who are fortunate enough to be able to pay for their tuition which frequently costs them several times their regular college fees, spend hours every day being crammed by tutors who equally overstrain themselves to eke out in this way their meagre salaries as masters. It is not usually for lack of industry, though often grievously misdirected, that young Indian aspirants to academic honours can be with any justice blamed.

Most disastrous of all was the abundant crop of private schools that sprang up like mushrooms to accommodate the overflow from Government or State-aided schools. The majority were Indian counterparts of "Dotheboys Hall," conducted solely for gain and often by men who were themselves the failures of the University system. As recently as 1918 a member of the Sadler Commission reported as follows his visit to a high-school of that type :

"The school occupies less than one-quarter of two stories of a quadrangular house. It is approached by a very dirty and dilapidated stair-case, the corridors are in such disrepair that one must be careful of one's steps, and the dreary dinginess of the rooms can scarcely be exaggerated. On the lower floor are 4 narrow class-rooms round a dark little office and library ; on the floor above, 5 rooms have been made immediately under the slates, in two cases by the simple device of putting up movable screens of dirty patched sackcloth.   The largest room might perhaps seat 24. It is used for a class of 50. The smaller rooms should at the most hold a dozen ; they are used for classes of 20 to 40. For Rs322 (£21 10s.) a month, a staff of 14 masters is maintained, including the head master himself and two of his brothers.   The head master draws Rs60 (£4), the two brothers Rs20 (£1 6s. 8d.) apiece. The second master draws Rs33 (£2 4s.) ; his qualification is that he is a plucked B.A.   One master, a law student reading for his degree, draws Rs30 (£2). Of the teachers on Rs15 (£1) one has been on the staff since 1886 and another has served for 14 years. We next visited the hostel which houses 5 or 6 masters and 45 boys. It consists of 2 fair-sized rooms at the top of an old, rather broken-down house, together with several small cells opening off the main rooms. Here we found a row of strips of matting at right-angles to the wall all round each room, at the head of each strip of matting a rolled-up blanket, and seated on each blanket, with his back to the wall, a boy ; all of them absolutely idle, without books or any other resources, staring before them. They cannot always sit there, and, when they are not in the dirty and cramped class-rooms, their only refuge must be the street. There is no kind of safeguard against the evilest influences. Imagination fails to picture what they do in the rains or in the hot weather.   Last year from this seat of learning 15 boys took the matriculation examination out of a class of 25 : 9 passed and 3 obtained a first division. This institution for ' affording *mofussil* (up-country) boys the advantages of a Calcutta education ' is recognized by the University of

Calcutta as a suitable place in which to obtain preparation for admission to the University."

How profound a sense must both teachers and students have acquired in such surroundings of the elevating influence of Western education and of the Western civilization behind it. How deep must have been their gratitude to the British *raj* to which they owed these blessings!

In the same year the Department of Public Instruction itself made the following admission :

" Such parts of education as are most necessary but not understood by the parents, *e.g.*, good discipline, social life, good physical condition, a reasonable standard of work in the classes, not being demanded, are not supplied, and to maintain their popularity concessions and exceptions are granted which a self-respecting institution would refuse."

It was late in the day to realize all this, for the conditions so forcibly described in 1918 had been growing up ever since the appeal of the Education Commission of 1882 to private enterprise had taken effect in this baneful multiplication of the private-venture schools which have invaded many other seats of learning besides Calcutta. Secondary schools and colleges were swamped with the *bhadralok* element which ultimately preponderated in the proportion of 3 to 1 over the urban element. Up-country boys were let loose in thousands amidst appallingly unsanitary conditions and all the temptations of a great crowded city without any of the old restraints which home life under the watchful eye of their own narrow community had previously provided. They were expected on the other hand to assimilate through the medium of a foreign language a whole order of new ideas equally foreign to that in which they had been brought up in their own homes. This is one of the inherent difficulties of

Western education in India, even when conducted on the most approved lines. In England boys from all the different social strata have some common fund of beliefs and experience and traditions upon which their schoolmaster in every grade of school can build. We have always been able to assume, too, that the training of the intellect for which our boys are sent to school and afterwards perhaps to college, is carried on, broadly speaking, in the same religious and moral atmosphere which they imbibed at home in their early childhood and which they continue to imbibe there during the holidays. Not so in India, but the very opposite. The Indian boy when he goes to school to be taught English and to obtain a Western education finds himself plunged with his very first primer in an entirely new world as far removed as the poles asunder from everything that he has ever seen or heard of at home. This is so especially if he comes from a rural or even an urban class that has never been brought into any sort of contact with Western ideas and customs. His home life has done nothing to prepare him for the schoolroom. It is the life to which his forbears have been bred for countless generations. It is determined by his caste which is his *Karma*. Some of his caste laws, though not the more essential, he may find it impossible to observe during his school years, but he can make the proper atonement. Fresh, perhaps, from a lesson in English history he may be seen proceeding with some of his schoolfellows to seek purification by sacrificing a goat to Kali or by begging for miraculous *mantras* from the Brahman attendants at the less terrifying shrine of the monkey-god, Hanuman. During his holidays he reverts with a sense of relief to the old traditions and habits, though with possibly a slight sense of superiority over those who have never had a chance of becoming " literate in English."

But it is not only his caste laws and all the
cherished beliefs of his childhood that he has to
leave behind him at the schoolroom door, but often
every picture of life such as he has learnt to see it
in his early surroundings from the moment he has
watched things growing in the fields and on the
trees, and the animals and birds and the many
phenomena of Nature so different from those he is
often made to read about in his textbooks, sometimes imported without any regard to latitude and
longitude. What can an Indian boy in the hot-
house plains of Bengal make of a wintry scene in
England with the snow lying deep on the ground
and the bare branches of our deciduous trees glistening
with hoar-frost ? Or what can a boy in the south
of India who sees the huge *durian* fruit growing
on lofty trees but has never seen an oak tree or an
acorn, be expected to make of the story of the
farmer's little son asleep in an English wood under
an oak tree and awakened by an acorn falling on
his nose, and his father solemnly pointing the moral
as an illustration of the Creator's wisdom and loving-
kindness in ordaining that pumpkins should grow on
the ground and only little acorns on the big oak
tree ? The dull-witted boy scarcely gets to understand the meaning of the English words in which
he has to learn his lessons, and least of all when,
as in many cases, his teacher, who may be a failed
B.A. or an even earlier failure by the wayside, is
only a few removes less ignorant. Given that he
surmounts these initial difficulties by dint of
application and the use of his memory to supply
or disguise his lack of understanding, he wanders on
in a growing bewilderment of mind with fresh batches
of painfully fingered notebooks under his arm,
through the labyrinthine maze which leads from one
examination to another.

The curse of the private-venture schools which

lowered all the standards, including those of matriculation itself, was that it induced relay after relay of
misguided youths to start in the educational race
who could never reach the winning-post. Their
intellectual and physical stamina, and their parents'
resources broke down under the strain. Many fell
out in the first or second lap, either failing even to
matriculate or else to pass the intermediate examination, or they were hopelessly plucked for their
degree; and those who managed at last to scrape
through frequently did so merely to discover too
late that the supply of such as they were already
far exceeded the diminishing demand. Government
offices were overstocked. The expansion of Indian
commercial and industrial enterprise was still proceeding slowly. The Bar was frightfully congested.
Even the value of a degree, and still more that of
a mere " failed B.A.," in the Hindu matrimonial
market, had depreciated. For occupations involving
manual labour their education, such as it was, had
rarely done anything to train them, and, as they
claimed at any rate to rank now amongst the
educated classes, they affected the contempt which
the learned castes had always entertained for those
who worked with their hands. They could not
bear the prospect not merely of encountering the
reproaches of their parents whose expectations they
had disappointed, but of returning to the drudgery
of their humble homes that had satisfied their
fathers and forefathers before them. They formed
an intellectual proletariat ripe for any mischief, and
the crashing of all the hopes which had induced
them to toil and suffer so much during several years
of squalid school and college life embittered them
towards an alien system that had caught them in
its toils and then cast them out on to the streets,
and towards the alien *raj* which they held responsible for it. Is it a wonder that they appealed for

vengeance to the great gods and goddesses upon whom they had been inclined to turn their backs, or that, in a period of angry revolt against the West, they listened eagerly to skilled agitators or fanatics who taught them that an alien domination was the root-cause of all their woes, and that its overthrow, even if it meant rivers of blood, was the only hope of salvation for them and for the whole of India that was suffering in other ways, but not less grievously than they, from the common oppressor.

These dangerous forces, though at the time strangely unobserved or carelessly ignored, had been growing up before Lord Curzon went out to India. He was far too able an administrator and took his duties as Chancellor of the Calcutta University far too seriously not to realize that there was something radically wrong in the state of Western education. But his mentality was attracted rather to the intellectual than to the moral effects of its deterioration, and above all in the higher education which he regarded as his particular sphere. In 1902 he appointed a Universities Commission, whose recommendations formed the basis of his new Universities Act of 1904. But for a man of his great intelligence and thoroughness, he quite unaccountably failed to realize that the causes of deterioration were not to be sought merely within the framework of the Indian University system, but largely if not chiefly in the terrible conditions prevailing in many of the secondary schools which fed the Universities. Schools were practically excluded from the purview of the new Commission, just as the University had been excluded from the purview of the 1882 Commission, which had been confined to the schools. The piecemeal handling of two such closely interrelated aspects of the whole problem of Western education was as unfortunate in the second as it had been in

the first case. As was to be expected under a Viceroy
who was a great autocrat with an overwhelming faith
in the efficiency of Government machinery, the chief
purpose of the Act of 1904 was to tighten the hold of
Government on the Universities and in the first place
on the Senate, which was still retained as the ruling
body, by reducing its total numbers whilst increasing
to an overwhelming majority the proportion of those
nominated by the Chancellor and giving *ex officio*
seats on it to the Provincial Directors of Public
Instruction.   In the Syndicate, which was the
executive body, provision, at first sight effective,
was made for a large number of college teachers,
but none was eligible who was not already a member
of the Senate. Increased powers of supervision over
existing colleges and the imposition of more stringent
conditions for the affiliation of new ones were steps
in the right direction, but they came too late and
made no attempt to deal with the fungus-growths
which, in so many schools, were rotting the foundations on which sound college education could be
built up. New faculties were to deal with the college
curricula and with the methods of University
examinations, but these were also to be mere
emanations from the Senate.   Practically nothing
was henceforth to be done without the approval of
Government.

Indian opinion, which Lord Curzon made no serious
attempt to consult, protested against such a comprehensive scheme of officialization, and in Calcutta
especially, where the large majority of the Senate
consisted of Indians who owed their seats on it to
many different considerations, but rarely to any
intimate acquaintance with educational matters, the
Act was attacked as a political blow deliberately
aimed at its independence. The Viceroy was even
accused of wishing to strangle Western education
because the new generation of Indians it had

produced possessed the courage and ability to criticize
and oppose him. The heated controversy over the
Act was the forerunner of the fierce outburst which
the Partition of Bengal was about to provoke, and
Lord Curzon left India before there was time to
carry out the more beneficial features of a reforms
scheme which in any case failed to strike at the roots
of the evil. Even such a urid "writing on the
wall" as the explosion in 1908[1]of murder conspiracies
invoking the sanction of ancient beliefs but bred in
schools and colleges that were the products of British
rule, did not call forth for many years any serious
searchings of heart amongst those responsible for
a system over which the State had never ceased to
claim a large measure of control. The moral usually
drawn by shallow critics was that it was now proved
up to the hilt that the introduction of Western
education had been from the very beginning the worst
blunder ever committed under the British *raj*.

Western education has been for India "the tree of
knowledge of good and evil." The evil often jumps
to the eye, but to the good only those Englishmen
can be entirely blind who distrust the superiority
of our civilization, though they may be loudest in
boasting of it, and at the same time ignore the finer
features of the Indian civilization with which it
comes into conflict. In ancient India education
was based on the bedrock of authority—the social
authority of the Brahman and of caste, the domestic
authority of the father or other male head of the
family, and, next to his, of the mother, who submissive as she was to her husband knew how to
claim the obedience as well as the affection of her
son, and, in the castes which enjoyed the monopoly
of learning, the authority of the *guru* or teacher to
whom the *chela* or disciple surrendered himself
with implicit faith for long years of study, sacred
rather than profane. Western education recognized

the principle of authority and upheld it, perhaps as firmly as Indian education, in the dark ages, but has tempered it with a growing spirit of inquiry since the Renaissance, and the Reformation set up the right of private judgment and in its train the whole conception of individual rights upon which Western society is still chiefly based; subject solely to their surrender within appointed limits to the one supreme authority of the State. Education in Europe has therefore developed individual character and initiative in a way that Indian education could not and never aspired to do, since it aimed at serving a social system which was neither an aristocracy nor a democracy nor a theocracy, but a communal organization of households within the larger organization of castes. Western education, it may be noted, achieved its greatest triumphs in India in the early days when the number of Indians who sought for it was small and the relations between them and a relatively small band of European teachers who threw themselves into their work as a vocation rather than a profession, were almost as close and intimate, and firmly rooted in authority— though the new authority was that of Western and not of Hindu learning—as those between the Hindu *chela* and his *guru*. Amongst the older generation of Western-educated Indians and even amongst those who have lost much of their faith in the West, one hears many who still speak of their Western *gurus* with the deepest affection and gratitude ; for the Indian, often over-sensitive to criticism, and above all to slights, real or imaginary, is singularly responsive to genuine kindness and consideration, A bureaucratic atmosphere is generally deadening. and never more so than where education is concerned. The Educational Service did not escape its influence as it became more and more highly officialized, though it never lacked many admirable exceptions, and it maintained a creditable level of professional efficiency. Nor was it professional efficiency that the Indians lacked into whose hands passed more and more largely, even in the higher schools and colleges, the task of educating their young fellow-countrymen on Western lines. Education does not consist in the mere reading of books. It is their interpretation that matters, and most of all in India where the medium is a foreign medium, foreign in language and foreign in spirit. With the best Indian teachers the angle of vision for all that stands behind Western education can seldom be quite the same as with the best English ones. The power of interpretation can seldom be quite the same. At first some balance was preserved between the European and the Indian element, but when the number of students increased by leaps and bounds, the European leaven was inevitably greatly diluted and tended to disappear altogether. Moreover, the provision of adequate training colleges for an Indian teaching staff had been gravely neglected. It became quite possible for a young Indian to complete his course of studies without having any opportunity in the ordinary course of things of hearing English spoken by an Englishman, still less of catching from the lips of an Englishman the spirit of an English education. When this happened in the colleges of the University it happened *a fortiori* in the high-schools, and if the type of Indian teachers remained relatively efficient there, it fell in many of the lower-grade schools to a very low standard until in most private-venture schools it sank to the nadir of moral as well as of scholastic worthlessness.

Yet with all its shortcomings and in spite of the many blunders which must be laid to the door of those, whether Europeans or Indians, who controlled the system, Western education cannot be called a failure when it has produced an intellectual élite capable of playing such a part as it does to-day in modern India. It has shown that Indian brains, when given a fair chance, are no whit inferior to European brains. They have succeeded in wrestling with and overcoming the tremendous initial difficulty of learning everything through a foreign tongue. The *babu's* high-flown and eccentric English may lend itself to the cheap ridicule which unfortunately too often wounds him to the quick. But we are not as a rule such proficient linguists as to have the right to scoff at others. The real wonder is the mastery of our language, and not only of our language, but of large fields of Western thought, which Western-educated Indians, many of whom have never left their country, display every day in public and official life, in lecture-rooms, on the Bench, at the Bar, in legislative and in municipal assemblies. The proportion of those who come to England to complete their studies has steadily increased, but, even when they are most successful, much of the credit rightfully belongs to the Indian Universities in which they have first graduated. It is perhaps to be regretted that until quite recent times those Universities concentrated almost exclusively on literature as the basis of a liberal education, whereas the young Indian, usually endowed with a plentiful imagination and a dangerous facility for loose generalizations, needed even more than British youths the wholesome intellectual discipline of a science course. But this was probably inevitable, since the framing of the curriculum as well as the teaching was originally in the hands of Englishmen who had themselves been for the most part brought up on the humanities. It was also inevitable that, when the best young Indian minds were fed upon the masterpieces of English literature, and when the history of English social and political evolution taught them to seek the secret of England's

10

greatness in her ancient love and achievement of freedom, they should have begun to apply all these lessons to the condition of their own country. The philosophic conception of freedom has usually taken in India the more negative shape of an escape from servitude, a liberation from the evils of human existence. Under the inspiring guidance of the first teachers who introduced them to Western education, there grew up in the last century a generation of Indians who saw in Western influence the liberation of Indian society from the thraldom of a religious and social system for which, when they were once touched with the Western spirit of inquiry, they ceased to find any rightful sanction. But when that stimulating guidance slackened and failed, and Western education, having grown largely mechanical, retained upon them an intellectual rather than a spiritual hold, other generations followed upon whom the old beliefs resumed their authoritative sway. It was the line also of least resistance. Stability and self-reliance are not amongst the virtues most conspicuous in the Indian character. The Indian who wants to apply the lessons of his Western education to social reforms at home comes at once into conflict with a mass of opinion still untouched by Western education, and often with the cherished beliefs of his own kith and kin. How much easier it is for him to apply them to criticism of an alien system of government and to gratify the aspirations to freedom which his receptive mind has absorbed from Burke and Shelley and Byron and Mill and all the Western apostles of democracy, by preaching the liberation of the Indian nation, as his vivid imagination conceives it, from an alien and therefore oppressive yoke. This was notably the line of least resistance upon which the Indian National Congress fell back, when its founders who had been brought up under the best influences of Western education in its earlier stages resigned themselves to its dissociation from the unpopular cause of social reform.

Quite as instructive has been the less fruitful history of Western education amongst Indian Mohammedans. Owing to the rigidity of Islamic dogma, the philosophy of Islam has almost always been much less catholic than that of Hinduism, and as its creed is essentially one of force, the fall of the Moghul Empire which had won India by the sword alone, was a blow that left the Indian Mohammedans plunged in fatalistic lethargy. For nearly half a century after the introduction of Western education they held, with few exceptions, entirely aloof from it. Not till the inflowing tide of Western influence was beginning to slacken amongst the Hindus did a great Mohammedan leader arise who, touched with the spirit of the West, sought to bring home to his people the disastrous consequences of their educational backwardness. They were not only a minority but an almost inarticulate minority in a new India in which, thanks to Western education, the Hindus who were extremely vocal were rapidly assuming a long lead. Sir Syed Ahmed Khan laboured with infinite courage and perseverance, and in the teeth of fierce opposition, to find a synthesis for Mohammedan orthodoxy and Western learning, and he at last found sufficient support amongst his more enlightened co-religionists to found in 1875 the Anglo-Mohammedan College of Aligurh as a worthy centre of Western education for the Mohammedan youth of India, whilst he extended the sphere of his personal influence by means of annual educational Conferences which attracted many Mohammedans from all parts of the country. By making Aligurh a residential college and by laying stress on religious and moral training, he hoped to avoid some of the pitfalls which beset Indian University students, and he was able to enlist the co-operation of English teachers and principals whose enthusiasm for their work was as keen and disinterested as that of the great pioneers of Western education in Calcutta and Madras and Bombay. The emphasis which he laid upon absolute loyalty to the British *raj* was calculated to appeal not only to the sentiment of his people whose faith is rooted in the principle of authority, albeit the authority should in theory at least be Mohammedan, but also to their self-interest, as he saw a much better guarantee for the preservation of their religious and communal rights under British rule as then by law established than under any revival of Hindu rule or any form of Hindu political ascendancy. As long as he lived he set his face consistently, and on the whole successfully, against any Mohammedan participation in such movements as the Indian National Congress. But when he died in 1898 he left no one who could quite fill his place. It may well be ascribed to the influence of his teachings that not a single Mohammedan was implicated in the first outbreak of murder conspiracies amongst the young Hindus who put their ill-directed Western education to such sinister uses. The impulse given by Sir Syed Ahmed to Western education amongst his co-religionists has survived in so far as it makes for material advancement, but the spirit which he sought to infuse into it has steadily evaporated, and whilst Mohammedan orthodoxy has perhaps a stronger hold than ever upon the fanatical masses, a Mohammedan *intelligentsia* has grown up who, whilst sometimes ostentatiously broadening their phylacteries, are much more disposed to join hands with Hindus in a common hostility to British rule than in striving to convert their own people to a more liberal and tolerant interpretation of their ancient faith.

Amongst Hindus, however, as well as amongst Mohammedans, there has been one formidable obstacle —perhaps the most formidable of all—to the achievement by Western education of the high purposes of its pioneers. They did not aim merely at the creation of an intellectual élite. Their hope was to lift the social and religious life of the people of India on to a higher plane by bringing to birth a new type of Indian mind saturated with Western ideals whose influence would filter down through the weight of example as well as precept. But can a new type be born of men alone without the co-operation of women ? That co-operation Western education has barely ever enlisted. Dalhousie, as we have seen, saw the urgent need of it three-quarters of a century ago, and the Bethune College for Women, founded in 1849 by one of the members of his Council, still bears his name and perpetuates one of the earliest efforts made to arrest the lopsided growth of an educational system restricted to one of the two sexes. Even in Western countries the State has been slow to recognize the importance of including girls as well as boys in any educational system that is to build up a nation. It was still more tardily recognized in India where even the practical difficulties are infinitely greater, and greatest of all amongst the very classes that it was hoped to draw within the orbit of Western education. First and foremost is the *zenana*. Even if Indian parents do not succeed in marrying off their daughters when they are still children, they impose upon them the strict seclusion of the *zenana* at an age which must break off primary education long before it can have any permanent value and rules out any possibility of secondary education. Fathers, whose chief concern is to provide dowries for their daughters, naturally grudge even the smallest amount of money spent on an education which, if they do marry, seems to them

to have been merely thrown away, whereas the
money invested in the education of sons is expected
to prove a good investment from which they may
themselves derive some benefit in their old age.
Add to these important considerations the intense
prejudice of the mother and all the female relations
against the Western woman's ideas and habits of
freedom and everyday contact with men which
they regard as degrading, if not morally wrong, and
one can understand that a much greater effort is
required to promote female than male education.
No such effort was forthcoming. There was no
demand for it from the Indians themselves, except
from a few enthusiasts, chiefly amongst the Brahmo
Samaj. Government and missionaries created and
maintained almost all the very few high-schools for
girls which drew only a small number of their pupils
from the better classes of Hindu and fewer still of
Mohammedan society. The Education Department's
statistics have shown from time to time an increase
in the number of girls' schools that does not look
unsatisfactory until comparison is made with the
overwhelming proportion of girls who receive no
education at all though they belong to the same
classes as the boys who flock to schools and colleges.
A very serious impediment is the dearth of women-
teachers and especially of women-teachers of a class
that might to some extent disarm the hostility of
the *zenana*. No system of female education can be
successful in which the teaching staff has to be
recruited almost entirely amongst men, and in India
less than elsewhere, and least of all when the small
minority of women-teachers are drawn from the
native Christian and lower-caste women, who, well
educated though they may have been by missionaries, bear in Indian eyes the stamp of degrading
inferiority. Again, the high-schools for girls were
dominated by the same fetish of examinations which

the Universities had set up for male education, and there was no differentiation between subjects more suitable for men than for women. Girls were even less amenable than boys to all ideas of hygiene or physical exercise or open-air pursuits. Primary education, *i.e.*, 99 per cent of female education altogether, was equally mechanical, and only by a few rare English-women with the gift of sympathy was any attempt made to adapt the rudiments of a practical education to the home life to which the Indian girl was destined to revert. Endeavours to carry even elementary tuition into the *zenana* by means of house-to-house visitations were in most cases dismal failures, and only very few of the highest and wealthiest classes indulged in the luxury of introducing resident governesses into their families, and sometimes in the teeth of such stubborn resistance from the *zenana* that life was made intolerable for the despised interlopers.

With such a disparity between male and female education in the classes whose whole outlook on life Western education, it had been hoped, would simultaneously enlarge, the deepening gulf, even if only an intellectual one, between the two sexes added a fresh complication to the problem of marriage, already beset with all the difficulties resulting from the rigidity of caste laws, as inexor-able as ever in regard to the *jus connubii*. Indian youths whose horizon had expanded with Western education looked in vain for suitable and congenial helpmeets, and their reluctance to wed the old-fashioned girl from behind the *purdah* merely stiffened the ignorant conservatism of the *zenana* into bitter hatred of foreign innovations subversive of all the inherited traditions of family life and of the sheltered sanctity of Indian womanhood. The same feeling of hostility was generated behind the still more impenetrable veil of the Mohammedan *purdah* when Mohammedan women saw their men-folk being caught, though much later, in the impious meshes of Western education. But in spite of all these peculiar difficulties, Indian women, if still in very small numbers, have already shown that they are no less capable than Indian men of doing credit to the most advanced forms of Western education. There are Indian ladies whose homes are centres of the same culture and refinement that we associate with the best type of English homes, and it is to the honour of Indian womanhood that when they decide to enter a liberal profession, it is medicine that they seem most frequently to select, doubtless because, as women, they are painfully familiar with the amount of human suffering and avoidable mortality due in India to the lack of the most rudimentary knowledge of hygiene and sanitation. Just as at the dawn of Western education it was a school of medicine at Calcutta that first attracted even the young Brahmans of Bengal, the Lady Hardinge Medical School at Delhi now attracts students from many different castes and races, and amongst Indian women who come over in increasing numbers to complete their studies in Europe, medical students are growing more and more numerous. None can realize more fully than educated women that education is the great social problem of India, and that until female education has made up a great deal more of the leeway which it has lost under the restraints imposed upon it by Indian social traditions, India cannot attain the place to which she aspires as a modern nation.

Not even the most extreme protagonists of the superiority of Indian over Western civilization deny the essential value of Western education or the service which it has rendered to India in rousing her out of her lethargy to a new sense of nationhood.

None talk of deposing Western education, for there are few of them who do not owe and are not conscious that they owe to it a great personal debt. Most Englishmen will admit that its methods have been often grievously at fault. As soon as, owing to the ready acceptance it at once met with, it outgrew the capacity of a small band of devoted Englishmen with a special vocation for the work, it was forced into an artificial mould, shaped more according to the letter than to the spirit. There was more mechanical control than helpful guidance, and the spirit was often starved in a vain attempt to stuff the brain with undigested knowledge. But the greatest source of weakness was the lack of any solid substructure of elementary education. Gokhale was the first great Indian who saw this clearly, but extracted nothing from official wisdom, or parsimony, beyond a frigid *non possumus*. Both Government and public opinion have, however, moved since then, partly under the increasing pressure of religious forces which have compelled the State to depart so far from the old principle of religious neutrality as to agree to the creation of a Hindu University at Benares and a Mohammedan University at Aligurh. Economic forces have worked at the same time in favour of broadening the basis of education. Four times as much public money is spent now on education as 20 years ago when Lord Curzon was Viceroy, and nearly half goes to primary education. Official control has been immensely relaxed and decentralized under the recent reforms which have included education amongst the subjects transferred from the Central to the Provincial governments. The demand for higher education on Western lines has not slackened. Almost every province that did not already possess a University is bent on having one for itself. The number of high-schools continues to increase. But the popular cry all over India is for elementary education. The sincerity of the cry has yet to be tested by the willingness of the parents to foot the bill, which must be a very heavy one, and the great practical difficulty of supplying a huge army of teachers has yet to be overcome. But it rests now mainly with the Indians themselves to solve the tremendous problem of Indian education as a whole. That they have been compelled to confront it and to realize that education is the greatest of all national problems is not the least valuable service that Western education with all its shortcomings has performed for India. There are Indians to-day who in a temper of unreasoning reaction imagine that the only "national" solution of the educational problem lies in an absolute divorce from the West. But against the possibility of such a divorce they themselves are the living witnesses. For inasmuch as they profess to believe that India can attain, and has indeed already attained, to the full stature of a modern nation, their conceptions of Indian nationhood clearly bear the impress of one hundred years of Western education, and the English language, which has been the gift of Western education to Indians, provides them with the one medium in which those conceptions find the widest and fullest range of expression amidst the jarring confusion of India's own countless tongues.

CHAPTER IX

THE GREAT WAR

By the time the Great War broke out in 1914 the storm which had swept over India after the partition of Bengal had almost entirely died down. Even so stern a Radical as John Morley, with all his hatred of coercion and his public record in Ireland behind him, had been fain to sanction repressive measures for curbing the inflammatory violence of the revolutionary Press and reaching the mainsprings of a murder propaganda that was devastating the younger generation. But he had refused to believe that in India any more than in Ireland a permanent remedy was to be found in a policy of mere repression. His views were shared by Lord Minto, though it was the Conservative Government then still in office at home that had appointed him in 1905 to succeed Lord Curzon as Viceroy, and a balanced scheme of reforms, commonly known as the Morley-Minto reforms, was embodied in the Indian Councils Act of 1909. It did not touch the British framework of Government, and Morley indignantly repudiated any intention of paving the way for a parliamentary system of government in India which, "if my existence either officially or corporeally were to be prolonged twenty times longer than it is likely to be, is not," he said, " at all the goal to which I would for a moment aspire." What he did was to enlarge the Indian Legislative Councils by introducing into them a considerable elective element, and whilst maintaining their purely consultative character to give them the opportunities of discussion and criticism for which the Indian National Congress had hitherto afforded the only popular platform. Another significant step was the introduction of an Indian into the Viceroy's Executive Council, the citadel of British rule, and of two Indians into the

Secretary of State's Council in Whitehall. Had the Indian Councils Act of 1892 made anything like the same attempt to satisfy the aspirations of an older generation of Western-educated Indians the growth of irreconcilable forces might have been arrested. It was only temporarily checked by the Morley-Minto reforms. They were at first generally welcomed as an instalment of what India was entitled to claim. The reforms did not in fact invest the new Councils with any powers of control, and they carefully provided for the maintenance of a majority of official members who were expected to vote to order and could therefore always override the Indian un-official minority. For a time, however, the new Councils overshadowed the National Congress, already seriously discredited by internal feuds and the scandalous scenes at Surat at the end of 1907, when the rowdiness of the extremists broke up the session in wild confusion.

No British reigning sovereign had ever visited his Indian Empire until King George went out at the end of 1911 with his Consort, Queen Mary, to hold in person a great Coronation Durbar at Delhi. It was an event which appealed to the imagination of India and to her traditional spirit of reverence for kingship. The Sovereigns had already visited India as Prince and Princess of Wales when their presence lulled the first storm that followed the partition of Bengal. The enthusiasm with which they were now received far exceeded their former experiences, and often took the form of almost semi-divine worship. The transfer of the capital from Calcutta to Delhi, the ancient seat of the Moghul Empire, which was perhaps chiefly intended to gratify Mohammedan sentiment, and a resettlement of Bengal with the creation of a new province of Behar and Orissa, which went far to heal for the Hindu population the old sores of Lord Curzon's partition, have been subjected since then to much criticism both at home and in India. But at the time they were hailed as impressive manifestations of the Sovereign's omnipotence entirely in consonance with Indian tradition. The attempt just one year later to kill Lord Hardinge by hurling a bomb into the howdah of the State-elephant which was carrying him and Lady Hardinge on his first State entry as Viceroy into the new capital was an alarming proof that the revolutionist's faith in murder had not yet been stamped out, and some time elapsed before the conspiracy was traced back to the actual perpetrators of the crime. But the immediate effect was to heighten the popularity which Lord Minto's successor had already earned for himself, and many hearts were permanently touched when, as he recovered from wounds that had nearly been mortal, he gave to the people of India a warm assurance that his confidence and affection for them had suffered no change.

Lord Hardinge's diplomatic experience and personal contact with the German Emperor before he went to India had convinced him that Germany's boundless ambitions would ultimately plunge the world into war. He was not unprepared for the catastrophe when it came in August, 1914, and he believed that the crisis would strengthen the forces of attraction which bound India to the British Empire. The event proved him to be right throughout the first two years when he was still Viceroy. None could then foresee that the ordeal would be so prolonged and severe that it would end by giving a fresh impetus to the forces of repulsion which tend to estrange India from the West. To most Indians the Great War came as a bolt out of the blue, for few of them, even amongst the best educated, studied the international situation which had lost its chief interest for them when the Anglo-Russian understanding removed the old apprehensions of a

appreciation of the fine part which India was playing when he declared that " henceforth Indian questions would have to be approached from a different angle of vision."

Had the war ended within two years all would have been well, but in India even the strongest waves of emotion are apt to subside suddenly. Tenacious as Indians are of their ancient beliefs and customs, their moods often change as rapidly as children's. The war lasted too long and it was too remote from them. Some of the Indian Princes went to the front with their own contingents, but few of the educated classes had any personal interest in the war. They had little or no connection with the Indian army, and it had indeed been one of their political grievances that no facilities had ever been provided for training their sons to join the army under conditions consistent with their self-respect. The fighting races which provided the bulk of the Indian army were for the most part illiterate and their humble kinsfolk who remained behind were quite unable to follow the doings of their sons and brothers on battlefields with unfamiliar names far away across the " black water." Only the casualty lists filtered down to them slowly, and the calculated optimism of official publications was gruesomely offset by the return of the sick and wounded of whom the steady stream from Mesopotamia brought home too often tales of mismanagement and defeat, startlingly corroborated by the thunderbolt of the Kut surrender, just after Lord Hardinge had handed over the Viceroyalty to Lord Chelmsford. If England had been reluctant at first to credit Kitchener's prophecy that the war would last three years, Indians were still more at a loss to understand why victory should be so slow to come to Great Britain and her powerful allies, and they began even to doubt whether it would come at all. Whilst with the exception of a few notorious agitators the Indian Mohammedans felt no compunction about the war with Turkey, and to the very end Mohammedan sepoys fought as staunchly against the Mohammedan Turks in Palestine and Mesopotamia as against the German Unbelievers in France, their religious feelings were genuinely disturbed when the Sherif of Mecca himself joined the Allies and hoisted in the Holy Places of Islam the standard of Arab revolt against the Sultan of Turkey, whose spiritual authority they still dissociated from his action as a temporal ruler.

The politicians of the extremist wing were the first to give signs of impatience as time passed without any practical attempt in England to give effect to Mr. Asquith's promise of "a new angle of vision." Lord Hardinge's farewell advice to his Legislative Council was to remember that self-governing institutions could only be developed by slow if steady processes of evolution, and not by any magical wand of statesmanship. But he was going away and his voice fell on ears that were growing less receptive. All the old forces of political discontent were again astir and they quickly responded to the vehement appeals of two leaders who were strange but not unnatural allies. Tilak's term of imprisonment had expired just before the beginning of the war and he at first observed with creditable self-restraint the covenant on which he had been allowed to return to his home at Poona. But in 1916 he emerged from his retirement and resumed his old propaganda for *Swaraj* as the only means of redeeming India from slavery to the West. Mrs. Besant, who professes to believe as firmly as any Hindu, and has indeed constantly taught Hindus to believe, that the gods and the philosophies and the customs of Hinduism are far holier and wiser and better than those of Western nations, launched in her paper, *New India*, the slogan of "Home

11

Rule " for India, and she was soon able to claim that her Home Rule League numbered fifty branches. If it was at first in schools and colleges that this propaganda provoked the most tumultuous enthusiasm, it soon swept the Indian National Congress once more off its feet; and when Tilak in company with Mrs. Besant stepped on to the platform for the first time since his six years' internment in Mandalay they were both acclaimed almost like incarnations of the Deity. A veteran Bengalee schoolmaster, Mr. Mozumdar, was in the chair, and in the course of a long and passionate oration, delivered as usual in high-flown English, he dragged in a reference to the Mutiny which was perhaps the most glaring of his many perversions of history. According to him " The East India Company after a hundred years of misrule was at last," he declared, " overthrown by a military rising which transferred the government of the country to the Crown ! " Then followed an emphatic demand for Home Rule, hot and strong, and a resolution embodying it was carried *nem. con.* Within a year Congress had travelled far from the sane temper in which, under Mr. Sinha's presidency and following his urgent advice, political controversies were postponed to the successful prosecution of the war. It was swayed once more by the Extremists who had broken up the Surat session of 1907. The voices of moderation and goodwill were almost silent. That of Gokhale had been hushed for ever. He had died very prematurely in the first year of the war, after a last and vain endeavour to restrain Tilak from breaking the war-time truce to political feuds. The British Government, absorbed in the desperate pre-occupations of the Empire's struggle for life, seemed to the impatient Indians to have forgotten Mr. Asquith's pledges. Lord Hardinge was known to have taken home with him a scheme of constitutional reforms,

and his successor, Lord Chelmsford, was also known
to have set to work as soon as he arrived in India
on another scheme in consultation with the members
of his Executive Council.   But Whitehall continued to preserve an enigmatic silence until the
Government of India implored it to put war-maps
aside for a moment and make some definite pronouncement that should stem the rising tide of
political unrest in India.

At that juncture Mr. Montagu became Secretary
of State for India.   He had already made himself
familiar with Indian affairs not only as Parliamentary
Under-secretary at Whitehall, but by the more
unusual method of spending several months leave
in India whilst holding that office.   He owed
perhaps to his Semitic origin a peculiar sympathy
with Asiatics, and to his English Liberalism a firm
belief in the virtue of representative institutions all
the world over.   He scarcely deserved, however,
either the praise or the blame heaped on to his name
for the famous declaration which he made in the
House of Commons on August 20, 1917.   The
principles enunciated in it had already been settled
whilst Mr. Austen Chamberlain was Secretary of
State for India before his quixotic resignation on
the findings of the Mesopotamian Commission, and
no other than Lord Curzon himself had a large hand
in framing its terms.   The responsibility in any case
was that of the Cabinet as a whole, whose mouth-
piece on such an occasion it was Mr. Montagu's
duty to be as Secretary of State.   It was undoubtedly
a momentous pronouncement, more momentous
indeed, though in the stress of war the country and
the House itself were slow to perceive this at the
moment, than any that had been made in Parliament
since the days of Burke and Pitt.   It was to the
effect that British policy was " not only the
increasing association of Indians in every branch

of the administration, but also the granting of self-governing institutions with a view to the progressive realization of responsible government in India as an integral part of the British Empire."

Even with the reservation of the British Government's right to determine periodically the stages and the measure of Indian constitutional advance it involved in the mere promise of responsible government a signal departure from the old principle of Indian governance as a trust exercised by Great Britain under the sole responsibility of Parliament. Viewed merely as a necessary concession to Indian sentiment in fulfilment of Mr. Asquith's promise, it was certainly announced in too perfunctory a fashion. Had it been made earlier and in the solemn form of an Imperial proclamation it would perhaps have made as profound an impression in India as Queen Victoria's proclamation after the Mutiny. But British statesmen, obsessed with the shallow and certainly now obsolete notion of an "unchanging East," have seldom been willing to believe that nowhere is it more true than in India that, "if it were done when 'tis done, then 'twere well it were done quickly"; and many at home and in India could not at first take quite seriously so important a declaration of policy dropped, as it were, casually across the floor of the House by a new and almost unknown Minister. The British Cabinet, however, meant it seriously, and Mr. Montagu most of all. He proceeded in person a couple of months later to India to draw up in consultation with the Viceroy, Lord Chelmsford, an exhaustive report upon the general situation and on the most practical way of carrying the new policy into effect. It was a formidable task, for the old inquiries into the state of India which before the Mutiny had been conducted by Parliament whenever the East India Company's charter came up for renewal, had been curiously

enough dropped ever since Parliament's responsibility had become far greater and more direct with
the assumption of the government and administration of India by the Crown without the buffer which
the East India Company had hitherto provided.
The inquiry had now to be conducted and the report
drawn up in haste, and, what was still worse,
amidst the din and turmoil of political agitation.
For whilst the Indian moderates dared not say
publicly that the declaration of August 20 fulfilled
and more than fulfilled their expectations, the
Extremists had from the very first condemned it
root and branch as totally inadequate; and just
before Mr. Montagu landed in India the Indian
National Congress, with Mrs. Besant in the chair,
which it had long been her ambition to occupy,
renewed in almost threatening terms its imperious
demand for immediate Home Rule. The Montagu-
Chelmsford Report was nevertheless an extremely
able document, as exhaustive as it could be made
within the time, and its recommendations were the
outcome of consultations not only with the chief
officers of Government in every department, but
with representatives of all political parties including
the most extreme. It was laid before Parliament
in April, 1918. As far as India was concerned it
was a singularly unfortunate moment. The great
German push in France had just then moved the
British Government to make a fresh appeal to India
for further help and especially for intensified recruitment for the Indian Army and into that appeal
many Indians read a cry almost of despair. In
substance India's response was again splendid and
recruits flowed in more abundantly than ever and
notably from the fighting races of the Punjab. The
Indian Assembly voted another contribution of
£45,000,000 sterling to the Imperial exchequer for
war purposes and showed its appreciation of the

Once

gravity of the war crisis by maintaining a sober and temperate tone in the discussion of Indian internal questions. But there was less restraint elsewhere. The Extremists clearly thought the time was ripe to make their own terms for acquiescing in war measures which they did not openly venture to refuse, and they poured out undisguised scorn upon the reforms foreshadowed in the Montagu-Chelmsford Report, Mrs. Besant taking the lead, with her declaration that they meant "a perpetual slavery which can only be broken by a revolution."

Whilst political agitation waxed fast and furious, the masses whom it might still have left untouched had new and very real causes of discontent, and their "angle of vision" too had been changed by the war which had for the first time brought them in considerable numbers into close contact with the white man. The war which had begun by restoring concord and goodwill between the ruling and the subject race in a great common effort, failed in the end to draw them together, as many had hoped, in the consciousness of sacrifices borne and victory achieved in common. Its aftermath plunged them into fresh conflict, with a fresh intensity of racial feeling.

CHAPTER X

THE SILENT MASSES

THE world war has left nothing quite unchanged in the world—not even the " silent masses " of India, whose life had been scarcely touched by the inner struggle between the old and the new, confined almost entirely to the educated classes of the great cities, which had been the most vital part of Indian history during the XIXth century. The war was not yet at an end when the Montagu-Chelmsford Report made bold to interpret their silence as " a pathetic placid contentment " which would have to be disturbed for their own good. Their contentment was already being fast enough disturbed, if indeed the term would not always have been a misreading of a mute resignation to the conditions under which it was the will of the gods, and of that other inscrutable power known as the *Serkar*, or Government, that they should live.

Those conditions are harder than they, perhaps, fortunately for themselves, could ever fully realize, having had no experience or knowledge of any others, and therefore no standard of comparison. The vast majority of the population of India have always lived and still live by agriculture, and of that vast majority the greater part have always lived and still live on the edge of hunger—submissive to the immutable laws of Nature and climatic conditions peculiar to India, and the almost equally immutable laws of India's social and religious evolution through the ages.

Out of India's 320,000,000 the urban population, including within that term many villages of even less than 5,000 inhabitants, numbers only just over 10 per cent and shows a very slow rate of increase. Of towns with over 100,000 inhabitants there are only 35 with an aggregate population of eight and a-quarter millions, and of these only two, Bombay and Calcutta, have each over one million. Within the towns, and mainly within the few larger towns amongst them that can be called cities, is confined almost exclusively so much of the life of India as has been directly influenced by the impact of the West and can be called in any way modern. Nine-tenths of the whole population are scattered in small villages and hamlets almost innumerable where they follow the same agricultural and pastoral pursuits as their forbears for countless generations past, and reproduce in our own times immensely ancient conditions of life which have survived all the vicissitudes of India's political history. The general aspect of an Indian village—of sun-dried mud with thatched roofs in the dry atmosphere of the great plains and plateaus of Upper India, and of wattle and bamboo and palm-leaves in the more humid regions near the coast and the more tropical hills and jungles of Central and Southern India—presents at first sight much less variety than the features and complexions and the dialects and local peculiarities of the multitude of different peoples that are born and live and die in them dependent always on the fruits of the soil which vary as greatly as the nature of the soil itself, and the incidence of rainfall which in most parts is the sovereign factor that makes or mars its fruitfulness. But just as the country as a whole is one vast and often rich field of agriculture, so the life of the Indian *ryot* presents nearly everywhere certain features common to this vast agricultural population, and the most universal feature of all is poverty.

That this is so is an unpleasant admission to have to make after a century-and-a-half of British rule, which has done little so far to quicken the dead waters of ignorance that have stunted the moral and intellectual development of the Indian peasant.

But in so far as his outlook on life is largely governed by a ceaseless struggle for existence with the forces of Nature, in some respects more capricious and cruel than in any other part of the world, British rule may well claim to have done a great deal to ease the strain upon him, and in many ways which he only dimly apprehends. First and foremost save for the Mutiny, which was short-lived and confined to a relatively small area, it has given him for a whole century complete immunity from the ravages both of internal warfare and of foreign invasion. Throughout the whole of India under direct British administration, and, indirectly and in a lesser degree, in the Native States, it has reduced the pressure of taxation on his land and the even greater pressure of arbitrary exactions, and it has taught him entirely new standards of justice and humanity often finely exemplified in the personal influence which a single Englishman can exert over the whole of a huge district entrusted to his charge, though only the merest fraction of the people may ever come into close contact with him. If British rule has been slow to evolve any large co-ordinated policy for the scientific development of India's agricultural resources, the construction of 38,000 miles of railway, and of great irrigation works that have added over 20,000,000 acres to the cultivable area of the country are only the most striking amongst the many material advantages which have enured not least to the benefit of India, and which are almost wholly due to the initiative of the State and to the influx of British capital confident in the stability of British rule.

On the other hand, the very stability of British rule and the reign of law and order which it has established over the whole of India have indirectly conduced to the enormous growth of population which is one of the most easily demonstrable causes of India's poverty. Within the fifty years for which trustworthy statistics are available the total population of India has grown from 200,000,000 to more than 300,000,000, and of this enormous increase the largest proportion has been in rural India. The principal reason is not far to seek. The *Pax Britannica* has permitted the undisturbed fulfilment by the Indian people of the most sacred duty imposed upon them by their social and religious system—viz., the procreation of children for the paramount purpose of leaving a son or sons to carry on the ancestral rites essential to the salvation of all generations past, present and to come. To quote an Indian writer on the Population Problem— " Everybody marries, fit or unfit, and becomes a parent at the earliest age permitted by Nature. For a Hindu, marriage is a sacrament which must be performed regardless of the fitness of the parties to bear the responsibilities of a mated existence." Under the far-reaching influence of Hinduism early marriages are almost equally common in non-Hindu communities. This huge increase has, moreover, taken place in spite of a death-rate twice as high as that of Great Britain, and largely due to infantile mortality and the prevalence of many diseases which are regarded as preventable in other countries and might be prevented in India but for the Indian's dense ignorance of hygienic laws and the insufficiency of medical services to deal with such vast populations. The other side of the picture is that there has been no sufficient increase in production to keep pace with this fifty-per-cent increase of population in fifty years, and that there is not enough land to-day to yield a living wage to those who labour on it, so long as their own social customs and their ancient methods of cultivation remain unchanged and block or hinder the way to new avenues of economic development. Conditions vary to some extent in different parts of the country. In Bengal, for instance, the Hindu laws of inheritance and subinfeudation have broken up the land into such tiny parcels for the individual holders that according to the Census of 1921 with 24,496,000 acres under cultivation in that province, giving employment to 11,000,000 persons, the average amount of land for each worker was under 2¼ acres. In England the average is 21 acres—almost ten times as much—for each agricultural worker ; in the self-governing Dominions and the United States far more. In other provinces the overcrowding of the land is not quite so appalling, but there are few in which there is enough land under cultivation to provide under existing conditions and present methods of cultivation sufficient sustenance for the cultivator, or even—and this is an almost equally important factor—enough work to keep him usefully occupied. It is often said that though the Indian *ryot* can and does work hard at intervals, he is naturally very indolent. But if he is indolent he has many excuses. Not only has he very often too little land to keep him constantly at work, but the work he has to do does not need to be continuous, for owing to the peculiarities of the Indian climate the amount of work that has to be done in the fields is largely conditioned upon the seasonal periods of drought and rainfall. In some parts of the country if the rains fail he can do nothing but sit and starve, whilst if there has been a good monsoon he has merely to scratch the soil and it will yield an abundant harvest. Work as he may he cannot control the rainfall on which ultimately depends his chance to keep body and soul together.

There are, however, many other opportunities of work besides merely ploughing and sowing and harvesting from which he is shut off by caste law or immemorial custom. He lacks, too, one of the chief human incentives to work. He may by greater industry or intelligence better his material condition within the caste into which it is his *Karma* to have been born, but he cannot hope and he is indeed forbidden to hope that by any effort of his own he can rise out of it, and the only laws he has to observe for his salvation are his caste laws which are immutable. He does not as a rule repine. He takes things as they are because he cannot conceive them otherwise. The temperament of the Indian peasant is by no means the same all over India. It varies with the immense variety of races and beliefs and natural surroundings. If his life is generally tinged with a hue of melancholy fatalism, it is seldom a gloomy fatalism. He is often light-hearted and merry and not devoid of a rough sense of humour. But his range of experience is very narrow. He rarely gets a glimpse of any other forms of social life than those to which he is tethered. Take rural England, on the other hand, where the landed gentry, and the sporting squire, the lady bountiful, the country clergy, the schoolmaster, the doctor, the general shopkeeper, the cricket field or football ground, the local hunt, even the public-house with its sometimes very seamy side, all help to vary the monotony of village life. In the Indian village there is nothing to stir the *ryot's* mind to any curiosity of the outside world with which his only concern is the marketable price of his produce, and the amount of taxes he has to pay, both ruled by mysterious powers as inscrutable to him as those of his household-gods and even more difficult to propitiate.

The Indian village community was in ancient times the basic social unit. At its best, it was absolutely self-contained, having its own hierarchy of castes, its local gods and its Council of Elders, its Brahmans and its sorcerers, its scribes and its artisans, its barbers and its washermen, all born like the cultivator to their hereditary avocations, all paid in kind either in actual produce or by the assignment of small plots of land. One of the modern grievances against British rule is that it has disorganized the ancient village community, and its economic life has certainly been seriously affected by the introduction of manufactured articles which have increasingly displaced those that used to be supplied on the spot by the village craftsmen. From this point of view there is something to be said in favour of Gandhi's propaganda for the *Charka*, or domestic spinning-wheel, and the wearing of the homespun *Khaddar* as the means of reviving domestic industries and keeping many hands busy that would otherwise be often idle in an Indian village. It may be that the decay of the ancient village system has left us little on which to build up new rural District Boards of the Western type. But the reproach comes ill from Indians who look for the building-up of India as a great united nation. For Hindu writers themselves recognize and sometimes even boast that the system led to the complete detachment of village life from the larger life of the State. Like the whole social system of Hinduism of which it was an integral part, it tended to repress the spirit of co-operation in the service of larger national ideals, just as the narrow restrictions of caste repress all individual initiative and effort.

At the particular seasons when his experience tells him he must be up and doing, the Indian peasant will work as hard and with as good a will as any peasant in the world. But he fights against heavier odds than any other, and, if at other seasons he is prone to indolence, what incentive has he to industry? If also he is thriftless, what incentive has he to thrift? It may seem absurd to talk of economy and extravagance, of thrift and of improvidence, when the Indian peasant finds it hard enough to escape starvation. Yet he manages to

indulge, if only on rare occasions, in forms of extravagance that seem to us worse than futile, as they
frequently cripple his meagre resources for the whole
of his life. To him, however, it is not futile extravagance since the occasions on which he is so recklessly
lavish are chiefly religious festivals, marriages and
funerals, which are the only great events that break
the monotony of his existence and which the doctrines
of his religion, the laws of his caste and the hungry
appetites of his Brahmans require him to celebrate
regardless of all cost. The village usurer, himself one
of the village institutions, is always at hand and
ready to help—at a price—and the price is often
promised with little or no thought as to the possibility
of ever paying it; and when the appointed date arrives
and payment is impossible, the price is raised and
raised again until the land to which he clings with
all the passion of a peasant-race has to be mortgaged
and finally passes out of his hands into those of the
moneylender. How can it be otherwise when he
will often spend many years rental on the purchase
of a wife for himself or for his sons and on the gifts
and festivities which immemorial custom pre-
scribes as an essential part of every wedding, and
when at the same time it is to the moneylender
alone that he has usually been able to turn
for credit?

The Indian politician, who has been generally
town-bred and has little personal contact with rural
India, prefers to lay stress on the heavy taxation of
land. But long before British rule, land was always
the chief source of revenue for the rulers of India;
and if the taxation of land is still a heavy burden,
it has steadily diminished, its incidence is regulated
by periodical assessments carefully and fairly conducted, and it is tempered in seasons of great
distress by not ungenerous abatements and sometimes
by complete remission. Of the two great systems of

land tenure obtaining in different parts of India, and in the aggregate in about the same proportions, the *ryot-wari* under which the revenue is derived from individuals who are the actual occupants or are accepted as representing them, is generally regarded as less onerous and less open to abuse than the *zemindari* system under which the revenue is derived from individuals or communities owning the land but not necessarily or usually cultivating it them- selves and occupying a position identical with, or analogous to, that of a landlord. Where great Indian landowners, such as the *Thalukdars* and *Zemindars* of Oudh and of other parts of the United Provinces and Bengal, had their rights solemnly safeguarded when they came under British rule, they are for the most part absentee landlords who take little interest in their tenants except in order to extort the highest possible rents, often with many abusive " cesses " piled on to them, which the tenant does not refuse. When motors came into fashion some landlords found it convenient to levy a special " cess " in addition to the ordinary rent in order to pay for the purchase of the coveted Rolls-Royce. As for the mere agricultural labourers, their position is everywhere very precarious, especially if they are at the further disadvantage of belonging to the " depressed " castes.

That the agriculturist in British India is never- theless on the whole better treated than in the Native States under the direct administration of their autonomous rulers is very clearly shown by the opposition that the suggestion of a transfer of any small district from the former to the latter almost invariably provokes. The most recent and striking instance has been the general protest in the Berars against their retrocession by the Government of India to the Nizam; and, though he is a great Mohammedan ruler, the Mohammedans of the

Berars made their protest heard, though perhaps less publicly, as earnestly as the Hindus.

The real burden on agriculture is not taxation, but indebtedness which frequently amounts to many times the revenue derived from the land by the State. In the Punjab, a province of small landowners where indebtedness may perhaps be rather greater than in other parts of India, recent inquiries have shown that over eighty per cent of the landowners are in debt, and that the debt represents twelve times the land revenue paid by all concerned, whether indebted or not. All that burden of debt is moreover quite unnecessary, for it is estimated that nearly the whole of it could be at once discharged if India had not in the course of the last fifty years hoarded £500,000,000 of gold, instead of putting it to reproductive use. Gold and precious stones and jewels were regarded in the old days of devastating wars and general insecurity as the most portable form of wealth and also the most easy to conceal. The tradition has survived into the new era of security that British rule brought with it, and as in olden times India continues to absorb annually enormous imports of gold which vanish mysteriously in secret places. Much of it no doubt also goes to adorn the ears and the noses, the wrists and the ankles of Indian women not merely for the gratification of their vanity but as the safest investment against the sudden changes of fortune with which the position of the highest and the lowest amongst them may always have to reckon. In the Punjab, the last great province to be brought under British rule, the sense of security which came with it has even promoted the growth of indebtedness, and not least in the " Canal Colonies " which owe their existence to a series of great irrigation works. The enormous appreciation of land led straight to a corresponding enormous increase of indebtedness, as the landowners

too often merely improved the occasion to borrow
proportionately larger sums from the moneylender,
concerned of course only to get a better security for
his loan. But, if on a larger scale in the Punjab,
the same thing was happening in most parts of
India. The rapidity with which land was passing a
quarter of a century ago by foreclosure on un-
redeemed mortgages into the hands of non-
agriculturists led Government to pass such measures
as the Punjab Land Alienation Act, the Deccan
Relief Act, the Tenancy Acts for Bengal and the
United Provinces which all aimed at protecting
landowners from the pitfalls with which the moneylender beset their improvidence. But legislation
alone proved as usual in such cases only temporarily
effective. Urban politicians were quick to suspect
the motives of Government interference with freedom of contract, and the ingenuity of the lawyers
conspired with the resourcefulness of the money-
lenders to defeat any substantial improvement.
A more practical line of approach has been found
in the Co-operative movement. It was a sun-dried
bureaucrat, Sir Frederick Nicholson, who first pointed
the way in 1895 when he said that if she could find
a Raffeisen rural India would be saved. The idea
was followed up by other great administrators and
notably by Sir Denzil Ibbetson, perhaps the greatest
of that period, and in 1904 Lord Curzon stood sponsor
to the Co-operative Credit Societies Act which gave
the first official *imprimatur* to the movement. It
languished, however, until further Government action
was taken during Lord Hardinge's Viceroyalty on
the report of a representative committee appointed
in the autumn of 1914 to explore the whole subject.
It has had ever since the enthusiastic support of a
number of young and able officials who have carried
many Indians of good position and influence along
with them. It is in the rural districts and as an

agricultural movement that it has achieved the most remarkable success and not least in a backward province like the Punjab, where the Mohammedan population has shown unexpected receptivity and keenness, and the membership of primary Societies has been only exceeded in the Bombay Presidency. Co-operative Credit Banks have helped the peasant to realize the value of capital and with it the value of thrift, whilst the value of team-work has been brought home to him by the pooling of produce for sale and frequently in a still more convincing fashion by the consolidation for the purposes of co-operative cultivation of the many small and often widely-separated patches of land into which individual and family holdings have come to be endlessly sub-divided.   A very hopeful feature of the Co-operation movement is that it has not been arrested by the political turmoil of recent years, not even in the sorely troubled Punjab, and it is gradually creating an entirely new and fruitful order of moral and social ideas.

The practical work done by the Agricultural Department of the Government of India, created, rather late in the day, in the same year as the Co-operative Societies Act, must not, however, be underrated.   To it is mainly due whatever progress has yet been made in the improvement of antiquated methods of production, in the amelioration of the qualities of produce by careful investigation and selection of seeds and strains and by the study and destruction of parasitic pests, etc.   The research work done at the headquarters of the Imperial Department of Agriculture at Pusa—which India originally owes, however, to the munificence of an American visitor—and in like provincial institutions, the agricultural colleges, the experimental farms, the local instruction given by trained experts have all had excellent results within the relatively small

areas they have been able to reach in such an
enormous field. Even for the better breeding of
cattle and for the improvement of dairy produce
with more and better varieties of fodder, much has
been done through similar Government agencies in
spite of the inherent difficulties of touching anything connected with so sacred an animal as the cow.

Directly or indirectly these are all at the same
time educational agencies in so far as they stimulate
the peasant's natural but dormant intelligence, and
even his superstitions are liable to yield to his
material interests when he is made to see clearly the
conflict between them in which he is the loser.
But until education even of the most elementary
character—and indeed it cannot at first be kept too
simple—has begun to permeate the masses, it will
be impossible to reduce the dead weight of long-
descended social and religious custom which hangs
like a mill-stone round the Indian peasant's neck.
It is responsible for the heavy burden of over-
population. It is responsible also for depriving half
the population—the female half—of the opportunity
of contributing its legitimate and indispensable share
to the economic productivity of the country. Not
only have whole castes been taught to regard any
form of manual labour as a badge of humiliating
inferiority and to relegate their womenfolk to rigid
seclusion and enforced idleness, but, except in the
lowest social strata, tradition demands that woman
shall confine herself to the purely domestic duties
of her household, and female labour, which in its
many various forms plays so large a part in all
the progressive communities of the modern world,
is, if not forbidden, almost universally discountenanced and banned. Religious beliefs also oppose
insuperable obstacles to the development of economic
resources from which the land might easily derive
great benefit. The Hindus worship the cow, and an

Indian writer has recently estimated the loss which
that worship involves every year for the whole
country at more than four times the land revenue.
The killing of a cow is a heinous crime. That is one
of the chief reasons for the wretched condition of
the cattle, for it is mistaken piety quite as much as
mere ignorant callousness that keeps enfeebled and
half-starved beasts at the plough long after they are
past work and encumbers the land with an enormous
excess of economically-useless cattle. Even their
bones and hides are too sacred to be utilized for
ordinary commercial purposes, and the industries
connected with them have been only recently
taken up by the Mohammedans who, on the other
hand, have an equally uneconomic, if less costly,
religious abhorrence of the pig. Incredible quantities
of animal manure are wastefully consumed as fuel
for the baking of the peasant's bread instead of
being used to fertilize his fields. Equally extravagant
is the consumption of *ghee* or clarified butter,
and, as it is used for sacrificial as well as for
household purposes, its place is too holy to be
taken by the oil of the immense Indian coconut
groves of which the produce is exported to Europe
for conversion into margarine. Nor is it only the
worship of the cow which is immeasurably wasteful.
Monkeys and other animals and birds are scarcely
less sacred, and must not be destroyed though they
swarm in such numbers that they destroy enough
valuable produce of fields and orchards to represent
another great economic loss to the country. Often
the way of progress is blocked, not by any ascertain-
able religious inhibitions, but by the obstinacy of
inveterate traditions of which the origin and per-
sistency are equally unaccountable.

What has the British *raj* stood for in the obscurely-
working minds of these scores of millions since it
ended the Great Anarchy of the XIXth century and

ultimately gave the whole of India the immense
relief of peace ?   They have felt themselves dimly
enveloped by the all-pervading power of the *Serkar,*
the Government, whose orders filtered down to them
from on high through many different agencies and
in many different forms which they only dimly
apprehend.   The vast majority seldom have an
opportunity of visualizing it for themselves in the
white man who with all his strange ways is in their
eyes its one human embodiment.   Their opportunities
of contact with him have slowly increased in the
small areas directly affected by the construction of
railways, by modern irrigation works and by the
educative influences recently brought to bear upon
many different branches of agriculture.   But in the
more remote parts of the country their opportunities
have actually grown less frequent since the increasing
burden of office-work has compelled the British
official to curtail the touring season in which he used
to shift his camp from village to village and lend a
patient ear to their grievances and petitions.   In
many parts of the country, instead of pitching his
camp amongst them, he is apt nowadays merely to
flash past them in his motor. The periodical reassess-
ment of the land revenue still brings the Settlement
Officer very near to them for as long as his special
work lasts, for it has to be done chiefly on the spot,
in the villages and fields and in close touch with
the owners of each separate parcel of land.   That
there is no settlement work to be done where, as in
Bengal, a permanent settlement was made in the
early days of British rule, has tended to increase the
distance which separates the rural masses and their
rulers. One irritating factor has been the multiplication of petty rules and regulations under a centralized
bureaucracy which in India, as elsewhere, has
developed an unholy partiality for red-tape, and
even when strict regulations are required, as under

the Forestry Department, for the protection of new plantations, the restrictions placed upon old grazing and other customs have often been needlessly chafing. The main cause of trouble in the exercise of the *Serkar's* authority, even for the most laudable purposes, is that, in the last resort, it is brought home to the masses through petty village authorities and the rural police, whose inherited traditions of oppression and corruption were not likely to be checked so long as the parsimony of Government blinded it to the inevitable consequences of scandalously low rates of pay.

It is perhaps in their hours of most acute distress, in famine and in pestilence, that the British official has most frequently appeared to the masses as the *deus ex machina* in their midst. It is then that they have seen at close quarters the civil officer and the doctor working quietly, methodically and with indomitable courage—sometimes even unto death— to help them where they know they are incapable of helping themselves. One cannot, of course, generalize from the case of a primitive tribe who once fashioned a crude image of the British Collector in a tall hat and placed it in the front rank of their beneficent gods, whilst another figure, that of his turbaned native clerk, was placed in the front rank of their maleficent deities ; but there is ample evidence to show that the individual Englishman's sense of justice and natural kindliness have won for him in normal times a large measure of confidence and often of genuine affection from the "silent masses" that have come more or less directly into contact with him, and have humanized the more remote sense of awe universally inspired by the far-reaching power of the British *raj*.

Whether the state of mind of the "silent masses" before the great war could be accurately described as "placid contentment" or was proof against the incitements of political agitation may well be doubted, as they had already shown in some parts of the country, in Bengal less than ten years earlier, and yet another ten years earlier in the Deccan, that their " contentment " could be easily disturbed by great gusts of religious and racial passion. But towards the end of the great war at any rate times had ceased to be normal in India. With greater intensity than in the first years of the century the distrust and resentment which superstition breeds in a terrified population swept over the whole of India with the awful visitation of influenza which, following upon a serious recrudescence of the bubonic plague in 1917, carried off in 1918–19 between 12,000,000 and 13,000,000 people, depopulating whole villages, and dangerously lowering the vitality of scores of millions. Altogether 125,000,000, or nearly three-sevenths of the total population— and mostly in the prime of life—were affected by the malady, which did more havoc in less than a year than the plague since its reappearance in modern times in India, *e.g.*, during nearly three decades. The low standard of living to which ignorance and poverty condemn the bulk of the agricultural population of India deprives them of the normal power of resistance to disease which more fortunate communities possess, and leaves those who are not actually struck down, a prey to a sullen sense of despair which any accident may translate into a violent movement of revolt. Everything conspired just then to promote that dangerous temper. The failure of the monsoon in the summer of 1918 with the consequent failure of harvest was more than usually disastrous at a time when India was feeling the economic pressure of the war in the rapid rise of prices for many necessaries of life usually imported from Europe. The few cotton rags which the poorest *ryot* wears became almost unpurchasable.

Everything, including very often the peasant's only means of bringing his produce to market, had to yield to the exigencies of the war, and it was the rural districts that suffered most from the disorganization of the Indian railway system which, though it withstood on the whole the tremendous strain of the war years, has been shown since then, in the report of Sir William Acworth's Committee of Enquiry, to have been always inadequate and administered on short-sighted and inefficient lines even for peace-time purposes. The war poured a great stream of wealth into India, but flowing, as in other countries, chiefly into the pockets of a few, whether British or Indian, it did not relieve the poverty of the masses, and there were other features of the war that profoundly modified the reverence in which the ruling race had been generally held by them.

India made from first to last a fine contribution towards the winning of the war. But when it was won Englishmen and Indians were apt to draw very different conclusions from its final issue. Englishmen saw in it chiefly a fresh proof of the vigour and tenacity of their race. With the secret bitterness of the racial feeling which had grown up in India before the war still in their hearts, the chief impression which its horrors ended by producing on many educated Indians who watched it from afar was one of amazement at so barbarous and almost fratricidal a struggle between the great white nations of the world; and they read into the ruin in which it seemed to have plunged victors and vanquished alike the impending bankruptcy of Western civilization. Some were genuinely shocked at the spectacle which a distraught Europe presented, some gloated over it as an assurance that the time was nearly ripe for a great revolt against the white man's supremacy which would have to be fought out not only in India but all over Asia, and, indeed, all over the world. Upon the unsophisticated minds of the silent masses the war had a different effect, but scarcely less injurious to the prestige of the ruling race. It was from them that the large Indian armies, about 1,000,000 men altogether, had been chiefly drawn, and the majority had been supplied by the martial races whose loyalty to the British *raj* has always been held least open to question. To the great majority of these men who had fought our battles on many fronts and even in Europe, the war had brought their first glimpse of Western conditions and habits of life, and, when they came home, they had many tales to tell and often of the seamy side of the things they had seen. Some of the more intelligent who had been in France were able to draw pictures of the French peasants' independence and prosperity which contrasted cruelly with the miserable life of the Indian *ryot*. They had had their share of the common victory, and if they returned not a little proud of their own achievements, they were not reluctant to convey the impression that without them the war would never have been won for England ; and those who had remained at home nodded approvingly, bearing in mind the urgent appeal made to India for more and still more recruits during the last phases of the war, and the intensive campaign of recruiting officers who towards the end would seldom take a denial. All these stories, often no doubt embellished with lively touches of Oriental imagination, travelled from village to village and into remote jungles and highland valleys which had hardly ever seen a white man, and just at a juncture when many other circumstances conspired to produce a ferment of unrest and racial jealousy. Nothing could have been better calculated to spread further and deeper the psychological change in the Indian attitude towards the ruling race which had begun with the Japanese victories over Russia and which the outbreak of the great war had only for a time arrested.

Events were quick to follow that showed how dangerously far that change had spread even amongst the silent masses.

CHAPTER XI

THE INDUSTRIALIZATION OF INDIA

WHILST the more obscure reactions of the great war thus reached even the silent masses of rural India which represent all that is oldest in India, all that British rule has least tended to disturb, it affected still more directly the new labour proletariat that has grown up in the most modern cities of India as the offspring of Western industrialism of which the transplantation to India has been one of the most striking phenomena of the later stages of British rule. It is in fact only within the last quarter of a century that India has taken rank amongst the great industrial countries of the modern world and it is the great war that has given her industrial development an unprecedented impetus.

Foremost amongst her industries stand her textile industries which were the first to be introduced into India and actually employ a larger number of hands than in England. With his passion for historical inaccuracy, Gandhi has asserted that Lancashire built up her industrial prosperity on the ruins of Indian industries. But if this is putting a very large cart in front of a very small horse, few Englishmen will contend that the long and tangled history of British economic policy in India constitutes a blameless chapter in the annals of British rule. So long as the East India Company was a merely trading corporation, it was naturally governed by its own immediate interests. At first the competition with which it had chiefly to reckon was that of rival interests at home, as well as of the other European countries engaged in the long struggle for the trade of the Indies. When it had once securely established its own monopoly, it was like all great monopolies, prone to abuse its position, alternately promoting the native industries which yielded it large profits, and laying a heavy hand on others that did not. But when Parliament deprived it in 1833 of its trading monopoly, it finally ceased to be in fact a trading corporation at all, and was transformed into a great agency of Indian Government, directly controlled from London in all matters of policy, including economic policy. That was the time, too, when the application of steam-power to industry was giving an entirely new orientation to British economic policy, of which one of the chief purposes was henceforth to secure enlarged markets for the exportation of rapidly expanding manufactures. Steam navigation was also bringing the Indian markets much nearer to England, and her new power-looms and spindles were bound to make havoc of many of the ancient domestic industries of India which still relied on unorganized manual labour for production and on slow, creaking bullock-carts for transport. Not till after the Mutiny was the construction of railways and good metalled roads to feed them undertaken on any large scale in India, and then they served quite as much to facilitate the introduction of foreign manufactures into the more remote parts of the country as to stimulate Indian exports. Satisfied that with her abundant natural supplies of coal and iron the manufacturing supremacy of Great Britain was safe against all outside competition, the Manchester school flourished at home with its economic watchword of *Laissez-faire, laissez-aller,* and the Government of India followed suit. Though, in his masterly survey of what England had done and still had to do in India at the close of his own long tenure of office in 1856, Lord Dalhousie had included the development of her vast economic resources as an important part of the duties of our trusteeship, little or nothing was done until the American Civil War deprived Lancashire of her chief supply of cotton. Attention was then directed to India as a cotton-growing country, but in the first place only for the purpose of providing the raw material for one of England's greatest manufacturing industries. Few then foresaw that British enterprise would soon perceive the advantage of utilizing cheap native labour by transplanting modern industrial processes out to India and spinning and weaving her cotton on the spot.

To-day the two greatest industries which British brains and British capital have created are the cotton industry in Bombay and an equally flourishing jute industry in Calcutta, though many others only less important have sprung up elsewhere. Jute grows hardly anywhere in the world except in Bengal and the industry has not developed in competition with any home interests. But it was otherwise in Bombay where the cotton-mills were so successful that others in due course sprang up not only in Ahmedabad, in the northern part of the Bombay Presidency, but also in the Central Provinces and Madras. England had to import all her cotton from abroad. India could produce the raw material herself and export both cotton-yarns and manufactured piece-goods able to compete in a good many lines with Lancashire both in the Indian market and in some of the foreign markets of Europe and the Far East. Free Trade was a British creed imposed on India, as she was repeatedly assured, for her own good. All the greater was Indian resentment when England herself imposed upon India a departure from the sacred principles of Free Trade as soon as Lancashire began to feel the pinch of Indian competition. At the behest of Whitehall the Government of India imposed an excise duty on Indian cotton manufactures equal to the customs duty on British imports of similar goods. It was a thinly-veiled measure of protection for Lancashire at the expense of India, and the sophisticated arguments by which it was defended rankled as deeply as the thing itself.

There were complaints, too, not altogether unfounded, from the British trading community as well as from Indians, that commercial questions did not receive much attention from the Government of India. A department created in 1866 to deal with such questions languished and was finally abolished in 1879 under the financial pressure resulting from two Afghan wars which India ascribed rather to Disraeli's ambitious Imperialism than to mere zeal for the safety of her north-western frontier. Its work was transferred to the Finance Department, then and for many years afterwards absorbed in the still unsolved problems of currency and exchange. Moreover, Treasury officials in most countries are more concerned with balancing the year's Budget than with the representations of a commercial community that may take longer but more expensive views. The British had first gone to India solely for trade, but the Civil Service that governed India and governed her in many ways with great efficiency during the second half of the XIXth century, was inclined to pride itself, like the class from which it was chiefly drawn at home, on having no connection with trade, and to treat with good-humoured superiority the English " box-wallahs " of Bombay and Calcutta, merchant princes though they often were. Nor were Indian politicians of the Western-educated class specially qualified or disposed to deal with economic questions. Their strength was drawn, it is true, from the cities, but mostly from the Bar and from the liberal professions, and they also had little connection with trade. They concentrated their attacks on military expenditure and the " drain " upon Indian revenue of the " home charges " or remittances to Whitehall for the service of Indian loans and the cost of European administration. It was chiefly for the political capital to be made out of it that the repeal of the cotton duties found its way regularly into the set speeches and "omnibus" resolutions of the Indian National Congress during the first two decades of its existence.

Indian manufacturing industries and the general trade of the country forged none the less steadily ahead, and a genuine demand arose from Indians themselves for technical education to enable them to take a larger share in this new development. One of the most welcome measures taken by Lord Curzon was the creation in 1904 of a separate department of commerce and industry in exclusive charge of a member of his Executive Council, Sir John Hewitt, who had unusual aptitude for economic questions. In spite of the political turmoil of the following years, India was already beginning to play an important part as an industrial and commercial country when the great war broke out. It was a bolt from the blue, and at first there was consternation and depression, but only to be followed by such an outburst of activity as India had never known. For with the increasing strain upon the material resources of the whole Empire it became necessary to explore and develop them in every part of the Empire, and this was done in India with a thoroughness and energy which Government had not been hitherto wont to display. During the war years the production of cotton piece-goods was doubled, that of the jute-mills and of the woollen-mills was nearly trebled, leather factories multiplied more than tenfold. The Tata Iron and Steel Works, perhaps the most remarkable achievement of Indian enterprise and Indian capital—aided however by American expert advisers—had been completed shortly before the war, and they produced, apart from other valuable output, the whole of the rails required for

laying down the military lines in Mesopotamia and
from Egypt into Palestine and Syria without which
the operations against Turkey could never have
been brought to a decisive issue. The work of a
Munitions Board established in 1917 showed con-
clusively what an enormous economic asset India
was to the Empire for purely war purposes, and at
the close of the war an Industrial Commission was
appointed to carry on in peace time the exploration
and development of Indian resources initiated under
the stress of war. Under Sir Thomas Holland's
lead it probed pitilessly the official lâches of the past,
and its exhaustive report disclosed the deplorable
backwardness of the country, the inadequate provision made for technical and scientific training, and
its still quite inadequate equipment in regard to
fundamental industries. It did not shrink from
recommending the active participation of the State
in industrial development, the grant of State aid to
private enterprise and the creation of a scientific
all-India service to conduct research work and to
co-ordinate industrial activities. To give effect to
these recommendations a separate Ministry of Industries was forthwith constituted.

Then came a sudden and tremendous reaction.
The wave of largely artificial prosperity on which
Indian trade and industry were borne along during
the war and soared to an inordinate height during
the great post-war boom receded to make room for
a period of extreme depression, partly due to similar
phenomena in Europe, and partly to other causes
special to India, namely the recrudescence of fierce
political agitation and the acute stringency of the
financial situation revealed by a succession of
Budget deficits. To other forms of unrest, the
distress amongst the poorer classes in the cities who
had suffered in many respects even more than the
agricultural population from the enormous rise in

the cost of many necessaries of life with which the rise in wages had wholly failed to keep pace, added labour unrest in a form and on a scale hitherto quite unknown in India.

There are essential differences between the vast agglomerations of industrial workers that collectively constitute Labour in England and those to which the same name has come to be applied in India. The latter are of relatively recent growth, and if they suffer even worse hardships from their frightful congestion in the few centres in which they are collected, 'they show this distinctive feature, viz., that they have not yet been completely severed from their connection with the land. The mill-hands, whether in cotton-mills or jute-mills or woollen-mills, and the large army of railwaymen and the miners in the more important coal mining districts make up the bulk of what is called "Labour" in India. They have been recruited more or less casually as the demand grew up from the agricultural population who were willing to leave their fields for portions of the year to earn higher wages in the cities, but who, nevertheless, as soon as they had made some savings, generally wanted to return to their villages, and almost always insisted on going back to look after their fields at the most important seasons for sowing and reaping. This practice may be less universal to-day, but there has not yet grown up in the cities an industrial population wholly divorced as in England from rural life. Still less has it learnt to develop any solid organization under its own leaders. It is for the most part unskilled, illiterate and profoundly ignorant. It has many grievances. But one must distinguish between two classes of grievances, those arising out of the conditions under which it works and those in which it lives. As to the latter they have been and often still are appalling. They were nowhere brought more

13

fully to light than in the hideous overcrowding of the insanitary *chauls*, or huge industrial tenements, in Bombay at the time of the first great plague-epidemic about thirty years ago, when the police had to search for corpses concealed out of sheer panic or superstition in dark, foul rooms tenanted sometimes by a single family of ten and even more. The owners of these appalling slums were Indians and it is from their vested interests that in one shape or another opposition to municipal improvements has almost constantly proceeded, and it required the energetic impulse of Sir George Lloyd, a strong Governor with business capacity, to launch a great city improvement scheme which is transforming almost beyond recognition the most congested of modern Indian cities by reclaiming its valuable foreshores, extending its habitable area and opening up new quarters where there will be light and air and wholesome water for all classes of the population. In Calcutta, where the jute industry is still almost entirely in British hands, and the lie of the land offers fewer obstacles to the expansion of the city, many of the companies have laid out long lines of sanitary tenements for their operatives with suitable bazaars at which they can purchase all the necessaries of life; and schools and spacious playing fields for their children; all in convenient proximity to the mills that stretch for several miles along the upper reaches of the river. An equally good example has been set by the European millowners in Madras and in Cawnpore and followed by many Indian millowners, notably in Nagpur, whilst the new model city laid out by the Tata Brothers at Jamshidpur round their steel and iron works shows what Indian captains of industry can do if they will. Much, however, still remains to be done before the conditions under which Indian labour lives cease to resemble those that obtained in England towards the

middle of the last century rather than those that
prevail at home to-day, unsatisfactory as these still
often are.

As to the conditions under which the Indians work,
the majority of employers, Indian and European,
have now fully recognized the importance of providing not only highly-equipped but healthy
factories well ventilated and well lighted, and
generally well up to modern requirements. To
compare Indian and British scales of wages is
difficult, for even given equal skill, which is very
rare, the physique and the habits of the average
Indian make him incapable of the same output of
work in the same number of hours as the average
Englishman. He does not work so continuously or so
hard. That Indian labour has in the past been often
grievously underpaid and overworked is nevertheless
generally admitted, especially Indian female labour,
itself a novel feature on so large a scale in Indian
social and economic life in which woman has
hitherto been allowed only a very subordinate part.
Children, too, have been employed for excessively
long hours with little or no regard for sex or physical
maturity. The Government of India was slow to
legislate for the new labour conditions resulting from
the growth of great manufacturing industries, but
there has been a great improvement within the last
few years, due in no small degree to the fact that
being a member of the League of Nations, India has
been intimately associated with the work of the
International Labour Bureau. A new Factory Act
has been passed in accordance with the recommendations of the Washington Conference, and in some
directions the Indian Act is in advance of Washington.
It contains important provisions for safeguarding
the health of working women, and, instead of plead-
ing the special difficulties which a statutory limit of
age for juvenile work presents in India where

physical development is more precocious than in
Western countries, it courageously raises the limit
not to fourteen but to fifteen years, whilst permitting
the employment of younger children only on
special and very stringent conditions. Legislation
has also been introduced to place trade union
rights and compensation for accidents on an
assured basis.

But no amount of legislation can do what Indian
labour must do and has so far been quite unable to
do for itself, namely, to build up its own organization.
That must inevitably be a slow and difficult process.
Trade unions have grown up like mushrooms, but
in the dearth of any leaders produced from their own
ranks, they have not been organic growths. They
have generally been the artificial creation of professional agitators who have made it their business
to take up with more passion than knowledge the
grievances, legitimate or otherwise, of Indian labour,
still incapable of formulating them for itself or of
seeking any other remedy than turbulent manifestations of its discontent.

The first Congress to style itself the " All-India
Trades Union Congress " met in 1921 in Bombay, and
though it boasted of representing ninety-two trades
unions, Sir George Lloyd, who received its principal
spokesmen and listened courteously to their high-
sounding address, failed to elicit any information
from them as to the status of the unions, their
method of formation, their internal constitution or
the actual experience of the leaders in the trades
they claimed to represent. They were not men
who had risen to the leadership of labour out of its
own ranks by superior industry and knowledge.
Indians of the type of Mr. Joshi, trained in Gokhale's
Servants of India Society to devote themselves
unselfishly to social service of any kind, are still
few and far between. Legislation may help, but

not much real progress can be looked for until labour throws up its own responsible leaders, and this can only happen when the level of education has been raised. Even amongst ordinary skilled labour, it is still lamentably low and the gulf has yet to be bridged between the new industrial proletariat and the small but growing class of industrial employers possessing both capital and education, and conscious of the need for genuine co-operation if a class-war is not to be numbered amongst the results of India's industrialization.

The influence of Bolshevism cannot in this connection be entirely ignored, for though it is with the extreme forms of Indian nationalism and its terrorist organizations that Bolshevist propaganda has hitherto sought contact, it might find a yet more promising field for the intensive propaganda it has started all over the East in these large agglomerations of industrial workers, as emotional and credulous as they are ignorant, whom the growth of Western industrialization has for the first time crowded together within a few Indian cities in an atmosphere not altogether uncongenial to racial and to class hatred.

Gandhi himself was to find out too late how much easier it was for him to rouse the passions of a mob of mill-hands in Bombay than to restrain them when once roused ; and Indian labour may conceivably fall into the hands of far more dangerous leaders than a Gandhi and with none of his religious scruples about the use of violence. Nor can Gandhi or any-one else now drive industrialism out of India. It has come to stay, and to stay in Indian rather than in European hands. Already the Bombay cotton industry has passed to a very large extent out of the latter into the former, the number of European companies having sunk to only 17 out of 193. Less marked elsewhere, the tendency is the same

almost everywhere except in the Calcutta jute
industry, and the change is none the less significant
because Indian captains of industry, wiser than
many Indian politicians, are not as a rule too proud
to retain the services of European managers and
technical experts.

Hopes have been widely entertained that the
commercial and industrial development of India
would help to draw Englishmen and Indians together
by creating outside the heated sphere of politics
new ties of common interest, even if sometimes
inevitably competitive. Nowhere, certainly, has
healthy competition between them been keener than
in Bombay, and nowhere also have there been
friendlier relations. But in the present political
ferment economics and politics tend to become more
and more interlocked, and the demand for protection
with all its far-reaching implications, put forward
not altogether unreasonably by Indian manufac-
turers, has been taken up in a very different spirit
by Indian political parties who see in the complete
economic independence of India chiefly a stepping-
stone for her to national independence. The first
idea of attacking British rule through British trade
goes back to the *Swadeshi* movement originally
started by Tilak in the Deccan, and carried into
Bengal during the anti-partition agitation. It was
then that the boycott of all British imported goods
was passionately preached for the double purpose of
encouraging native industries and of hitting the
British people where it was asserted they would feel
it most, viz., in their pockets, and compel them to
relax their grip on India. But the opportunity for
developing a comprehensive protectionist policy had
not come when the great war drew to a close in
1918. The industrialization of India had, however,
proceeded far enough to produce at a critical
moment the beginnings of a labour movement which

combined with the new stirrings of the silent masses
and the political turmoil amongst the educated
classes to bring about within six months after the
war was over the greatest upheaval since the Mutiny,
none the less formidable because it was an unarmed
revolt.

CHAPTER XII

THE NON-CO-OPERATION MOVEMENT

It was in the lurid after-glow of the great war that Gandhi stood forth as the Man of Destiny and launched against British rule and Western civilization his fervid appeal to the ancient religious forces of India and, at the same time, to all the racial and social passions aroused by the impact of the West. He possessed the special characteristics of saintliness which all Indians revere as infallible signs of divine inspiration. He was the Mahatma upon whom had descended the wisdom of the Vedic sages. But his voice might not have carried so much or such widespread weight if he had not been already famous as confessor and martyr to the cause of India in South Africa where at the time when racial feeling was growing acute in India, the white man had publicly stamped a large Indian community with the brand of racial inferiority in a great Dominion of the British Crown.

To understand the deep sense of injustice created by the treatment of Indians in British possessions outside India one must remember that the trouble owes its origin, not to any spontaneous impulse on the part of Indians to emigrate, but to the need in some of our colonies for cheap labour to develop their natural resources. In South Africa, for instance, it was Natal that approached the Government of India as far back as 1860 for permission to recruit Indian coolies as indentured labourers on the land. Permission was granted ; Indians were recruited ; they went out, worked hard and to the satisfaction of their employers, and, when their indentures expired, often remained in the country as " free " Indians to become small farmers and pedlars and traders. Other better-class Indians then followed who were not indentured, but went out to seek a legitimate livelihood by supplying the needs of the growing Indian communities and doing business on a small scale which the native could not and the white man would not do. The Indians spread to other parts of South Africa and as they were industrious and thrifty and content to live on a lower economic scale, the white man, though unable to do without them, began to regard them as at least potentially inconvenient competitors, as well as in other respects somewhat undesirable neighbours, to be kept in their place as an inferior race. It was in the Boer Republic of the Transvaal that the Indians were first subjected to extremely harsh treatment, and, on representations made by the Government of India, their grievances figured prominently in the British indictment of President Kruger's policy which led to the South African war.

It is at this juncture that we first hear of Gandhi who had had occasion to go out to South Africa professionally soon after he had been called to the Bar in London and had returned to practise in Bombay. All his sympathies were at that time with England, and because he felt very keenly the position of his fellow-countrymen he gave his active support to the British as soon as the Boer war broke out. He even earned the thanks of Government for his loyal service in raising an Indian field-ambulance corps and leading it to the front. He was convinced that once British supremacy was firmly established in South Africa, the influence of the Imperial Government would be exercised to right the wrongs of the Indian community. But when his hopes were disappointed and South Africa under the British flag adopted a number of measures designed not only to check future Indian immigration but to impose racial disabilities and curtail the existing rights of the Indian population already settled in the country, he did not shrink from initiating a policy of passive resistance with hunger-strikes and mass marches as public demonstrations of protest in order to rouse public opinion not only in India but in England, where he still trusted the British people's innate sense of justice. British public opinion was, however, swayed by the argument of the South African whites that in order to maintain the purity of their race and its accustomed standards of life, restrictions had to be placed both upon further Indian immigration and upon the indiscriminate extension of Indian settlements in the country. India on the contrary had ears only for the grievances of her own people, and Lord Hardinge owed much of his personal popularity and great influence as Viceroy, which stood the Empire in such good stead during the great war, to a speech at Madras on November 24, 1913, expressing "the sympathy of India, deep and burning, and not only of India but of all lovers of India like myself, for their compatriots in South Africa in their resistance to invidious and unjust laws." Such an emphatic and almost sensational protest from the head of the Government of India, backed by earnest representations from Whitehall, induced the South African Government to display a less unyielding spirit, and as the result of a Commission of Enquiry, an Indian Relief Act was passed, whilst in direct correspondence with Gandhi, General Smuts gave further conciliatory assurances. When Gandhi went home just after the outbreak of the great war, the Government of India identified itself once more with Indian sentiment by awarding him the *Kaisar-i-Hind* gold medal. The truce in South Africa only lasted, however, for the duration of the war, and when it was followed by fresh anti-Indian legislation the feeling in India was more intense than ever, as the action of the South African Government conflicted acutely with the British

Government's recognition during the war of a higher status for India, actual and potential, within the Empire. Not only had Indians fought side by side with British troops even on European battlefields, but India had been admitted on an equal footing with the Dominions to the Imperial War Councils in London and to the Peace Conference in Paris, and even as an original member to the League of Nations. More than that, she had been promised, as the ultimate goal of British policy, her promotion to full membership in the British commonwealth. To Indians it might well seem intolerable that they should continue to be penalized anywhere in the Empire for the colour of their skins.

Yet there was no direct connection between that issue and the one that drove Gandhi, on the morrow of the war, to set the spark to an explosion of which the after-shock has not yet spent itself. Deeply as he resented the treatment of Indians under the British flag in South Africa, where he had also conceived a profound aversion from Western materialism, he never doubted that, in the war into which German ambitions had forced her, England was fighting for righteousness. Passing through England at its outbreak on his way back to India from South Africa, he offered to raise an Indian ambulance corps as he had done during the Boer war. All through the war he kept up very friendly relations with Englishmen in India, often addressing English as well as Indian audiences on the foundations of religion common to all creeds. In the last year of the war, he attended and spoke at the great gathering at Delhi in March, 1918, when the Viceroy appealed for another great Indian effort. In a district where he happened to have great personal influence he urged every village to contribute twenty recruits, so that Khaira alone should furnish a contingent 12,000 strong. He already had visions of *Swaraj* for India, but as a partner in the Empire with the same rights as the self-governing Dominions, and the surest way of achieving it, he said, was not to talk about it during the war, but to join with the rest of the Empire in winning the war. Always ready to espouse popular grievances in regard to taxation, or to labour conditions in Bombay, or to the treatment of coolies in the planting districts, his action was not always wise, but his influence, when as in Champaran he was invited to join an official commission of enquiry, was admittedly exerted to promote not strife but concord. He had a genuine admiration for the great qualities of Englishmen, if only, as he used to say, they would not allow their hearts to be hardened by an over-weening pride of race and love of power.

Viewed from any normal standpoint there was no analogy whatever between the circumstances which had driven him to preach passive resistance in South Africa as the only weapon left to a small and helpless community labouring under a sense of cruel injustice, and those which moved him to transplant his old South African plan of campaign into India. But his emotional temperament was seldom governed by reason alone, and he was not only a Hindu mystic but he had borrowed from a long study of Tolstoy a curiously un-Hindu belief that authority was the source of all social and political evils. The exercise of authority which stirred his indignation was a legislative measure which raised no racial issue. There still lurked in some parts of India the spirit of violent lawlessness unloosed ten years before in Bengal, and a special Committee, presided over by Mr. Justice Rowlatt, a Judge of the Court of King's Bench, sent out to India for the purpose, had been appointed to inquire into the whole history of the terrorist movement. It concluded with a strong recommendation that Government should be invested with additional powers for dealing with criminal conspiracies. Such powers were accordingly embodied in two Acts commonly known as the Rowlatt Acts. Gandhi had himself condemned all violent conspiracies as a flagrant denial of the Hindu doctrine of *Ahimsa* which forbids the doing of any hurt to others. But when the Rowlatt Acts were passed it was these that he denounced as measures of odious oppression directly violating the first principles of *Ahimsa*. Government pointed out rightly enough that the Acts threatened the freedom of none but evildoers actually engaged in criminal conspiracies to commit violence. They bore in Gandhi's sight the apocalyptic mark of the beast, and he adjured his people to place a religious ban upon them by taking with him the vow of *Satyagraha*, to oppose their enforcement by every means in their power, short of any breach of *Ahimsa* by violence to life, person and property. The form of passive resistance which he prescribed was termed " civil resistance " and assumed a little later the shape of " Non-Co-operation," *i.e.*, the treating of Government and of everything proceeding from Government as morally no less " untouchable " than the lowest castes of Hinduism are to the " twice-born " castes.

This was a Hindu conception which on its own merits was unlikely to commend itself to Indian Mohammedans. But no sooner had peace been concluded than some of their leaders resumed the pro-Turkish propaganda which they had been compelled to suspend for the duration of the war, and they were ready to welcome any agitation that might weaken the British power which they held mainly responsible for the crushing defeat of Turkey. Other influences operated at the start in Gandhi's favour with the Mohammedan masses. The worship of ascetic saintliness is one of the many ancient traditions common to Mohammedans and Hindus.

Gandhi's appeal was addressed to all without
distinction of creed. Nor was there anything in the
wording of the *Satyagraha* vow to alarm the scruples
of the most orthodox followers of the Prophet.
Exceptional distress and disease had combined with
the effects of the war to produce conditions of
nervous depression and excitability which made the
silent masses singularly receptive to any message
that breathed a spirit of rebellion. When Gandhi
travelled all over India preaching *Satyagraha* and
administering the vow, Mohammedans and Hindus
flocked in their thousands to hear him, and, though
they knew little or nothing of the Rowlatt Acts, they
readily succumbed to the magnetism of the frail and
emaciated figure which, even to those who could not
understand his words, seemed to tell the cruel story
of his long suffering for those of their own race in
South Africa at the hands of the white man who
had just exploited India and brought untold suffering upon her in a terrible war fought for the greater
glory and profit of her alien masters. The *Satyagraha*
movement spread like a prairie fire, and even Indian
legislators who had helped to pass the Acts took
fright and joined in the popular outcry against them.
To many who were not prepared to go as far as
Gandhi, the Acts were extremely obnoxious and
seemed at least highly impolitic because they were
being forced upon India at the very moment when
she was looking for some very different demonstration
of the reality of the new era of reforms that was to
give effect to the Montagu-Chelmsford Report.

Government, however, showed no signs of yielding,
and Gandhi proceeded to proclaim the 6th April,
1919, as *Satyagraha* Day, on which a complete
hartal, or abstention from all ordinary business and
the demonstrative closing of all bazaars, was to be
observed throughout India and mass meetings held
for the taking of the vow. On that day occurred

in the capital city of Delhi itself the first collision
between a turbulent crowd of Gandhi's followers and
the police, whose instructions were to maintain order
in the streets. Of the sincerity of Gandhi's injunctions to refrain from violence there is no reason to
doubt, but no one can work up ignorant and
emotional masses to a high pitch of religious frenzy
without creating a temper which the slightest
incident will provoke to violence, and behind Gandhi
there were many who did not share his aversion from
violence. There were only a few casualties at Delhi,
and Gandhi, throwing the whole responsibility on
the police, merely urged his *Satyagrahis* to steel
their hearts. Worse things were quick to follow.
In Bombay, in Ahmedabad and all over the Punjab,
Satyagraha became the signal for wholesale rioting
with pillage and arson and in some cases murderous
outrages on Englishmen, and even on English
women, and the movement assumed the undeniable
character of an organized revolt against the British
raj. Sir George Lloyd was able to quell the disturbances in the Bombay Presidency without having
recourse to a general proclamation of martial law and
Gandhi was moved to condemn such outbursts of
violence as *Duragraha*, or the inversion of *Satyagraha*.
But it was too late. The Punjab was aflame. He
was forbidden to enter a province in which there
was the added danger of proximity to the unruly
North-West Frontier and the menace of an Afghan
war. Nowhere were more revolting outrages committed by Indian mobs than at Amritsar, where
five Englishmen, two of them local Bank managers,
were killed with fiendish brutality, and a missionary
lady, known for her good works, escaped with her
bare life. Nowhere, too, was repression carried to
greater lengths. Order had been restored before
General Dyer reached Amritsar, but on an ill-
omened day he thought himself justified in opening

fire without warning upon a great crowd assembled in the Jalianwala *Bagh* in defiance of his orders prohibiting all public meetings. Only those, perhaps, who have visited the *Bagh* after studying the evidence given by General Dyer before a Committee of Enquiry presided over by Lord Hunter, a former Solicitor-General for Scotland, can realize the full horror of the tragedy enacted there. It was to dig so sinister a gulf between the ruling and the subject race that the story of that black day in the annals of British India cannot be ignored. The *Bagh*— once a garden—has long been, save for one clump of old trees, an open space covering perhaps the area of Trafalgar Square, enclosed on every side by mud walls with tall houses rising in many places close up against and above them. The approaches are few and extremely narrow. By one of them, leading on to the highest ground in the *Bagh*, General Dyer with a party of fifty Ghurka entered the *Bagh* and saw, at a distance of perhaps a hundred yards, a dense crowd, variously estimated at from 6,000 to 10,000, most of them engaged in listening to speeches. General Dyer assumed, rightly enough, that this was a public meeting in contravention of his orders and a seditious one. Without a word of warning he opened and kept up upon them a fusilade that did not stop until, as he himself said, his party's ammunition was almost exhausted, though the panic-stricken multitude broke at once, struggling to escape through the narrow exits or attempting vainly to climb the walls, or in despair throwing themselves flat on the ground. General Dyer, according to his own statement, personally directed the firing to the points where the crowd was thickest. The " targets," he declared, were "good" and by the time he and his men went off by the same way they had come, they had killed 379, according to the official figures given some months later by Government, and they left about

1,200 wounded on the ground for whom he did not consider it his " job " to provide any help whatever. General Dyer was convinced that the sternest measures were necessary to spread terror through the Punjab and scotch a great revolutionary movement. He followed up his action at the *Bagh* by a " crawling order " compelling all Indians to go on all-fours who wanted to pass through a certain street in which an Englishwoman had been nearly done to death by the mob in one of the previous days' rioting. The Lieutenant-Governor, Sir Michael O'Dwyer, insisted on the withdrawal of this order, but nothing could wipe out the memory of it. Throughout the Punjab martial law was enforced with the utmost rigour and sometimes by quite unprecedented methods.

Opinion amongst Englishmen will probably always differ with regard to General Dyer's action. A great many, naturally infuriated by the excesses of the Indian mobs and with the recollection still in their minds of what English women and children had suffered during the Mutiny, hailed him as the saviour of the Punjab, and large sums were raised by public subscription at home as well as by Englishmen in India to be presented to him with a sword of honour. Official inquiry in India was belated, but ultimately the British Government placed their severe censure on record in a published dispatch to the Government of India, blaming more especially General Dyer's omission to give warning before opening fire as inexcusable, his failure to give medical assistance to the dying and the wounded as an omission of obvious duty, and his " crawling order " as an offence against every canon of civilized government. In a recent libel action tried in this country which turned upon Sir Michael O'Dwyer's action as Governor during that period, the Judge, Mr. Justice McCardie, took an opportunity to give

14

it as his considered opinion that General Dyer as the man on the spot who could best measure the needs of a very dangerous situation was entirely justified in taking the action he did. But the Labour Government, then in office at home, held that the learned Judge was not in full possession of the facts, and maintained and reiterated their predecessors' censure. There the question rests and may be left to rest. But it is difficult to believe that General Dyer's faith, however honestly held, in the expediency of preventive massacre in order to forestall possible or even probable and grave trouble, will ever commend itself to the British people.

But upon Indians of all classes and creeds and races with exceptions too rare to signify, Jalianwala Bagh and the Punjab events produced only one feeling, a feeling of horror and indignation which, amongst the masses, found vent in a great outburst of racial hatred. None would believe that such things would ever have been done in any English town or in any possession of the British Crown with a white population, whatever provocation an unlawful assembly or an unruly mob might have offered, nor that if, *per impossibile*, they had been done, British public opinion would not have been as unanimous in reprobating them as Indian opinion was in this case. To borrow the Duke of Connaught's own language when he visited India early in 1921 to open the new Legislatures on behalf of the King, " the shadow of Amritzar lengthened over the whole of India."

The Government of India Act, by which it was hoped to restore the internal peace of India, was passed at the end of 1919, just when most of the facts in regard to the Punjab tragedy, already widely known and in some quarters wildly exaggerated in India, were for the first time being reluctantly disclosed by the Secretary of State in England.

The Hunter Commission of Enquiry was appointed in consequence of those regretably tardy disclosures, but it came too late to mitigate Indian resentment wrought to a white heat in India by the passionately one-sided report of a committee hastily appointed on its own account by the Indian National Congress to prejudge the case. Gandhi was ready to do penance again and again for his followers' frightful lapses from *Ahimsa*. But could these, he asked, be reckoned for one moment against " the wrongs of the Punjab"? None but a "Satanic Government" could grudge the " redress " by which alone the rulers of India would show the " change of heart " he required of them. To the wrongs of the Punjab Gandhi already had added the wrongs of the Caliphate in order to secure Hindu-Mohammedan " fraternization " in one great Non-Co-operation campaign which was to wreck the whole scheme of reforms embodied in the Act before it could be put into operation, and paralyse British rule by a great national boycott. No Indians were to take part as candidates or voters in the elections for the new legislative Councils. No Indian was to use any article of British manufacture or importation, and, as a sign of the covenant, none was to wear any but home-spun clothes of native-grown cotton. All Indians were to resign their offices under Government and give up their orders and titles. All Indians on the Bench and at the Bar were to withdraw from the Law Courts. All Indian parents were to take their children away from Government and State-aided schools and colleges. All Indians were to flee the contamination of " a Satanic civilization " in its factories and counting-houses, and even in its savings banks and hospitals. Ultimately when by practising *Ahimsa* under whatsoever provocation from a Satanic Government the nation showed itself ripe for *Swaraj*, Non-Co-operation would enter on

the further stage of " civil disobedience " with an
organized refusal to pay taxes. Thus, and thus alone,
by the exercise of " soul-force " would India deserve
and obtain *Swaraj* within a period which Gandhi
first fixed at one year and subsequently extended
more indefinitely. What his own conception was of
the government or institutions or social conditions
of a *Swaraj* India he never revealed except in vague
promises of a return to the pristine simplicity of
the Vedic age, symbolized for the nonce in a return
to the domestic spinning-wheel and the hand-loom.
He struck, however, a more practical note when he
preached temperance and self-abnegation and the
spiritual need for peace between rival creeds and
communities, and though he never went to the
length of condemning caste as an institution, he
pleaded strongly for the removal of untouchability as
incompatible with real *Swaraj*, which, whatever else
it might mean, meant first and foremost, he declared,
freedom and brotherhood for all Indians.

Of the old Nationalist leaders few were at first
disposed to respond to his call. The moderates had
ranged themselves in the opposite camp by accepting
the constitutional reforms as a first stride towards
self-government. The Poona Brahmans and others
of the Tilak school—Tilak himself had just died—
distrusted Gandhi's orthodoxy even more than his
political strategy. Others again shrank from the
serious personal sacrifices required of them. His
wholesale denunciation of Western civilization still
alienated from him some of the more thoughtful
amongst the Western-educated classes. But he
carried with him the bulk of the Congress party
from which the less violent elements seceded and
ultimately formed themselves into a new Liberal
party. As an attempt to kill the new constitution
in the womb, Gandhi's great plan of campaign ended
for the time being in failure. His followers boycotted

the elections, and were therefore not represented in the new Legislatures, but the Legislatures came into being without them. The boycott of British goods was very partial and ineffective. Mr. Motilal Nehru was almost the only prominent barrister to sacrifice a lucrative practice and all the amenities of a refined and almost luxurious Western manner of life, and, as Sir Subramanya Eyar had long since retired from the High Court of Madras, his resignation of his knighthood was an ineffective gesture and he found no imitators on the Bench. The boycott of schools and colleges derived far less support from teachers and professors than from schoolboys and students, for whom it meant a spectacular display of patriotic independence and a succession of somewhat turbulent holidays. They went out " on strike " in large numbers and if the educational life of the country was thrown only for a short time into confusion, a lasting blow was dealt at the principle of authority essential to the sound training of youth at the most critical and receptive age, always rigidly enforced under India's ancient system of education.

But if Non-Co-operation attracted only a section of the Western-educated and hardly any of the propertied classes, Gandhi acquired a personal hold, unexampled perhaps since Buddha, on the masses both in the congested slums of the modern cities and in the stagnant backwaters of agricultural India. For if he was a reckless agitator, the saint that was also in him was moved like the founder of Buddhism by a great compassion for the poor, the humble and the sinner. To all these he made his own special appeal, even to the prostitutes, who, flocking to hear him at his bidding, took with much wailing and tears the vows of repentance he exacted from them and passed up their gold and silver bangles to be laid at his feet as an earnest of their " change of hearts." Thousands of miserable *ryots* in remote rural districts tramped for miles to hang on to his words as he discoursed on the beauty and freedom of village life in the old Vedic times and foretold the return of that halcyon age when *Swaraj* should have swept away the rack-renting landlord and the insatiable tax-gatherer. Few doubted that the gods had lent him the gift of prophecy and that the days of the British *raj* were numbered. His words were as the holy *mantras* through which the gods worked great miracles. Though he did not cease to condemn violence, there were many amongst his followers who did not share his scruples. Local Non-Co-operation Committees were formed and recruited youthful bands of "volunteers" sworn to take orders from them which purported to emanate from Gandhi. In many districts Government officers found themselves confronted with organizations in secret or open opposition to them and more readily obeyed. One symptom was the revival of the old prejudices against vaccination and inoculation. Villages sullenly refused the local transport required for Government officers travelling on duty—even for medical officers deputed to plague and cholera areas. Forest regulations, especially those curtailing old grazing rights for the better protection of young plantations, have always been unpopular, and in the Central and United Provinces where Non-Co-operation held sway, State forests were burnt down over many square miles in circumstances which only arson could explain. For such things Gandhi could not be held directly responsible, but it was in his name that the reckless spirit in which they were done had been evoked out of slumbering depths of ignorance and superstition.

Gandhi's name was one to conjure with equally amongst the industrial masses in the cities. When he preached temperance they attacked the liquor shops, and when he condemned the drinking of tea

because it was a detestable foreign custom, they
marched more peacefully to some popular shrine and
solemnly destroyed their teapots and their teacups.
Gandhi denounced industrialism as the most hateful
of all Western importations into India, and in all
industrial troubles his sympathies were invariably
with labour. The strike was the only industrial
weapon which Indian labour was then capable of
borrowing from the trades unions of the West.
Under the exciting influence of Gandhism, even when
not directly incited by his more reckless disciples,
strikes of all kinds became as common in India as
in England, not only amongst industrial workers in
the big cotton-mills and jute-mills and other large
manufacturing industries, but amongst the workers
employed by the municipalities and the State,
postmen, railwaymen, tramcar drivers, and even
city scavengers. Many of them were lightning
strikes often started on most frivolous pretexts.
Some lasted a few days, others for months. They
often presented the most unpleasant features of
our own strikes, not merely picketing, but gross
intimidation and even violence. For such things
also Gandhi could not be held directly responsible,
and he could even persuade himself, but not his
followers, that by proclaiming a boycott of the
Prince of Wales' visit to India he was only giving
an exceptionally impressive form to " non-violent
non-co-operation " with the Satanic Government
under whose auspices the young Prince was coming
out. But the formidable riots in Bombay on the
day of the Prince's landing, which were only quelled
after heavy loss of life, showed how very different
was the interpretation placed on his injunctions by
the blind masses who imagined they were following
his lead. In vain did he again do penance and
declare that " the *Swaraj* he had just witnessed had
stunk in his nostrils." Murder and arson and riot

too often dogged the footsteps of the fervent apostle of non-violence. The culminating horror was reached at Chauri-Chaura on February 4, 1922, when, in the centre of agrarian disturbances fomented on soil no doubt specially well prepared for a revolt against indigenous landlords as well as against a foreign *raj*, a frenzied mob of rioters discovered that faith in Gandhi was of no avail to stop rifle-bullets, and, having borne down a small force of local police by sheer weight of numbers, did them brutally to death, and cast not a few of them, still living, into the flames of the burning police station. Gandhi, who had been meanwhile maturing his plans for starting " civil disobedience "—which in this case meant the refusal to pay land revenue—in the Bardoli district of the Bombay Presidency, was once more stricken with horror and remorse, and sorrowfully confessed that India was not yet ripe for any further step towards *Swaraj* since there were Indians still lacking enough " soul-force " to refrain from unutterable deeds of violence. But what he could not or would not see was that even more irreparable than the worst deeds of violence was the intense racial hatred engendered or stimulated by the whole Non-Co-operation movement, with its chorus of vituperation and calumny and falsehoods poured out daily in platform speeches and in the columns of a vitriolic press and circulated by word of mouth in secret gatherings against a Satanic Government and the Satanic civilization of which it was the appointed instrument. It was not the British oppressor of India but the white man who was held up to the execration of the Indian as the common oppressor of all the coloured races of the world.

Racial hatred was indeed the strongest connecting link between the original Non-Co-operation movement started by Gandhi with the vow of *Satyagraha* which appealed primarily to the Hindus and the

Caliphate movement which made its own distinct
appeal to the militant spirit of a creed that had always
relied upon the sword. Of the two movements which
for a time were fused almost into one by Gandhi's
personal influence the Caliphate movement in support
of Turkey was perhaps the more peculiar. For
though the Turks were their co-religionists the
Indian Mohammedans had during the greater part of
their history known little and cared even less about
Turkey. The Moghul Emperors had at rare intervals
exchanged ceremonial correspondence with the
Ottoman Sultans; but the *Qanoon-e-Islam* which
described less than a century ago the beliefs and
customs of Indian Mohammedans never once mentions
the Turkish Empire or the Turkish Caliphate.
How little Indian Mohammedan opinion was formerly
affected by British policy towards Turkey was
shown when Delhi, the old capital of the Moghul
Emperors, resounded with the religious war cries of
Mohammedan mutineers within two years after
England had waged the long and costly Crimean
War against Russia in defence of a great Mohammedan Empire. It was strangely enough
England herself who did most to magnify Turkey in
the eyes of the Mohammedans of India. For a long
time during the XIXth century it was her policy
to bolster up the Ottoman Empire against Russia
for many other reasons besides the danger which
Russian expansion in Central Asia seemed to portend
for the safety of the Indian North-West Frontier.
That policy culminated in the dispatch of Indian
troops as far as Malta in 1878 when the Russian
armies were at the gates of Constantinople, and
Beaconsfield was ready to risk another war with
Russia in order to save Turkey once more. It
remained nothing but a gesture, for war was at the
eleventh hour avoided, but it was a gesture that
brought Turkey nearer to India than she had ever

been before, and nearest of all to the Indian Mohammedans, upon whom Englishmen themselves then took great pains to impress the close community of interests between Turkey and India, often even talking about the British Empire as the greatest Mohammedan Empire in the world because its population included far more Mohammedans than did Turkey.

The Sultan Abdul Hamid who had succeeded to the throne when the very existence of his Empire was threatened by internal commotions and foreign wars, knew how to play with great adroitness on this chord of British friendship, until Lord Salisbury realized that in backing Turkey England had backed the wrong horse and threw British influence into the scales against Turkish misrule of the Christian subject-races to whom the Treaty of Berlin after the Russo-Turkish war had brought little real or permanent relief. Abdul Hamid's resourceful mind was travelling in quite another direction, for he had conceived a far-reaching plan to seek compensation for the territorial losses inflicted upon his Empire by reviving and extending over the whole Mohammedan world the spiritual leadership which in theory at least attached to his position of Caliph as well as Sultan. It was to India that he first turned his attention as a promising field for his Pan-Islamic propaganda in reprisal for the lead which England was now taking in pressing upon him unpalatable reforms for the benefit of Infidel Bulgars and Greeks and Armenians. But the moment was ill-chosen for any attempt to estrange Indian Mohammedans from the British *raj*. During the greater part of the XIXth century they had held entirely aloof from Western education, and of those who had tardily recognized its value if they were to hold their own under modern conditions in competition with Hindus, the majority were still under the influence of the one great leader, Sir Syed Ahmed, who had sought to teach them that Western learning could be reconciled with the tenets of Islam and that only in unwavering reliance upon the British *raj* could they find any permanent safeguard both for their faith and their communal rights against the menace of Hindu ascendancy which he detected in the political aims of the Indian National Congress. Pan-Islamism made no serious headway in India in Abdul Hamid's days, though the crushing defeat of the Greek armies in Thessaly in 1897 when for the first time for two centuries Turkey could claim to have waged a victorious war upon a Christian power, sent a thrill of pride through the whole Mohammedan world, and substantially enhanced the Sultan's prestige as a great Islamic potentate, whose name was more and more frequently introduced into the Friday prayer in the Mosques of India. The creation of the All-India Moslem League in 1905 in almost open opposition to the Indian National Congress at the moment when the latter was being swept off its feet by the storm that had burst out in Bengal was a fresh affirmation of Sir Syed Ahmed's political creed, of which the partition of Bengal seemed itself to be a striking vindication. For, if it provoked the wrath of all Hindus, all Mohammedans rejoiced at it as it created in Eastern Bengal a new province in which Mohammedan influence predominated.

Gradually, however, even Indian Mohammedans began to take alarm at the general trend of European policy towards Turkey, with the one important exception of Germany, who had quickly stepped into our shoes at Constantinople as her only wholehearted and indulgent friend. All the Mohammedan states of North Africa had passed under British or French ascendancy and the remnants of Persian independence were being swept away by an

understanding between England and Russia. Then
came Italy's high-handed occupation of Tripoli, the
last of Turkey's African possessions, and immediately
afterwards the Balkan wars which reduced the
Ottoman Empire in Europe to little more than
Eastern Thrace and Constantinople and the Straits.
It was easy to persuade Mohammedans that most
of the European powers were engaged in a deep
conspiracy to destroy Islam, and there was in India
a new school of " Young Mohammedans," who
professed to believe that England was the prime
mover in that conspiracy. They had outgrown
Sir Syed Ahmed's faith in British rule and joined
hands with the Hindu Extremists in the Indian
National Congress, and some were in direct touch
with the " Young Turks " of the Committee of
Union and Progress at Constantinople.

It was, perhaps, fortunate that when the great
war broke out Turkey did not go into it until three
months after India had thrown herself fully into the
Empire's struggle against the two Germanic Empires.
By entering into the war just when she did as their
subordinate ally, Turkey lost her chance of capturing
the Indian Mohammedans, many of whom had sons
and brothers already fighting or on their way to
fight side by side with British armies at the front.
A few of the most prominent champions of Turkey,
such as the two brothers Mohammed and Shaukat Ali,
both of them Western-educated men of no mean
ability, were interned for the duration of the war
because they refused to give any assurance that they
would refrain from an actively disloyal agitation.
But the vast majority of Indian Mohammedans never
swerved from their allegiance and indeed furnished
the largest quota of recruits for the Indian armies
in the field. Only when the war was over did they
begin to display any special concern for the fate of
Turkey. Then the brothers Ali, released from their

internment, saw their chance of rousing their co-religionists far more effectively than they had ever succeeded in doing before the war, and their success affords a striking illustration of the rapidity with which a blaze of religious passion can be kindled in India. They were shrewd enough to see that no pro-Turkish agitation would really stir the masses unless it could be given a religious sanction. So the cry they raised was " Save the Caliphate of Islam." The Sultan and Caliph, they alleged, would no longer be able to discharge the religious functions if his territorial power as a temporal ruler were curtailed. The war waged against Turkey by the Allies, and notably by England, was in effect, they declared, a war against Islam itself and it was the duty of all true Mohammedans in India as elsewhere to set the higher loyalty they owed to the Caliph above the secondary and spurious loyalty which their British oppressors sought to impose on them. The agitation was at first largely artificial, but it sufficed to spread great alarm amongst the advisers of the Government of India with some of whom the obsolescent tradition still survived that the British *raj* should rely on the loyalty of Indian Mohammedans who knew how to fight, as a counter-weight to the Congress sedition-mongers, mostly Hindus, who knew only how to talk. Government received and seemed almost to welcome Caliphate deputations, even when they were headed by a man whose antecedents were as fully known as Mohammed Ali's, and he was allowed if not encouraged to head a deputation to England to lay the views of the Caliphate Committee before British Ministers. Though Mr. Lloyd George, as Prime Minister, gave them a very cold reception, they found some influential well-wishers, and chief amongst these Mr. Montagu who, like many Jews, had an instinctive tenderness for Turkey in recollection of the tolerance extended by her to their race when it was proscribed by Christendom. In such circumstances the Caliphate agitation could but gather increasing momentum, and it assumed such menacing proportions that it ended not only by overawing the Government of India but by deflecting British policy towards Turkey from its primary and legitimate war purposes. If the terms of the Treaty of Sèvres were severe, they merely redeemed Great Britain's war pledges to the oppressed subject races of Turkey, Mohammedan as well as Christian, that they would never again be allowed to relapse beneath the Turk's infinite capacity for misrule. The revival of old jealousies amongst the Allies and England's intense war weariness no doubt contributed also to the final surrender to Turkey at Lausanne, but the Caliphate agitation was one of the decisive factors. Whatever views Englishmen may entertain of the Lausanne settlement on its merits or in the peculiar circumstances of the case, there can hardly be any question of the gravity of the precedent set when for the first time in matters of high policy affecting the whole Empire British Ministers yielded to the turbulent religious agitation, under openly disloyal leadership, of a relatively small minority in the Empire—a minority even in India.

The story of the Caliphate movement, even allowing for a certain leaven of genuine religious feeling, was a squalid and often tragic one. One of the most pathetic incidents for which it was responsible was the emigration of large bodies of ignorant Mohammedan peasantry who deserted their lands and homes in the North-West Province at Mohammed Ali's instigation in order not to live any longer under Infidel rule, and sought but did not find a refuge on the Mohammedan soil of Afghanistan, whence the wretched and half-starved survivors gradually filtered back to India as the poor ruined dupes of unscrupulous leaders.

When Gandhi threw his mantle over the Caliphate movement in the belief, as he said, that it was essentially a splendid demonstration of religious faith, he gave the brothers Ali, who scarcely professed to share his meekness of spirit, the most striking proof of his unbounded confidence by parading his intimate association with them as an example of the brotherly relations between Hindus and Moslems without which, as he admitted, there could be no real *Swaraj* even in an independent India. But the fraternization was superficial and of short duration. Popular demonstrations were held to the new-fangled cry of " *Hindu Musulman ki-jai,*" and, sometimes to the scandal of orthodox Mohammedans and Hindus alike, the fraternization stretched so far as to allow the Hindu "brothers" to address Mohammedan congregations in the mosques and Mohammedan "brothers" to bring pollution into the innermost shrines of Hinduism. But the Hindus soon began to note that joint Hindu and Mohammedan demonstrations against the British *raj* were apt to end in the looting of the Hindu quarter by their more pugnacious Moslem brothers, and they finally had a frightful object-lesson in the rising of the fierce Mohammedan Moplahs of the Malabar coast in 1921-2. Directed at first against the British, it soon turned into a savage onslaught on the Hindu population, recalling the worst days of the early Mohammedan invasions of India. Helpless Hindus were ruthlessly plundered and slaughtered, and their women ravished, the only alternative given to them being to embrace Islam at the point of the sword.

British troops at last put down the outbreak, but as it was clearly traced to the Caliphate agitation a Hindu member of the Legislative Assembly made bold to ask how long such men as Mohammed and Shaukat Ali were to be allowed to go on preaching the doctrines which the Moplahs had carried into brutal practice. The career of the two brothers was, however, only interrupted by their sentence to two years imprisonment for tampering with the loyalty of Mohammedan Sepoys. It was in the house of their friends that their influence ultimately received a far more severe blow when, at the very moment when two members of the Angora National Assembly were to be welcomed at a monster Caliphate meeting in Delhi, the news came that the Angora Assembly had just abolished the Caliphate and sent the Caliph into exile. Their stock-in-trade was gone, and most of their personal influence ; but not the legacy of racial and religious hatred they have left behind them, all the more dangerous as, in the case of a Mohammedan population, it is always liable to be suddenly charged with the dynamic energy of militant fanaticism.

But the Caliphate agitation, if fiercer and, owing to its political reactions at home, for the moment more successful, never ran so deep as the Non-Co-operation movement with its peculiar appeal to the ancient forces of Hinduism, translated later on into a Swarajist plan of campaign conceived on more practical lines. Both, however, were running full-tide whilst a new Constitutional charter for India, known as the Government of India Act, 1919, had been carefully and patiently enacted by the British Parliament, and preparations were being steadily made by the Indian Government for bringing it into operation. There could be no more striking contrast between the British and the Indian psychology.

CHAPTER XIII

INDIA'S NEW CONSTITUTIONAL CHARTER

IT was on such rough waters that the new Indian Constitution was launched when the Chamber of Princes, the Council of State and the Indian Legislative Assembly were opened at Delhi on February 9, 1921, by the Duke of Connaught, in the name of the King-Emperor. There was a great muster of Princes and Ruling Chiefs from the Native States arrayed in all their panoply of gleaming jewels and robes of many colours, though there were notable absentees, amongst them the Nizam of Hyderabad, who ranks as the premier feudatory of the Crown. But as the institution of a Chamber of Princes, though an interesting innovation, in no wise affected the peculiar and separate status of the Native States, it was not there that one had to look for the historical significance of the great pageant, but in the far less picturesque assemblage representing the new Legislatures of British India. The great majority wore European dress with only here and there the head-gear peculiar to their caste and race to introduce a note of local colour. But they claimed to stand for a new Indian nation and for new principles of democratic government, if also for reasoned loyalty to British rule—differing on this crucial point from the one political party conspicuous by its absence. In an uncompromising spirit of rebellion the Non-Co-operation party had of its own will excluded itself from representation in any constitutional assembly committed to acceptance of British rule. The demonstrative absence of a party for whom *Swaraj* meant a complete breach with the West contrasted violently with the generous spirit of the Royal message read out by the Duke which culminated in these weighty words: "For years—it may be for generations—patriotic and loyal Indians have dreamed of *Swaraj* for their Motherland. To-day you have the beginnings of *Swaraj* within my Empire and the widest scope and ample opportunity for progress to the liberty which my other Dominions enjoy."

The guns of the Fort boomed forth a Royal salute, but all the time a strange silence brooded over the ancient and populous city. Except for rare groups of sightseers who could not withstand the temptation of a brilliant spectacle, the streets were deserted. The people of Delhi, Hindus and Mohammedans, had gone out in their thousands to hear Gandhi deliver, a few miles away, a very different message of his own, calling upon India to strain her whole soul-force to throw off the Satanic yoke of an alien rule and an alien civilization. Striking, too, was the contrast presented by the two messages between the ancient India that goes back for thousands of years to the Vedic age, and the new India superimposed upon it by British rule. Gandhi's message was that of a dreamer appealing wildly to the passions of his people with vague visions of a coming millennium conjured up out of a largely mythical past. The King-Emperor's message gave its final *imprimatur* to the carefully-considered provisions of a great constitutional charter drawn up after long and careful deliberation by both Houses of the British Parliament, 6,000 miles away, in discharge of the trust first committed to them by Pitt's Government of India Act of 1784.

Parliament never contemplated terminating or surrendering that trust. What it enacted was a devolution to Indians of power and responsibility never before conferred upon them, and with a view to a further devolution if and when the experiment proved sufficiently successful to justify its extension. Ten years was the term appointed for the first stage, and before its conclusion a full inquiry into the results by that time achieved was to inform the judgment

of Parliament in pursuance of the Declaration of
1917 that " the British Government and the Government
of India on whom the responsibility lies for
the welfare and advancement of the Indian
people must be judges of the time and measure
of each advance." These and other reservations
for the maintenance of Parliament's control showed
it to be conscious of the gravity of the experiment,
though it was one which all its own traditions
constrained it to make. British ideas of political
advancement have been bound up for centuries with
the development of representative institutions. A
British democracy having been led to see in the
response of India to the Empire's call during the
war a proof of her maturity for a closer association
with a Commonwealth of free nations, the only
direction in which it could occur to them to look for
the means of promoting her advancement was in
the development of representative institutions
modelled as far as might be on those to which, as
they believed, their own country mainly owed its
liberties and its greatness.

Representative institutions were not altogether
new to British India and the Morley-Minto reforms
had put them for the first time on a partially-
elective basis. But the event had gone to show that
they could only be dead sea fruit if they lacked the
stimulus of some real power and corresponding
responsibility. This was the task to which Parliament
had to address itself. Any division of powers
and responsibilities, some to continue reserved as
before to the constituted organs of Indian Government
and some to be transferred, even tentatively, to
Indian Legislatures, was clearly seen to involve the
introduction of an element of dualism which came
to be known as Dyarchy. If Parliament's ultimate
responsibility was to be maintained—and of that
there was never any doubt—and if at the same time

Legislatures were to be created in India on as broad a basis of popular representation as her social conditions allowed for an essay in responsible government, some spheres of government and administration would have to be transferred under adequate guarantees to Indians in order that they should be made and held responsible for them to those Legislatures. Where were such spheres to be found ? Parliament after the most exhaustive process of inquiry and deliberation which it could possibly apply to the solution of this question came to the conclusion that only in the Provinces could the foundations be laid for any larger structure of responsible self-government. Agriculture and industries, education, public health, excise duties, public buildings and roads and local self-government were the subjects which affected and interested most closely a considerable part of the population, and on which Indian experience and Indian knowledge of popular opinion could, it was hoped, be most usefully brought to bear, especially as popular needs and desires are apt to vary from province to province. It is these subjects and a few minor ones that were selected for immediate transfer to Indian Ministers responsible in the Parliamentary sense of the word to the Provincial Legislature for their administration. These Indian Ministers were to be at the same time members of the Provincial Government which, as a whole, had still to remain responsible, not to the Provincial Legislature, but through the Viceroy and the Secretary of State, as in the past, to the British Parliament, whilst the Governor and his Executive Council continued in the same way to administer the Departments more immediately charged with the maintenance of law and order including Justice and Police.

Under this ingenious but delicate system of equipoise, the actual government of the province consists of two wings, the Governor and his Council dealing with the "reserved" subjects and the Governor and his Indian Ministers dealing with the "transferred" subjects, the Governor himself acting as the link between the two wings, and retaining definite powers of control to be exercised by him in emergencies over the Legislature to which only his Indian Ministers are responsible. Dyarchy was not, however, intended to be permanent. It is a temporary device for tiding over an admittedly difficult period of transition. For if and when the Indian Ministers have proved themselves competent to administer the departments first transferred to them, and the Legislative Council has shown the will and the capacity to act up to its own constitutional responsibilities, the transfer of further departments may come with the next period of transition, until, with the transfer of all departments of provincial administration, full provincial self-government is reached. With one vital reservation, the powers of the Provincial Legislature are such that they approximate already to those of a sovereign Parliament in regard to the "transferred" departments in charge of Indian Ministers, and even over the "reserved" departments it exercises considerable if limited power through its control, also within definite limits, of finance and legislation. The vital reservation is this, that at his discretion, but subject of course to the higher authority of the Government of India and the Secretary of State, the Governor is empowered to override the Legislature if he is prepared to "certify" that such action is essential to the discharge of his own ultimate responsibility to Parliament.

On the other hand Parliament decided that the time had not yet come for any such devolution of authority by the Government of India, which remains supreme. A new All-India Legislature has, however, been created, consisting of two Houses, the Legislative Assembly and the Council of State, both with a large Indian majority. But the Government of India is not responsible to it. Dyarchy has not been introduced into the Viceroy's Executive Council, and no separate departments of All-India administration have been transferred to Indian Ministers. But the number of Indian members of the Viceroy's Executive Council, *i.e.*, of the Government of India, each with his own portfolio and presiding over his own Department, has been so substantially increased that Indian influence must carry much greater weight than it ever did before in the very citadel of Indian Government. In the same way, though the Government of India is not responsible to the All-India Legislature whose powers in regard to matters concerning the army and foreign affairs and relations with the Native States are strictly limited by statute, the Legislature holds an extremely strong position, as it enjoys not only wide opportunities for discussing questions of general policy and criticizing the action of Government, but also every elastic power over finance and legislation. But the Viceroy's authority is fully safeguarded. Subject to the superior authority of Parliament represented by the Secretary of State, the right is given him to override either or both branches of the All-India Legislature in any matter which he is prepared to " certify " as vital for the peace, security and good government of India. Put into simpler terms, the All-India Legislature can exercise very great influence, but cannot exercise unlimited control.

If the spirit in which India's new Constitutional Charter was granted by the British Parliament is to be fully understood the Act of 1919 must be read in the light of the recommendations made by the Joint Select Committee of both Houses, virtually invested with the full authority of Parliament itself, and also of the " instruments " to the Viceroy and to Provincial Governors, respectively issued under the Royal Sign Manual when the Act was first brought into operation. The Joint Select Committee for instance clearly realized the difficulties likely to arise in the normal conduct of affairs by a Government consisting of two separate wings, and it expressly desired " the habit to be carefully fostered of joint deliberation between members of Council [*i.e.*, Executive Council] and Indian Ministers sitting under the Governor as Chairman." The Committee held that " there cannot be too much mutual advice and consultation," but they also held that, when once opinions had been freely exchanged, it should be definitely established on which side of the Dyarchy the responsibility for a particular decision rests.

To reduce the risk of conflicts between the All-India and the Provincial Legislatures, it has been laid down that they should severally confine themselves in the exercise of their legislative functions to the respective spheres assigned to them by the classification of Central and Provincial subjects under the new rules of devolution, though no statutory change has curtailed their rights in principle to concurrent jurisdiction. The larger administrative autonomy granted to the provinces has necessarily involved a larger measure of financial autonomy. The assignment of particular revenues to the provinces follows the same lines as the " transferred " subjects, with the addition of certain proportions of other All-Indian revenue encashed in the provinces. On the other hand—and this is a provision which has given rise to heated controversies—the provinces have to make out of their revenue important annual contributions to the Central exchequer, of which the aggregate amount was set down at about £10,000,000, and whilst hopes were held out of a speedy reduction, the right of the Government of India to increase it as required in cases of emergency is distinctly reserved.

The constitution of Indian assemblies that might be fairly regarded as representative was a problem of peculiar difficulty in the present state of a country still in so many different stages of evolution and with such an immense variety of peoples. How were the constituencies to be formed and what was to be the electoral franchise where election was possible ? Absolutely uniform constituencies were ruled out as incompatible with any equitable measure of representation for races and creeds and classes whose historical and actual importance could not be measured merely by their numbers. The principle of communal representation, reluctantly accepted by Lord Morley in the Indian Councils Act of 1909, has been retained, and given effect to by the creation of general constituencies for non-Mohammedans and Mohammedans and, in some provinces, for other distinct communities (Sikhs, for instance, in the Punjab, and Mahrattas in the Bombay Presidency), whilst special constituencies have been created for the representation of special interests, such as those of the large landlords, the Universities, and commerce and industry which would otherwise have been swamped in the general constituencies. The right of nomination to a certain number of seats both in the Provincial and in the All-India Legislatures has also been reserved, in the case of the former to the Provincial Governor, and in the case of the latter to the Viceroy, in order to provide for the presence of officials qualified to make statements and answer questions on behalf of Government, and also in order to enable individual selection to redress in some cases the balance in favour of any particular interests which would not have been represented at all, or quite inadequately represented, even in the special constituencies. These nominated members, however, are few in number compared with the elected members, and the official *bloc* by which Government could always secure a mechanical majority in the old Legislative Councils has entirely disappeared.

The qualification for membership of the different Legislatures varies, and even for the Provincial Councils it is not quite uniform in every province. But the differences are not material. The electoral franchise, except in the special constituencies, is based as a rule on a very modest property qualification. Illiteracy is no bar, for though barely more than ten per cent of the population attain even to the lowest standard of literacy, there are many men of intelligence and substance, whose opinion is worth having, even if they are unable to read or write. The registers at the first general election in the winter of 1920–1 contained over 6,000,000 names, or altogether 2½ per cent of the male population throughout that part of India to which the Act applies—a very small fraction, no doubt, of the whole population, but one which after all compares not altogether unfavourably with the proportion of the British population that enjoyed the franchise a century ago, before the Great Reform Bill. The total number of voters placed on the rolls was nearly 5½ millions out of a total population of 240,000,000 in British India, to whom alone the new Constitution applies. The total parliamentary electorate in England before 1832 barely exceeded 200,000, and was only 84,000 for the boroughs and Universities represented by an entirely disproportionate majority in the House of Commons. The comparison, however, must not be pressed too far, for the conditions which then prevailed in England differed widely from those that now prevail in India. The political education of the British nation as a whole was then far more advanced than is that of the Indian people to-day. Long before the masses got the vote in England they took a keen interest in politics and could exert a great, if indirect, influence upon Parliament. It was their pressure from below that gave an increasingly democratic character to our Parliamentary institutions. The masses in India are still far removed from that stage. What detracts from the authority of the new Legislatures in India is not so much the smallness of the electorate as that the Indian elected members are mostly drawn from one class only, very influential no doubt, but still numerically very small, and often, its critics allege, not much in touch with other classes, viz., the class which through Western education has assimilated the forms rather than the democratic spirit of British Parliamentary life. Whether that spirit could be acclimatized so quickly—or indeed ever—in India, as Parliament assumed when it enacted the new Constitution, was and still is a moot point. But it was only natural that it should proceed on that assumption. When, moved by the vision of a new era opening up for the whole world as the consummation of a heroic struggle for freedom, the British people determined that India too should have her reward for her loyal contribution to the common victory, what else could they reasonably do than make a serious attempt to set her feet on the path of responsible government, the path they had themselves trodden, more slowly and laboriously, it is true, but with no mean success?

Difficulties there were and clearly very great ones, and Parliament, not unmindful of them, sought to meet them by maintaining undiminished its right of ultimate control. But there was one difficulty, less immediate and therefore less apparent, but perhaps in the long run the most formidable of all, which it was beyond the power of Parliament to meet. Indirectly the new Constitution was bound to affect the whole of India, but directly it could apply only to that part of India which is under direct British administration. That for different reasons certain areas even within that part were excluded from its immediate application is of little importance. The point of paramount importance is that it could not be applied to the Native States that possess their own autonomous rights of government and administration. A fresh line of cleavage has been thus set up between the Native States and British India. The consequences may be minimized so long as the supreme Government is not made responsible to Indian Legislatures, but if, and as soon as, that happens, there will inevitably be frequent danger of conflict between any popular system of government in British India and autocratic systems of government in the Native States. In the meantime the only attempt made to link the latter up with the new order of things in British India has been the creation of a permanent Chamber of Princes which may bring them into closer corporate association with the Government of India in the form that it still constitutionally retains. But the link is a very slender one, as the Princes can only deliberate on matters concerning their common interests as rulers of the Native States. Nor can they be compelled to join the Chamber, and some of them, even amongst the most important, have so far held aloof.

Parliament still holds the Secretary of State and through him the Viceroy and the Provincial Governors responsible for the good government of India in all its vital aspects, and the Secretary of State still continues to be advised, and in some matters formally controlled, by the Council of India in Whitehall. But the Agency duties formerly performed by the India Office have been transferred to a representative of the Government of India upon

whom the title and status of High Commissioner have
been conferred on the analogy of the High Commis-
sioners maintained by the Dominion Governments
in London. For the first time, too, a long-standing
Indian grievance has been removed by the placing
of the Secretary of State's salary on the British
estimates instead of being charged to the Indian
revenue. The House of Commons has thereby
acquired a special opportunity of discussing Indian
affairs when the annual vote for Ministers' salaries
comes up, and an attempt has been made to revive
Parliamentary interest, which sank to a low ebb
after the periodical inquiries into the state of India
in the old Company days were dropped with its
disappearance in 1858, by the institution of standing
committees of both Houses to which definite functions
are assigned. On the other hand, it has had to
recognize that its interference in minor matters of
administration must be necessarily curtailed, and
the Speaker took an early opportunity of ruling out
certain questions addressed to the Secretary of
State relating to " transferred " subjects in the
provinces on the specific ground that it was highly
undesirable for the House of Commons to interfere
with the control of Indian affairs now transferred to
Indian Legislatures.

Side by side with great constitutional changes
which must react on the whole of India though
they do not directly affect the Native States, a
change of almost equally vital importance has been
initiated in the composition of the public services,
which must directly affect for better or for worse
the character of the whole administration in a
country where good administration is still, perhaps,
of greater consequence than any mere forms of
government. The object of this change is to carry
into effect that part of the British Declaration of
August 20, 1917, which promised an increasing

association of Indians in every branch of the administration. From the foundation of the Indian National Congress and even long before it the small proportion of Indians admitted to any but the subordinate public services has been a sore subject with Indians, who waited with growing impatience for the fulfilment of the fair promises held out to them by Parliament as far back as 1833 and solemnly renewed in Queen Victoria's Parliament in 1858. Those promises had, it is true, always been accompanied by a little saving-clause—" as far as may be " —and in the circumstances in which India had passed under British rule, it was inevitable that Englishmen should for a long time have enjoyed the monopoly of all the higher posts in the administration. But if it was unduly prolonged and tended to develop some of the defects inherent to all powerful and self-centred bureaucracies, Englishmen could legitimately claim that it was they who had in the course of less than a century introduced standards of integrity and justice and efficiency entirely unknown before the British *raj*. Indians of all classes, except the inveterate enemies of all Western ascendancy, were indeed not so long ago almost unanimous in recognizing their great qualities of character, though not many had the courage to pay them so frank and public a tribute as Gokhale did in the speech already quoted in a previous chapter. They may have often displayed some of the defects of their qualities, but they have always at least the peculiar advantage of complete freedom from those prejudices of caste and communal jealousies which often unavoidably militate against the impartiality and independence of Indian officials. They are not exposed to the strong personal pressure which can be so easily and often cruelly applied to Indians under their peculiar social system. Nor, if one bears in mind the need for men with a technical education which India could not for a long time herself supply in the many services requiring expert knowledge which were created in India after the transfer to the Crown in 1858, can it be contended that their numbers were ever excessive when compared merely with the huge population of India or with the army of Indian subordinates employed under them in a huge administration required to cover many large fields of work such as education, public works, irrigation, railways, civil, medical and veterinary services, etc., in England usually left by the State to private or municipal enterprise.

Ten years ago, according to official statistics, the number of Englishmen in Government employment holding appointments of more than Rs200 a month—and there were scarcely any below that grade—was just under 6,000, and amongst these the Indian Civil Service, the *corps d'élite* with the greatest powers and responsibilities, had a total strength of 1,371. Indians not unnaturally regarded these numbers as excessive when they themselves were qualifying in rapidly increasing numbers and on approved standards of education for most forms of Government service. It was not, however, so much of the actual numbers that the more reasonable representatives of Indian public opinion complained as of the enormous proportion of the most important and highly-paid posts reserved in practice, if not in principle, for Englishmen. In the above classification, taken as a whole, Englishmen were considerably outnumbered by the Indians, but in the higher grades the position was reversed and in the Indian Civil Service there were only ninety Indians altogether. Such figures, it was urged, were entirely out of relation to the great progress India had made in every field of modern life. Another Indian grievance was that not only were they not admitted in sufficient numbers into the services, but that when admitted into them they were apt to be treated by their British colleagues as inferiors unfit for any independent responsibilities and thus denied the opportunities of developing administrative qualities which they were assumed to lack because they were Indians. They insisted on the contrary with some force that, however valuable the work of British officials might be, the experience they acquired during their term of service was lost to India as soon as they retired, often still in the prime of life, to spend the rest of their lives at home, whereas the retired Indian official remained in the country and could go on serving it in other ways. After the Morley-Minto reforms the Government felt that the time had come to make a serious attempt to redress some of these grievances, whether material or sentimental, and two years before the war, when Lord Crewe was at the India Office, a Royal Commission was appointed to inquire into the Indian Public Services, which counted Gokhale amongst its Indian members and Mr. Herbert Fisher and Mr. Ramsay MacDonald amongst its British members. Under the chairmanship of Lord Islington it completed its protracted inquiries in India before the outbreak of the war, but it sat again in London in 1915, and before complete agreement could be reached between all the British and Indian members it lost Gokhale's much-needed services through his premature death, and the other Indian member, Mr. Justice (now Sir) Abdur-Rahim, drew up a minority report which on many points sounded a louder note of dissent than Gokhale would, perhaps, have insisted on. The majority report itself was, nevertheless, a genuine attempt to remove many legitimate Indian grievances and it at any rate abolished the invidious distinction drawn by the Aitchison Commission twenty-five years earlier between Imperial and Provincial services into which the Indians, practically relegated to the latter, had read a scarcely disguised form of racial discrimination. But the report for reasons connected with the war was not made public until 1917. Indian opinion, agitated by the renewal of political controversies, dismissed it as by that time already obsolete, and much of it was treated as such in the Montagu-Chelmsford Report in view of the great constitutional changes which it contemplated. When these were embodied in the Act of 1919, a policy definitely directed towards the training of the people of India to self-government, involved the early introduction of as many Indians as possible into every branch of the administration and not least into the higher public services. Steps were at once taken to that end, and on no niggardly scale. Even for the Indian Civil Service the percentage of recruitment of Indians was fixed in 1920 at 33 per cent increasing to 48 per cent in 1930, the date appointed for an eventual extension of responsible government. But this did not satisfy the growing impatience of Indians who were already beginning to clamour for an acceleration of the stages of constitutional advancement. They insisted equally that the "Indianization," as it was called, of the public services should be accelerated, and they rejected the Government scheme as wholly inadequate.

Other complications were meanwhile arising in quite another quarter. For a very serious danger arose that the chief sources of European recruitment would dry up so rapidly at home as to make it impossible before long to maintain even the minimum proportion of Englishmen still required as a leaven for the Indianized public services during the period of constitutional transition contemplated by Parliament. For many of the older British officials the constitutional changes represented an unpleasant and even intolerable breach with the old traditions of

service which had never required them to take orders
from Indian Ministers and seldom from any Indian
superiors, whilst the enormous rise in the cost of
living consequent upon the war had not only robbed
life in India of most of its former amenities but had
rendered it very difficult for them to make both
ends meet even by reducing their accustomed
standards of expenditure. In answer to this outcry,
those who wished were allowed to retire with
proportionately-reduced pensions at an earlier age
than the service regulations had hitherto required.
The numbers who availed themselves of these
facilities were considerable, but more serious still
was the effect produced upon recruitment in England
by their gloomy description of the changes and their
still gloomier anticipations as to the future—reinforced, too, by letters in the same strain from those
who still remained in India, often not unnaturally
exasperated by such an orgy of racial hatred and
abuse and calumny as the Non-Co-operation and
Caliphate movements brought forth. Even in less
stormy times it might have been hard for those who
had been accustomed to the old conditions and had
done excellent work under them to realize that
there might be equal if different opportunities of
doing excellent work under the new conditions.
But they might have remembered that the young
men who go out under the new conditions
would not be constantly obsessed as they were
with recollections of " the good old times," and
that, not only in India but all over the world, the
economic consequences of the war have generally
made things very much harder for the younger
generation of all classes in search of a suitable
livelihood. Rabid declamation in India against
predatory hordes of British parasites was scarcely
more unreasonable than the lamentation of despon-
dent Englishmen who declared that India was no

16

longer a country fit for white men to live in, or the
inspissated gloom of Jeremiahs who wrote of India
as already a lost dominion. But they produced
a cumulative effect in our Universities. At Oxford,
for instance, where in the past the competition for
the Indian Civil Service used to be particularly keen,
and in the five pre-war years an average of almost
twenty-four graduates passed out into the Indian
Civil Service, only ten altogether were recruited into
it in the three post-war years, 1921, 1922 and 1923.
The falling-off at Cambridge and other British and
Irish Universities was equally marked. At that rate
the moment seemed to be drawing very near when
the supply of young Englishmen of the high standard
required for the Indian Services would cease altogether, and with the passing of the present generation the British official would disappear entirely
out of India. The prospect was so serious that
resort was promptly had to the appointment of yet
another Royal Commission composed of four Englishmen and four Indians under the presidency of Lord
Lee of Fareham. The reception accorded in India to
that Commission and to its recommendations will have
to be considered in conjunction with other Indian reactions to the new Constitution. But it shows how
quickly things move in India to-day that the purpose
of Lord Lee's Commission was to inquire, not as Lord
Islington's Commission had done, ten years earlier,
how many Indians could be safely admitted into the
Indian Public Services, but how few Englishmen it
would be safe to retain in them, and what could be
done to ensure the continued recruitment of those few.
It marks as clearly as any of the provisions in the
great Government of India Act of 1919 how far and
how quickly England was prepared to travel towards
close and genuine co-operation on the road to equal
partnership if only Indians would not persist in
refusing co-operation, and rejecting partnership.

CHAPTER XIV

In other Oriental countries besides India the XXth century has witnessed the introduction, with only indifferent success, of Parliamentary institutions on a Western model. But they have sometimes owed their existence as in Turkey and in China to successful revolutions against Oriental despotisms and sometimes as in Persia and still more recently in Egypt they have grown up under severe international restraints on the political independence of the country. Only in Japan have they developed under fairly normal conditions, though there, too, they were born in a period of stress when the whole nation was suddenly bidden to exchange its mediæval armour for an entirely new and modern equipment. The Parliamentary experiment now being made in India is altogether different. It has the sanction and support of a firmly-established Government pledged under the authority of the British Parliament to encourage the political evolution of India towards the same forms of responsible government which our own Parliamentary institutions have promoted. There was little to guide us in prognosticating its success or failure in India, for the old Legislative Councils were merely consultative bodies with extremely limited powers, and when Lord Morley reformed their constitution in 1909 he repudiated most emphatically all idea of paving the way for Parliamentary institutions for which he considered India to be still quite unripe. Judgment cannot yet be passed upon an experiment which only began with the opening of the new Indian Legislatures at the beginning of 1921, but their record, for the first legislative period at any rate, was not altogether discouraging.

There were dark clouds on the horizon when the

Parliamentary curtain went up. The Non-Co-operation movement was raging furiously. But it did not directly affect the character of the first representative assemblies elected under the Act of 1919. Gandhi having absolutely banned the elections, they resolved themselves into relatively mild competitions between candidates of other parties who were at any rate agreed to accept the new constitution. They therefore passed off on the whole quietly with a fair attendance at the polls, and, except in the Madras Provincial Council in which a new non-Brahman party secured a surprisingly large majority over the Brahmans, the Indian elected members in the Provincial as well as in the All-India Legislature formed loosely-knit groups of moderate opinions inclined to be critical of Government but professing readiness to co-operate with it on reasonable terms. The majority were Hindus, and exercised an ascendancy due, as it must continue to be for a long time to come, not merely to numbers but to a higher average of education. Many of them were lawyers, and they mostly belonged to the Western-educated classes whose inveterate suspicions of the bureaucracy, still strongly entrenched on the Government benches, led them to be always on the alert to vindicate their independence against the opprobrious charge of " slave mentality " hurled at them by the Non-Co-operators who had boycotted the elections.

The chief interest centred in the Legislative Assembly, as it was specially created to reflect Indian opinion and Indian sentiment in the classes to whose co-operation Parliament chiefly looked for the success of representative institutions in India. It settled down to its work at Delhi in February, 1921, under the deep impression made by the Duke of Connaught's inaugural speech and the message read by him from the King-Emperor. The

first session began well. The Indian members felt
that, whilst the Punjab tragedy could not be passed
over in silence, it was their duty not to deepen a
shadow which had, in the Duke's own words,
"lengthened over the face of India," and after conciliatory assurances from Government an Indian
resolution, couched in sober and earnest terms
calculated to satisfy legitimate Indian sentiment
without provoking recriminations from the British
official or unofficial members, was passed unanimously.
The same spirit of mutual forbearance was displayed
in regard to other thorny questions raised by non-
official Indian members, for instance, as to the
"freedom" of the Press and the repeal of "repressive" legislation, by which the Rowlatt Acts were
chiefly meant. Another cause of dispute arose out
of the Esher Committee Report on the Indian army
which was construed into an attempt to place it
permanently and for all purposes at the disposal of
the British War Office. But the Assembly was
content to affirm that the purpose of the Indian
army was the defence of India and that it should be
controlled by no one but the Government of India,
and when a series of resolutions were moved for
placing it on a "national" basis, Government
showed a disarming readiness to refer this and all
other contentious subjects to Committees and Commissions for further investigation. The question of
fiscal autonomy was already decided in principle in
favour of India, and the creation of a Central Department of Industries and Labour helped to facilitate
the co-operation of the Assembly in practical
legislation on those subjects. Even a huge and
unprecedented deficit in the Budget which necessi-
tated new or increased taxation was dealt with on
both sides with great restraint, though this Cape of
the Tempests was not rounded without much
trenchant criticism of the heavy military expenditure

which largely accounted for the deficit, and a distinct warning, not confined to the Indian unofficial benches, that Government would have to mend its financial ways before drafting its next Budget. The danger of an immediate conflict was happily averted, and when Lord Chelmsford, whose term of office was drawing to an end, closed the first session, he was able to say with some legitimate pride as one of the joint-authors of the Reform scheme that it would " go far to dispel the doubts of those who have looked upon our new constitutional departure with gloomy forebodings."

The angry tide of Non-Co-operation was still however rising outside the walls of the Indian assemblies, and when the new Viceroy, Lord Reading, soon after his arrival, invited Gandhi up to Simla and remained closeted with him for several days, Indians began to wonder whether there were to be "two kings of Brentford." They wondered still more when, a fortnight later, Gandhi proclaimed a boycott of the Prince of Wales' projected visit to India for which the Viceroy himself had been ready to assume full responsibility, and greater still was their perplexity when nothing happened to the Mahatma after the open menace of such an outrage not only upon Indian loyalty to the Crown but upon all the traditions of Indian hospitality. Gandhi declared that the menace meant nothing more than an orderly but emphatic protest against the Satanic Government at whose invitation the Prince was coming out to India. But the sanguinary riots in Bombay on the very day of the Prince's landing gave it a very different complexion, and though Gandhi did public penance for the violence of his followers, vigorous measures had to be taken to avert a repetition of similar scenes in Calcutta. Hundreds of arrests were made and some of the foremost Non-Co-operation leaders, including Mr. C. R. Das, who was then

Gandhi's most active disciple in Bengal, were placed under lock and key before the Prince's arrival. The official programme was then carried out without any breach of the peace and the forces of disorder were kept in check within the popular quarters of the city. The most critical moment was over. English newspapers in India and at home, loyally taking their cue from official quarters, ignored or minimized the many unpleasant episodes of the tour, and the Prince, with his inborn tact and good temper, professed to make light of them though he could not but be conscious of the sullen atmosphere that prevailed in most of the large cities he visited. On some occasions, and in the Native States especially where short work is made of inconvenient agitators, there were plentiful and genuine demonstrations of enthusiasm. But they could not fully redress the balance. The Viceroy had doubtless hoped that the Prince's presence in India would pour oil on the troubled waters as other Royal visits had hitherto never failed to do, but the visit could hardly have been worse timed. So high was the tide of racial hatred then running that it almost submerged the ancient sense of Indian reverence for kingship which only ten years before had been so wonderfully demonstrated when a British Sovereign and his Consort stood for the first time on Indian soil. Such a change in the psychology of the Indian people has to be noted.

It was in the first year of Lord Reading's Viceroyalty that Gandhi's prestige with the masses reached its apogee, and though Non-Co-operation had no corporeal presence in the Assembly the pressure exercised by it from without made itself increasingly felt during the winter session of 1922. There could be no surrender to Non-Co-operation, for it was to fight Non-Co-operation that the Indian elected majority had entered the Assembly. But in the presence of a new Viceroy whose patience could easily be construed as weakness they were fatally tempted to vary their co-operation with more active and demonstrative interludes of opposition. For such support as they still felt themselves bound to give Government a heavier price had to be paid, *e.g.* in the repeal of the Press laws and of the Rowlatt Acts. As it was at the Viceroy's instigation that Mr. Montagu, by publishing the Government of India's dispatch in support of the Turkish plea for indulgent peace terms, had taken the particular action which offended against the canons of Cabinet propriety and precipitated his downfall, he could hardly take exception to the Assembly's enthusiastic tribute of sympathy for the ex-Secretary of State for India, though it was in effect a demonstration against the Imperial Government. Nor could Lord Reading resent the angry protests against Mr. Lloyd George's description of the Indian Civil Service as a " steel frame " which could never be dispensed with, or against Mr. Churchill's declared intention as Colonial Secretary to make Kenya a " characteristically British colony " when the Government of India itself seemed to favour a rapid Indianization of the superior services, and was actually engaged in doing battle for the Indians in Kenya against the Colonial Office. Government in fact accepted a stiff resolution emphasizing the right of overseas Indians to be treated as equal citizens with other subjects of the Crown, and if it demurred to a resolution demanding partial Home Rule in 1924 and complete Dominion Home Rule in 1929, it took the first step down a very slippery plane when, in spite of the definite provisions of the Act of 1919, it acquiesced in an amendment declaring that India had already made sufficient progress on the path to responsible government to claim an early revision of the constitution without waiting for 1929, the date named in the Statute. In spite of all concessions a very critical situation arose when Government had to introduce an even worse Budget than the preceding year's—with a still heavier deficit. Again it was largely due to military expenditure which was subjected to much more vehement and persistent attacks than in the previous session. These were warded off for a time by the tactful attitude of the new Commander-in-Chief, Lord Rawlinson, who was ready to give the Indian members both in public and in private the fullest possible information regarding the military situation. But Government had to promise that it would do its best to have military as well as civil expenditure submitted to an independent retrenchment Committee which could no longer be denied to Indian remonstrances. That Committee, over which Lord Inchcape presided, was expected to apply the axe in India as it had already been applied in England. The Assembly, nevertheless, proceeded to make automatic cuts in the civil estimates and rejected altogether nearly a third of the proposed new taxation, and, though it finally agreed to a partial compromise which still left a considerable deficit, it had the satisfaction of having established a precedent for subordinating the Upper House in regard to money-bills to the will of the popular Assembly when Government flinched from seizing the life-buoy thrown out to it by the Council of State who restored the salt duties proposed by the Finance Minister after the Assembly had emphatically rejected them. An open conflict was once more averted, but more grudgingly by the Assembly, and only after it had wrung from the Government a number of concessions which, whether wise or unwise, secured for the Legislature the honours of a session that had demonstrated its power to exert a very substantial measure of effective Parliamentary control in despite of the fact that Government was not constitutionally responsible to it. Only on one question did the Viceroy deliberately override the Assembly. He exercised for the first time his power of "certification" in order to enact a Bill, thrown out by the Assembly, for the better protection of the Native States against the irresponsible and calumnious propaganda conducted against them from British India and especially in the vernacular Press. As the Bill had been introduced to meet the representations of Princes and Ruling Chiefs who were alarmed at the repeal of the Press Acts in British India, this episode for the first time graphically illustrated the difficulty for the Supreme Government of running in double-harness a democratic India under direct British administration and a more or less despotic and often very mediæval India in the Native States.

The ghastly atrocities at Chauri-Chaura, which occurred whilst the Assembly was in session, startled even Gandhi into postponing the mass movement he was just projecting for "civil disobedience," and a few weeks later, on March 10, Lord Reading ordered Gandhi's arrest, for which several Provincial Governments had already for some time urgently pressed. When it failed to produce any serious upheaval he was entitled to claim that his long forbearance was justified by the event. Gandhi was brought to trial and expounded in court all his peculiar views at great length and with the utmost freedom, but never challenged the justice of his prosecution. He was condemned to six years' imprisonment, but he was released within a year on grounds of health after he had undergone a very severe operation. In his absence, disagreement soon crept in amongst his followers, many of whom had for some time past felt serious misgivings as to the success of

Non-Co-operation on the extreme lines laid down by
Gandhi though they suppressed them as long as his
magnetic influence could make itself directly felt.
As soon as it ceased, the situation was quickly felt
to have changed, but in what direction was not yet
clear.   In official circles it was assumed that the
Non-Co-operation movement would soon collapse
altogether.   But their optimism was not shared by
the Indian members of the Legislative Assembly.
Many of them owed their seats to the abstention
of the Non-Co-operators under Gandhi's orders at
the first General Election, and they came back to
Delhi for the third and last session in January, 1923,
with the well-founded belief that they would not
be given another walk-over at the next elections.
They saw little or no change in the spirit of Non-
Co-operation, but they apprehended a complete
change in their opponents' tactics.   They could best
meet it, they believed, by putting up a braver show
of opposition than they had hitherto done, and
instead of trying to educate their constituencies, they
sought to counteract the well-organized propaganda
of the much more active Non-Co-operators by
demonstrating in the Assembly that they, too, were
quite capable of " non-co-operating " with Government.   Almost the first thing they did was to refuse
off-hand the grant for the new Royal Commission
on the Superior Services appointed by Lord Peel
who, as Secretary of State in a Conservative
Government, was strongly suspected of holding
reactionary views in regard to India, though there
was nothing in the composition of that Commission
to confirm such suspicions.   Increasing stress was
laid on the urgency of " Indianizing " not only the
Civil Services but the Army, and on an early revision
of the constitution with a view to accelerating the
stages prescribed by Parliament for the development
of responsible government.   The Assembly was on

more solid ground in resisting some features of a
Budget which again showed a deficit, though a much
smaller one than its predecessors. An able Treasury
official, Sir Basil Blackett, had been sent out to set
India's financial house in order. He approached the
problem as an expert from Whitehall, impressed
only with the urgency of restoring Indian credit
by balancing revenue and expenditure, and he would
hear of no other way than an increase of the salt
duties which was precisely what the Assembly had
flatly refused to sanction in the preceding year.
The Assembly again refused. The proposed increase
was not large, but the salt tax had always had a very
bad name, and Indians could quote a great array
of British authorities who had often before condemned it as economically unsound and only to be
resorted to in case of dire necessity. Could dire
necessity be pleaded ? There were Englishmen as
well as Indians who contended that there were
other new or less objectionable sources of revenue
to be tapped, and, however halting had been their
own co-operation with Government, the Indian
Moderates had some right to complain that it was
Government that was itself playing them false
when, with a General Election in sight, and Non-
Co-operation ready this time to enter the lists, such
a Parliamentary veteran as Lord Reading insisted
on furnishing the common enemy with a formidable
electioneering weapon. The Assembly's rejection of
the salt duties was overridden by the Viceroy's
exercise of his exceptional powers, and with the
results which the Moderates had foreseen. At the
General Election at the end of 1923 they were badly
beaten, and Non-Co-operation *minus* Gandhi and
under the new name of the Swarajist Party
captured and dominated the second Assembly, in
which it made *Swaraj* a fighting issue.

It is easy to criticize the first Assembly. Whilst

Gandhi's boycott did not prevent it from coming into being as a constitutionally elected body, the fact that so popular a movement as Non-Co-operation was not represented in it at all created from the first an unfortunate atmosphere of unreality, and worse confusion followed when Indian members inside the Assembly succumbed to the temptation of looking for opportunities to compete with an irreconcilable party outside it. The Indian members who claimed to represent a new-born democracy themselves failed for the most part to discharge an essentially democratic duty. Few of them would give the time or take the trouble to visit and educate their constituencies, though this was a duty particularly incumbent upon them in a country still strange to anything like Parliamentary life. They preferred the lime-light of the Parliamentary stage. They still had the Indian National Congress weakness for resounding resolutions, often pressed for transparently theatrical purposes. From some of these artificial demonstrations they might, however, have been saved, had the Government bench, itself new to Parliamentary responsibilities, and Lord Reading, who was not new to them, spoken at times with a less uncertain voice and firmly reminded them of the statutory limits within which they were bound to keep their debates under the constitution to which the Assembly owed its existence. For the Indian Moderates, often left without any definite guidance from Government and lacking any leaders capable of maintaining effective discipline and cohesion, were apt to forget that they had been elected as avowed supporters of the new reforms, and instead of making the best of them and helping them along their first appointed stage, they constantly wanted to pull up the roots and see how they were doing, and then complained that they were desperately anæmic. They were on sounder Parliamentary ground when in presence of an alarming financial situation created mainly by an enormous military expenditure which absorbed half the revenues of the State, they insisted on exercising the limited power of the purse granted to them under the constitution. On such occasions the Indian unofficial members usually showed an undivided front in spite of the communal differences which have received statutory recognition in the composition of the Legislatures and must necessarily militate against the formation of strong and homogeneous political parties.

For solid work performed in less sensational fields than those of controversial politics, the first Assembly unquestionably deserved the praise bestowed on it by Lord Reading when in his prorogation speech on July 28, 1923, he referred to such measures as the Indian Factories Amendment Acts, the Indian Mines Act, the Workmen's Compensation Act, the Indian Emigration Act and the Criminal Procedure Amendment Act as evidence of constructive legislation likely " to have an important and beneficial effect upon the future interests of India." They were evidence also of much sound and unobtrusive work done on Committees by members of all parties and communities, including the European unofficial members between whom and their Indian colleagues the growth of friendly personal relations for which there had formerly been less opportunity, was one of the happiest results of their new Parliamentary intercourse. The debates were usually maintained on a high level of Parliamentary dignity and often of real ability and restrained eloquence, not only by Indian members who had sat in the old un-reformed Councils, but by the new members who had not had even that limited experience of the Parliamentary manner. They were quick also to acquire all the technicalities of unaccustomed forms of procedure, and in doubtful cases they were always ready to accept the guidance of the Speaker, Sir A. F. Whyte, who brought with him from Westminster some of the prestige and authority of the Mother of Parliaments.

If we turn to the Provincial Councils, their record during the first Legislative period tells as a whole no very different story, though it varies from province to province. The Indian representation in the Provincial Councils, from which also Non-Co-operation had stood entirely aloof in obedience to the Gandhi boycott, was generally drawn from the same classes as in the Indian Legislative Assembly and professed the same desire to co-operate with Government on terms of " give and take " in the working of the Reforms. The Provincial Councils had in this respect a more direct responsibility to discharge than the Legislative Assembly. For it was in the Provinces that responsible government was to be first placed on its trial in the shape of Dyarchy. But unfortunately, and not through the fault of the Councils alone, Dyarchy did not everywhere have a fair trial or any trial at all. The pivotal feature of Dyarchy as contemplated in the Act of 1919 is a sharply-drawn distinction of responsibility between the two wings of Government, the Indian Ministers in charge of the " transferred " subjects being directly accountable to the Provincial Council. But the intentions of Parliament were seldom carried out. In Madras, for instance, where the situation was, however, quite unique, the Council elections having resolved themselves into a straight fight between two parties, Brahmans and non-Brahmans, and the latter having obtained a sweeping majority, the Governor, Lord Willingdon, formed a non-Brahman Government of a unitary type and allowed it to eliminate almost entirely the distinction between reserved and transferred subjects. He believed he could dispense with Dyarchy by ignoring the rule specifically laid down for the guidance of Governors that, whilst they should encourage joint discussion of the transferred subjects between the two wings of their Government, the responsibilities of each wing should be clearly established and kept apart. Some other Governors for different reasons and in different circumstances adopted a similar attitude with the result that the dividing lines of responsibility disappeared or were hopelessly blurred. The Provincial Legislature never learnt to realize that it had the right and the duty to hold Indian Ministers to account, and Indian Ministers were never taught to render an account of their statutory stewardship to the Legislature. Haunted by the fear of being traduced by the Non-Co-operators for subserviency, the Legislature usually found it more convenient not to discriminate between the two wings of the Government, but to go on treating it as an indivisible whole, still the mere mouth-piece of a hateful bureaucracy, and as such always an appropriate target for attacks which, in the political atmosphere created by Non-Co-operation, earned easy popularity. But besides Indian inexperience and want of moral courage, the proverbial British belief in the virtue of muddling through contributed not a little to the general confusion. Such an innovation as to the dual form of Provincial Government raised no doubt different problems in different provinces, but the fundamental principles to be applied had been clearly laid down. Occasional conferences between Provincial Governors under the presidency of the Viceroy, to whom they are still responsible under the Act of 1919, would have provided an opportunity for comparing methods and results and securing the guidance of which all stood in need. Nothing of the sort was ever done. Each Governor did as seemed fit in his own eyes. The Ministers being human, were naturally inclined to throw any blame imputed to them upon Dyarchy. They sometimes acknowledged with a tinge of surprise the loyal support given to them by most of the British officials in the departments transferred to their administration. Their most frequent complaint, and the one which found readiest credence amongst their friends in the lobbies, was that they were not fairly treated in the allocation of revenue by the other wing of the dual Government. The Councils were thus tempted to attack not the "transferred" departments for which they were entitled to hold the Indian Ministers responsible, but the "reserved" departments, though the members of Government in charge of them were not constitutionally accountable to the Councils. An enormous amount of time was thus wasted in innumerable motions for the refusal or reduction of grants for the reserved departments, which under the Act could be nothing more than sham fights. In one session of the Bengal Council nearly 1,300 questions were asked and answered and 135 resolutions were debated which often raised general questions of policy lying beyond the range of its constitutional powers. This misdirected exuberance was largely due to the absence, except in Madras, of clearly defined political parties and to the anxiety of individual members under the pressure of the Non-Co-operation storm raging outside the Council doors, to advertise their political independence by public demonstrations of hostility to the wing of Government over which they had no statutory power of control. The cumulative impression produced on a public that had still less understanding for the refinements and delicate equilibrium of the new constitutional system was that the substantial measure of self-government conferred upon the provinces was a snare and a delusion. *Les extrêmes se touchent,* and the cry that Dyarchy had failed was

17

not raised more joyfully by the Indian Non-Co-operators than by the British Die-hards. For the latter it was proof positive that every attempt to develop self-government in India must end in failure and that salvation lies only in a return to paternal despotism. The Non-Co-operators used it also to damn the reforms, but for a different purpose. For them it meant that there could be no half-way house to *Swaraj*.

Dyarchy, it must be admitted, could not have been born under a more unlucky financial star. Not only was Non-Co-operation keeping the whole country in a state of turmoil singularly unfavourable to delicate constitutional experiments, but the same financial difficulties which led to the most serious conflicts between Government and the Indian Legislative Assembly were constantly straining the relations between the Central and the Provincial Governments. The Central Government could not abate a single farthing of the contributions to be made to its exchequer by the Provinces, and as the whole of India suffered from the same great wave of economic depression, every Provincial Government had to go through a succession of desperately lean years, just when a few fat years were most needed. Each Government had to provide first of all for the essential departments of administration dealing with the "reserved" subjects, and it was those dealing with the "transferred" subjects that were left to bear the worst pangs of starvation. Yet these were precisely the "nation building" departments, as Indians have learnt to call them, from which the Provinces expected the greatest and most immediate results when they were placed by the new constitution in the hands of Indian Ministers responsible to an Indian Legislature. People had been led to look for a rapid expansion of elementary education and road making and sanitation and local industries, and everything else that had begun to enlist a substantial amount of genuine public interest. But nothing happened because no money was forthcoming from the Central or Provincial Governments, and Indians, though they may carp at Government, still look to it for everything, and especially for the provision of ways and means, and are intensely reluctant to face the alternative of local taxation, even for elementary education, popular and widespread as the demand for it has everywhere grown.

Against the flood of misrepresentation to which Dyarchy was exposed there could be set off in almost every Provincial Council a number of practical and sometimes courageous achievements within the appointed framework of Dyarchy. Definite progress was made in the field of local and village self-government. The housing difficulty, as great in the new industrial centres as anywhere in England, was approached by great city improvement schemes, notably in Bombay and Calcutta, for which the Provinces and municipalities can now pledge their own credit. The inclusion of education amongst the subjects transferred to the Provinces acted as a stimulus to every branch, and not least to primary education, though willingness to bear the cost does not keep pace with the increased demand. Attempts have been made to transform and improve the older universities and new ones have been created or are contemplated in, perhaps, excessive profusion. In the Provincial Councils as well as in the Indian Legislative Assembly there were moments when the well-wishers of Indian reforms could point to the stirring of a new civic spirit, distinct from the political passions of the hour, and largely due to the existence of representative assemblies which, with all their shortcomings, were in closer contact than any bureaucracy, however efficient as a great administrative agency, with the intimate needs of the population.

But fresh and still heavier storm-clouds were gathering when the curtain rang down on the first legislative period under the new constitution, and when it rang up on the second period at the beginning of 1924 the Non-Co-operation movement had entered into possession of the Assembly at Delhi and of two Provincial Councils in a new and more clearly defined shape as the Swarajist party. Many of the older leaders of Indian Nationalism—even the veteran Surendranath Banerjee, once " the uncrowned king " of Bengal—had been left at the bottom of the polls simply because they had accepted the Reforms and honestly tried to make them work smoothly. Gandhi himself remained outside, but he had surrendered his leadership to Mr. Das who had formerly joined with him in his cry of " Back to the Vedas," but was now bent on arming the " soul-force " of India with the most modern weapons of Parliamentary warfare.

CHAPTER XV

THE REACTIONS OF WORLD-FORCES ON INDIA

EVEN before the great war and still more since its close India has felt as she had never done before the beginning of this century the reaction upon her of great world-forces over which she, herself, has no control. Whilst the revolt against Western ascendancy assumed in 1924 a new shape with the evolution of Gandhi's hectic Non-Co-operation movement into an organized and disciplined *Swaraj* party working inside the representative assemblies which he had banned, India knew for the first time the menace of the new world-force which Bolshevism had fashioned after the Russian revolution, and not for the first time the growing conflict between the white and the coloured races.

The latter has so far constituted the more pressing danger for India, and in view of the part which it had played in estranging Gandhi from the British *raj* with such still incalculable consequences, neither the British Government nor the Government of India could remain blind to it. The old bitterness aroused by the treatment of Indians in South Africa was only partially assuaged when the Imperial Conference of 1921 was induced to pass against the sole dissentient vote of the South African Union a resolution recognizing that " there is incongruity between the position of India as an equal member of the Empire and the existence of disabilities upon British Indians lawfully domiciled in some parts of the Empire," and expressing the opinion that " in the interests of the solidarity of the Commonwealth " it was desirable that their rights to citizenship should be admitted. It was something that South Africa, though in Indian eyes the worst and most formidable offender, alone stood out impenitent. For though in other Dominions besides South Africa Indians had been subjected to many disabilities a *modus vivendi* with them was already in sight, even with Canada, where, on the Pacific watershed at least, the feeling against Asiatic immigration is as strong in British Columbia as in the Western States of the American Republic. Except in South Africa the number of Indian settlers in the Dominions had always been small, and Mr. Shrinivasa Shastri, whom the Government of India deputed to negotiate with the Dominion Governments after the 1921 Conference, was able to arrive in most cases at an acceptable compromise which, whilst affirming the right of every Dominion to regulate immigration as it thinks best in the interests and according to the wishes of its own people, would at least secure the admittance of Indians who desire merely to travel for purposes of business or study or pleasure. Minor points remained over for subsequent adjustment, but Mr. Shastri's mission was on the whole successful. Indian labour had grievances, too, in several of the small Crown Colonies, such as Fiji and British Guiana, but there the Government of India was in a strong position and had in many cases its own remedy when the Indian communities could show legitimate causes of complaint. For it could stop all further recruitment of indentured labour in India, and the threat was effective with colonies that were greatly dependent upon it.

But there arose a much more serious situation from the Indian point of view than even in South Africa when Indian rights were threatened in Kenya, where Indians had settled of their own accord, and, according to the testimony borne years ago by Mr. Winston Churchill himself in his *East African Travel*, had done excellent spadework long before it became a British Colony and attracted an enterprising group of British settlers to whom immense tracts of land were conceded by the new British authorities, often with as little regard for the rights of the large native population as of the Indians who were already in the country. Anti-Asiatic legislation seemed bad enough to the Indians in a self-governing Dominion over which British Ministers could at least disclaim all control in such matters; but it was felt to be quite intolerable when a similar policy was adopted and carried to still greater lengths in a Crown Colony in East Africa directly controlled by the Colonial Office in London, and, at the instance of a small, but influential group of white settlers. The 30,000 Indians of Kenya were threatened with restraints on their right to the franchise, with the curtailment of free immigration and with segregation not only in the towns but throughout the country. They were also to be prohibited from acquiring land in the highlands, reserved for the white man as the most salubrious part of the country. Feeling ran high amongst the Indians in Kenya, and it ran equally high in India where every organized body of public opinion entered the most vehement protests and the Government of India was itself moved to make strong representations in London. But it ran even higher amongst the white settlers in Kenya, some of whom threatened to " cut the painter " if the British Government yielded to the Indians. In the hope of effecting an agreed settlement a Conference was summoned to meet in London in the early summer of 1923. It was attended by the Governor of Kenya with both a British and an Indian delegation from the Colony, and by an official delegation from India, which included Mr. Shastri. The white settlers enlisted in their favour such British opinion as was not entirely indifferent or pre-occupied with other matters by the usual appeals to Imperial interests and the maintenance of the purity of the race, and they even professed to stand for the interests of the native races of East Africa—a plea very hard to maintain in the presence of Dr. Norman Leys' grave and dispassionate indictment of our land and labour policy in those regions. " We get," he says, in his book on Kenya, " the extraordinary contrast of 10,000 square miles alienated to Europeans and populated by 1,893 ' occupied ' Europeans and 5,000 square miles reserved somewhat precariously to nearly 2,000,000 Africans," and he sets forth with conviction the disastrous results for all concerned, even for the land monopolists themselves and for the future of Kenya as a colony. The Indian delegates got little more than a formal hearing in London and were soon confronted with a " decision " which the Home Government called a compromise and the Indians a grievous surrender of their rights. But it was not a complete surrender. The franchise, though only on a " communal " basis, was conceded, segregation in the towns was dropped, and the door was not finally barred against immigration, nor even against the possibility of a reopening of the case " on a suitable opportunity." Though there was some hasty talk of retaliation in India, wiser counsels have for the present prevailed.

But the fresh assertion of the white man's superiority over the Indian as a coloured man, with the assent of the Imperial Government, in a Colony which ranks as a Crown Colony has estranged many well-disposed Indians from the British connection just as Gandhi was originally estranged from it by the anti-Asiatic policy of the South African Union. No sooner, too, is the fire damped down in one quarter than it blazes up again in another, when even the Municipal franchise is withdrawn from the Indians who have hitherto enjoyed it in Natal where they number 141,000 out of 161,000 in the whole of the South African Union, and fresh proposals to legalize the colour-bar for the protection of the white man's monopoly of skilled labour have elicited from General Smuts himself a new note of earnest warning.

To the demand for full *Swaraj* the colour question has brought, since it was raised once more so acutely in Kenya, many influential recruits who were hitherto firm believers in the advancement of India within the Empire. The Government of India, with the support in this matter of many Englishmen in India, backs up as far as it can at Whitehall the unanimous protests of Indian opinion ; but Indians know that whatever the constitutional theory may be, the Viceroy, as Lord Morley once declared, is only the agent of the Secretary of State, unless his personality is, like Lord Curzon's for instance, an exceptionally strong one and can impose itself upon Whitehall. They have only to contrast the vigorous and almost imperious tone Lord Reading adopted in pressing for a modification of British policy towards Turkey when he knew that the then Secretary of State, Mr. Montagu, was in complete agreement with him, and the submissive deference with which he conveyed the Indian Government's remonstrances against the Kenya decision, when there was no one in the British Cabinet ready to resist the pressure of the white settlers. *Swaraj* has now scarcely a more vigorous supporter than Mr. Shastri who has represented India with conspicuous ability and dignity on more than one occasion, not only at an Imperial Conference in London, but abroad in the League of Nations at Geneva, and at the Disarmament Conference at Washington, and who only a few years ago repeatedly expressed in addressing his fellow-countrymen a faith in the British people and the British Empire such as one rarely hears professed nowadays in India. He has joined those whom nothing will satisfy but the immediate grant of Dominion Self-Government ; for of what value, he asks, is any promise near or remote, of partnership in the British Commonwealth of Nations if England who claims still to act as trustee for India will not or cannot safeguard the existing rights of Indians in the self-governing Dominions of the Empire, or even in her own Crown Colonies directly subject to her control ? Only, he declares, when India is fully self-governing can she hope to have a government that will be able to uphold the rights of overseas Indians with the same determination with which a self-governing Dominion denies them to-day.

It is in the sense of racial injustice which rankles to-day in almost every coloured race that the destructive forces of Bolshevism find a weapon ready to hand all over the East ; and Bolshevism is at the gates, if not already within the gates, of India. With the Soviet revolution the old apprehensions, of a Russian military invasion of India, such as the Tsar Paul and again the Tsar Alexander I once dreamt of, have passed away. But just as Tsarist Russia, until she was threatened by a nearer German peril, looked upon England as the foremost obstacle to her Asiatic ambitions, Bolshevism now looks upon the British Empire as the foremost obstacle to its great scheme of world-revolution and is convinced that nowhere can it be more effectively attacked than in Asia. When a state of war still existed between Turkey and England before the peace of Lausanne, Moscow entertained the closest relations with Angora. The Soviet Ambassador at Teheran stepped into the position which the Englishman had held in Persia before Lord Curzon's Treaty was abrogated. The King of Afghanistan first used his independence, of which Great Britain's recognition removed the slight restraints formerly placed by the Government of India on his relations with foreign powers, to conclude with Soviet Russia a treaty of amity and alliance. In Central Asia where Bolshevist Russia rules to-day with a heavier hand than

Tsarist Russia ever did, she has a formidable base for revolutionary penetration in India. Bolshevism has the advantage of close kinship between the Russian mentality, itself semi-Asiatic, and the mentality of the purely Oriental peoples, and it has impressed into its service the fine schools of Oriental learning founded under the Tsarist regime. It sows most fruitfully in poverty and ignorance, and both unfortunately abound in India. Otherwise the soil might not seem at first sight suited to Bolshevist culture. The Bolshevists openly profess atheism and wage a relentless war against the orthodox national Church of Russia, whereas the spirit of rebellion in India deliberately appeals to the enduring forces of religion, whether Hindu or Mohammedan. But whenever religious fanaticism can serve their purpose outside of Russia, they are prepared to give any creed their blessing, and it was under Bolshevist auspices that a great Pan-Asiatic Mohammedan Congress was held at Baku in 1921 where England was singled out for fierce denunciations as the mortal enemy of Islam. The idea of a universal class-war such as Soviet Russia preaches is foreign to the Indian mind, for the caste system, whatever other disadvantages it possesses, precludes the passionate envy and hatred often provoked amongst the masses by the concentration of wealth in relatively few hands. Is not a Brahman a Brahman whether he be rich or poor, whether he occupies a high position in the State or whether he follows one of the many humble callings permissible to one of his caste ? Is not every Hindu born into the state of life and the caste appointed for him by his *Karma* ? For Mohammedans the class-war is almost equally difficult to reconcile with the Islamic conception of brotherhood in the Faith. But though class-war, including " the war against God," is the broad formula which Moscow generally uses to cover its activities, it displays great elasticity in adapting its methods to the different conditions that prevail among the different peoples whom it hopes to impress into its universal work of destruction. For Eastern consumption it starts schools, trains emissaries, produces a copious literature to preach revolt in diverse tongues to the down-trodden peoples of the Orient, and, though it claims to have risen far above a narrow Nationalism, it is quick to espouse any Nationalist movement in the East which it can saturate with its own hatred of the West. What it is doing in China, it hopes to do equally successfully in India, by inflaming the Indian's resentment of the white man's claim to racial supremacy. There are many channels through which it can penetrate to the Indian masses. The large agglomerations of Indian labour that have resulted from the industrialization of India provide a promising field for the creation of the " cells " in which it cultivates its own special virus for the destruction of "Western-bred capitalism." An organized Labour party hardly yet exists in India, but in its present embryonic stage, it has an active wing of a strongly Bolshevist complexion, which is at the back of many and often disorderly strikes that have little or no economic justification. Gandhi has marked his own abhorrence of Bolshevist methods of violence by refusing an invitation to visit Moscow as the guest of Soviet Russia, but, during the frenzy of Non-Co-operation, Chauri-Chaura showed that there is just as much inflammable material in rural India as there was in Russia when Bolshevism started by glutting the land-hunger of the Russian peasantry.

The revolutionary movements and murder conspiracies of which the marked recrudescence coincided with the birth of a new Swarajist party at the beginning of 1924 are naturally in communion with Bolshevism. The Swarajists formally disclaim any connection with them, though they admit their existence and make the admission an argument for *Swaraj* as the only remedy for an evil which they profess to reprobate but declare to be the inevitable consequence of England's refusal of freedom for India. The sequence of events carries a different interpretation. With the emergence from the General Election of a *Swaraj* party committed to a campaign of extreme political violence against the British *raj* as established by the Act of 1919, the revolutionary party that relies only on forcible violence for the subversion *sans phrase* of every vestige of British rule came once more to the surface. On January 25, 1924, after a long interval of ten years a dastardly murder took place in open daylight in the streets of Calcutta. The victim was an inoffensive member of the British mercantile community, and the murderer, Gopinath Sakai, cynically confessed that he had killed him by mistake for an inspector of police whom he had intended to murder. Other criminal outrages followed, but partially miscarried. A fully-equipped bomb factory was discovered in March and in August a serious bomb outrage took place. There was much clandestine importation of arms as well as of incendiary literature. " Red Bengal " leaflets were seized with the usual incitements to violence and there were other indications of Bolshevist propaganda and money. But as in previous periods of revolutionary activity convictions could not be secured in the clearest cases because terrorism was effectively employed to prevent witnesses from giving evidence in Court. Mr. Das, whilst protesting that deeds of violence were repugnant to him and his party, drew a strangely subtle distinction between the deeds themselves and those who committed them, when he moved and carried a resolution at a gathering of the Provincial Congress organization at Serajgunj extolling the patriotic ideals which had prompted Gopinath Sakai's deed, however deplorable the crime itself had been. To Gandhi as the constant apostle of non-violence such a resolution was detestable and his last Pyrrhic victory in his losing contest for ascendancy over the *Swaraj* movement was to get that resolution rescinded a few weeks later. But many *Swaraj* papers continued to follow the lead given them at Serajgunj in highly inflammatory articles in praise of the " heroes " who had practised murder in the earlier revolutionary movements, and the personal relations between the leading spirits of the new revolutionary movement which was closely modelled on them and some of Mr. Das's own followers, and even Mr. Das himself, were known to be most intimate. The Rowlatt Acts had been designed to enable the executive to cope with just such dangers as now confronted it, but their repeal had been one of the concessions which on his arrival in India Lord Reading had been induced to make to the politically-minded Indian's detestation of any legislation he can call " repressive," in the hope of retaining the often weak-kneed support of the first Legislative Assembly against the Non-Co-operation movement. With the Rowlatt Acts struck off the Statute book, the Government of Bengal felt itself powerless. Lord Lytton made urgent representations to the Viceroy, and finally, under his authority and, with the sanction of Lord Olivier and of his colleagues in the Labour Cabinet still in office in London, an Ordinance was issued which gave him the emergency powers he required. A large number of summary arrests were at once made chiefly in Calcutta under the new procedure just introduced or revived. Amongst the arrested persons were several members of the *Swaraj* party, some extremely close to Mr. Das. At once the old cry of autocratic interference with the liberty of the subject and arbitrary police persecution was

raised by the Swarajist party who declared that the
Ordinance was aimed at them, and it was taken up
more or less loudly by all the opposition groups,
whether from conviction or because they dreaded to
be taunted with a " slave mentality." It brought
Gandhi into line once more with Mr. Das whose
influence, nevertheless, remained paramount. But
Government was able to claim that the Ordinance
had fulfilled its purpose when overt political crime
soon ceased almost entirely, and a timely set-back
was given to revolutionary activity.

But Bolshevism has not dropped India and Indian
extremists have not dropped their faith in Bolshevist
Russia.

CHAPTER XVI

THE SWARAJIST PLAN OF CAMPAIGN

WITH the entry of a militant Swarajist party into the Legislatures at the beginning of 1924 the working of the Constitution, still barely three years in operation, was subjected to a far more formidable strain than during the life of the first Legislatures. For instead of having to deal with an Indian majority, always suspicious and sometimes in a fighting mood, but committed by the circumstances in which it had been elected to the principle of co-operation within the framework of the Constitution, the Government of India found itself confronted with a well-organized and resolute party, determined to use every power conferred by the Constitution to wreck it and produce a deadlock from which, in her weariness of strife, England would be fain to seek escape by the abdication, at any rate in all but name, of the British *raj*. The new Swarajist party had shed Gandhi, and partly because the non-fulfilment of his miraculous promise of *Swaraj* by a given date had broken some of his magnetic spell over the masses, and partly because two abundant harvests had relieved the acuteness of post-war hardships, the tumult of the Non-Co-operation movement had died down, whilst the Caliphate movement had lost its religious momentum when the men of Angora abruptly transformed Turkey into a lay Republic. But the new party contained the best brains of Non-Co-operation and pursued the same goal, and with greater strategic skill and greater concentration of purpose. It knew how to use India's young Parliament as a more resounding platform than the Indian National Congress for a sustained propaganda re-echoing all over the country at Provincial Congress conferences and through the ever-increasing host of vernacular newspapers tuned up to a key of almost incredible violence. Under the leadership of Mr. C. R. Das, Gandhi's lieutenant in Bengal when Non-Co-operation was flowing full-tide, and, like Gandhi, educated on Western lines and called to the Bar in London, but with more than Gandhi's intellectual ability and practical understanding of politics, the Swarajist party, though not in an absolute majority, succeeded in dominating the Legislative Assembly. By tactical superiority and by the importation of the racial grievance into every fighting issue, with Kenya constantly looming up in the background, it inflicted upon Government a series of spectacular defeats, which admirably served their purpose when they drove the Viceroy to fall back upon the exercise of his emergency powers to override the Assembly. For what more proof was needed that the Declaration of 1917 and the Act of 1919 were nothing but a fraud when the will of the people expressed by its constitutional representatives could be at any moment paralysed by an autocratic veto ? That in order to build up their case the Swarajists wilfully ignored the conditions and limitations placed by Parliament upon the representative institutions which were its creation was an argument which could not be expected to carry much weight with them as it was to the elimination of all such conditions and limitations that their plan of campaign was directed. There was less talk about a Satanic Government or about the miracles of mere soul-force. But whereas Gandhi had sometimes professed his readiness to forget and forgive if only the white man would show a change of heart, and to let the British stay in India if only they would become Indians in everything but the colour of their skins, the racialism of the Swarajist party was a racialism *à froid*. There was no room for the white man in India. He must go—bowed out politely, but inexorably.

This was the drift of all the long debates on the Indianization both of the civil services and of the Army, and notably of the three days' debate in the Legislative Assembly in November, 1924, on the Report of the Royal Commission on the Superior Services of which the appointment has been mentioned in a previous chapter. The principle of Indianization was explicitly conceded in the Declaration of 1917 which promised " the increasing association of Indians in every branch of the administration." Measures had been at once taken to speed up the recruitment of Indians for all the public services. The recommendations of the Royal Commission under Lord Lee went a long way further towards Indianization. But they included also a carefully considered and modest scheme for removing some of the chief material grievances of the English members of the services and giving them the moral sense of security which could alone ensure the continued recruitment of the reduced nucleus of Englishmen to be retained as a guarantee for the proper discharge of the responsibility still resting on Parliament. As the whole purpose of the Swarajists was to bring that responsibility to an end and release Indians from all British control, the retention of any such nucleus was the last thing the Swarajists would agree to. As has so often happened in India, little or no attempt had been made to enlighten public opinion beforehand on the object for which the Commission was appointed, and, in one of its non-co-operating moods, the first Legislative Assembly had rejected the necessary grants which the Viceroy had to restore by " certification." It was a bad beginning for the Commission which had the worst possible Press in India, even before it started from England, and the second Legislative Assembly made it clear that what was wanted was not " the increasing association of Indians " but the complete

elimination of Englishmen. The recommendations
of the Commission followed closely the lines of
constitutional reform laid down in the Act of 1919.
The Home Member, Sir Alexander Muddiman, put
them, as he said, " in a nutshell." " They amount
to this—that the Services should be controlled by
the authority which is ultimately responsible for the
administration of the subjects with which they
deal." The authority of the Secretary of State was
to remain unaltered in respect of the services operating in the field which had been " reserved " under
the Act to the Government of India's control,
notably, the Indian Civil Service and the Police
Service, though even for those services Indian
recruitment was to be so rapidly increased that a
proportion of 50 per cent Europeans and 50 per
cent Indians was to be attained in the Indian
Civil Service within fifteen years and in the Police
within twenty-five years. On the other hand, no
limit was prescribed for Indian recruitment into the
services operating in the " transferred " fields. As
these come under the Indian wing of the Provincial
Government, there was little doubt that henceforth
Indian Ministers would only appoint Indians, with
the result that, within a very short term of years,
there would be only 1,300 British officials left as
against 3,000 to-day in the All-India Services, and
less than 900 in the two "security" services which
are most directly responsible for law and order
amongst a population of 247,000,000 in British India
(*i.e.*, outside the Native States). Such proposals
Gokhale would have more than welcomed when he
sat on the 1912–15 Commission, and all the four
Indian members of Lord Lee's Commission subscribed
to them, including the veteran Nationalist, Bupendra-
nath Basu. But in 1924 the Assembly had no ears
for the argument that the interests of the public for
whom the services existed needed the best men even

if they had to be Englishmen, and that there were limits of safety beyond which neither the Government of India nor the British Parliament, to whom it was responsible, could go. An Amendment tantamount to rejection of the Commission's unanimous report was moved by Mr. Motilal Nehru, one of Gandhi's earliest converts to Non-Co-operation, and carried by a large majority composed of almost all the Indian non-official members. The vote was a foregone conclusion, but the speeches emphasized its significance. Some speakers disclaimed any desire to be unfair to Englishmen, and " Pandit " Mohan Malavya, who does not call himself a Swarajist, went so far as to admit that "the bulk of the Services is undoubtedly honest, efficient and incorruptible." But not even amongst the most moderate speakers was there a trace of the gratitude with which the founders of the Indian National Congress, patriotic Indians of the type of Ranade and Naoroji and Gokhale, had always acknowledged the debt which India owed to British rule and to British administrators. Not one even acknowledged that any attempt— let alone a generous attempt—had been made to meet the Indian point of view. A note of bitter animosity and scorn was seldom absent from their comments on the English Civilian's grievances. The one remedy they would hear of was to stop recruitment in England for a certain number of years; and that was no remedy, for if once recruitment was stopped in present circumstances there was not the slightest chance that it could ever be effectively revived. In fact they knew this perfectly well, and it was what they themselves wanted. It was reserved to a Swarajist member for Bombay City, which perhaps more than any other place in India owes its prosperity to British rule, to express in the most extreme form the racial feeling which a sense of Parliamentary propriety generally kept under restraint, when he wound up a violent speech by flinging at the British occupants of the Government benches: "The sooner you go, the better for the country."

The Indianization of the Army is a still more difficult question and all the harder to deal with now because the British military authorities never seriously approached it until it became a political as well as a military question. No attempt was ever made until quite recently to associate with the Indian Army the Western-educated classes which British rule has brought into being. That Army can in fact only be called Indian in this sense that it is recruited from Indians, chiefly of the races reputed for their martial qualities, and that it has a corps of native officers who are seldom more than glorified non-commissioned officers, promoted mostly from the ranks, and who, whatever their seniority may be, automatically take rank under and receive orders from the youngest British subaltern in the regiment. Not only the supreme command and higher administration of the Indian Army is exclusively British, but until the other day only its British officers held their commissions from the King, the native officers holding theirs merely from the Viceroy. The Indian Army has such a fine record of gallantry and loyalty that it would be invidious to compare it to a merely mercenary force, but it is essentially a great fighting engine, British-made, British-driven and British-controlled, for which India provides only the raw material of men. As soon as Western education produced a class of Indians qualified to claim a larger share in the civil services, they claimed to be likewise admitted to serve in the Army on a better footing than the ordinary native officers who, risen for the most part from the ranks, have little, if any, education other than that which they receive in the rudiments of their profession after they have joined the ranks. On the civil side, Government gradually made large, if somewhat belated, concessions to Indian sentiment. The military authorities remained adamant. Young Indians could be trained in India or go to England to be trained at British Universities for every civil career and take their chance side by side with Englishmen. For the Army they were given no such chance. There was no Sandhurst or Woolwich in India. In England they were not admitted. The creation of a Royal Military College at Dehra Dun whence those who qualify for a career in the Army may pass on to Sandhurst marked the first stage along a new road. A further stage came into sight when the late Lord Rawlinson whilst Commander-in-Chief in India undertook to Indianize completely eight units of the Army by gradually substituting Indian officers for British officers of every rank until the latter in due course should disappear out of the regimental cadre. This process however is too slow and confined to too narrow a field to satisfy Indian impatience. A more extensive scheme has also been sanctioned for raising an Indian territorial force consisting of University training-corps battalions not liable to active military service, and provincial battalions ready to accept full liability in that respect. But measures which might have been gratefully accepted a generation ago, are far from satisfying to-day the cry for Indianization which carries a special meaning for the Swarajists who are quite conscious of the dangers that British withdrawal would mean for a *Swaraj* India with no " national " Army behind her. But the racial feeling provoked by the question of Indianizing the Army is not confined to the Indians. Though the Army Department may wish now to approach it chiefly from the point of view of military efficiency, it has to reckon with the strong racial objections of British

officers to being placed in the position of ever having
to take orders from Indian officers. Nor can one
ignore the danger of personal friction between
British and Indian officers with their very different
outlook and social habits if they are made to rub
shoulders in a common messroom. But the feeling
goes far deeper, and responsible and experienced
British officers, not unnaturally proud of the confidence and even personal affection of their native
officers as well as of their men, are found to declare
that the Englishman's prestige with the native troops
themselves will be gone if they are ever placed under
other than British command. Indians whom education has trained to modern standards of self-
respect resent deeply such a stigma of racial
inferiority.

The whole question of the Indianization of the
Army is further aggravated by the fact that military
expenditure is itself much the heaviest of all the
burdens to be borne by the Indian tax-payer who,
under the new Constitution, still has no means of
controlling the amount or the purposes to which it
is applied. A series of unprecedented Budget deficits
gave the Swarajists an opportunity of which they
took full advantage to concentrate their attacks on
the disproportion of civil to military expenditure.
It is an old grievance, but an undeniably real one.
Even after the application of the axe by Lord Inchcape's Retrenchment Committee, military expenditure stands in the latest Budget estimates for 1924–5
for little less than half the total expenditure to be
defrayed by the tax-payer of British India (*i.e.*, by
240 out of 320 million inhabitants of the Indian
Empire, as the Native States do not, of course, come
here into account). The figures are close upon
64 crores for the military services out of a total of
131 crores. Even if these figures show a reduction
on previous years and are not quite as bad as they

look owing to the transfer of revenues which has taken place from the All-India to the Provincial Exchequers under the new reforms, one can understand the impression they make upon the Indians when they compare them with the total expenditure of public funds on education—not a fifth of what is spent on the Army, though Viceroys and Governors never tire of repeating that education is the greatest of India's needs and Indian public opinion is now more thoroughly awake to the truth of that fact than were sometimes those who stated it as a regular official *cliché*.   India no doubt has a turbulent north-west frontier to be kept in order.   Her position in the world has to be safeguarded outside as well as inside her natural boundaries, and for the part which the British Fleet plays in the protection of her far-flung shores she pays nothing at all. The presence of British troops in India constitutes, as most Indians themselves, however reluctantly, acknowledge, the best guarantee for the maintenance of internal peace between discordant races and creeds.   But even Indians who never grudged India's contributions to the great war, whether of treasure or of blood, carry their memories back to the succession of oversea expeditions during the last half-century to Egypt and the Sudan, to China and Somaliland in which Indian troops have been freely employed; and though Great Britain often wholly or partially relieved the Indian Exchequer of the extra cost incurred, they ask not unreasonably whether the Indian Army is not still chiefly maintained at its present strength in order to supply contingents for purposes which are more closely bound up with British Imperial interests than with any that can be justly described as Indian. Since the Esher Committee's Report, which could not be entirely explained away, Indians ask, also not unreasonably, whether India is not being unfairly

mulcted for the relief of the British tax-payer in the
share she is made to bear of the cost of the British
garrison as part of a great British military machine
which the conditions of Army service in England
render peculiarly expensive. At a time too when
India is being brought into close, and not always
very friendly, contact with the self-governing
Dominions of the Empire, and she has herself not
only had held out to her, though only conditionally,
the prospect of full Dominion status within the
Empire, but already formally enjoys it in Imperial
Conferences and in the League of Nations, Indians
want to know why she is subjected to a much
heavier burden than the self-governing Dominions
are required or expected to bear. All these grievances,
whether new or of long-standing, served the Swarajist
party as texts for denunciations, on public platforms
and in the Press, of British Militarism and Imperialism,
as fierce as the wildest imprecations launched at
them from Moscow.

The Swarajists even turned to their own account
the fiscal autonomy conceded to India not only in
principle but very largely in practice since the war,
though it was a noteworthy and perhaps so far the
most effective fulfilment of the promise of " the
beginnings of *Swaraj*" which the King-Emperor
made to India in his inaugural message to the new
Indian Legislatures in February, 1921. If England
had wished to see the development of Indian industries arrested for the benefit of British industries
after the great impulsion given to it under the
pressure of the Empire's war necessities, she would
only have had to stay the Government of India's
hand and insist on a reversion to its traditional
laissez aller policy. But, on the contrary, the response
made by Indian industries to the tremendous call
made upon them during the great war was held to have
established their claim to sustained encouragement

when the war was over, as a means of opening up for India a new road to prosperity in times of peace. At first the only measure of protection indirectly accorded to them was the repeated enhancement of Indian import duties, and this was in any case the easiest way to meet increasing revenue requirements. But India like the rest of the world was suddenly swept by the great wave of economic depression produced by the war after a brief interval of extravagant inflation. Not a few of India's nascent industries had owed much of their initial success to the temporary stimulus of war-prices and the absence of European competition, and there were signs of a general collapse. Political feeling reinforced the demand for a resolute policy of protection, Government no longer pleaded *non possumus*, nor could they do so, when, in accordance with the recommendations of the Joint Committee of both Houses of Parliament, the new and momentous principle had been conceded in England that in fiscal matters Indian were henceforth to prevail over British interests. A Commission appointed by Government concluded on the whole in favour of a cautious protectionist policy, and a Tariff Board was established to examine the conditions on which protection should be granted. It has already been freely granted to those industries which can show cause for it, and to none more freely than to the great steel and iron industry which a few years ago was believed to be standing securely on its own feet. All that Government attempts to do is steady the pace.

Protection has come in India and it has come apparently to stay, and whatever may be its merits as an economic policy, its ungrudging acceptance by the Government of India might have been expected to make for righteousness in the eyes of Indians of all political complexions. For free trade has hardly any friends amongst them. But the Swarajists have not been mollified. They seized hold of it, and never even disguised their intention to use it as a weapon for striking at England through her trade. Just as their campaign against political control has led to sustained attacks upon the authority of the Secretary of State in Council, they have singled out for obloquy the Stores Department of the India Office which purchases Government supplies in the English market, and on broader grounds they have resisted every suggestion of Imperial Preference as an attempt to exploit India for the benefit of the rest of the Empire. More openly avowed than in the Legislatures where the incidence of tariff protection has sometimes produced cross-currents of local and particular interests which have actually driven some Swarajist members to vote with the Government has been the anti-British animus in such municipal bodies as the Calcutta Corporation with the Swarajist leader, Mr. Das, as Mayor, and a Swarajist majority, where each member is pledged to act not in accordance with the wishes of the rate-payers to whom he is properly responsible, but in obedience to the decisions of a National Congress caucus that imposes a policy of which it bears none of the costs and consequences, however injurious they may be to the welfare of the city. Resolutions have been frequently carried for the purchase of such supplies as India must import from abroad in any foreign country, if possible, rather than in England, and when, owing to the better terms offered by them, British contracts have been unavoidably passed with them for work to be carried out in India, stringent clauses have been inserted enjoining the use of Indian in preference to British materials without regard for market prices. It is in a less crude form the old cry of economic *Swadeshi* revived in support of political

Swaraj with an added desire to find some means of retaliating against the Dominions as well as against England for their treatment of overseas Indians. Yet can the blame be laid exclusively at the Swarajist door when under the pressure of Lancashire, which no British Government can apparently resist, Sir Basil Blackett is made to say in the form common to all Finance Members of the Government of India for the last thirty or forty years, that financial stringency obliges him to retain the cotton excise duty, though Mr. Austen Chamberlain, when Secretary of State for India in 1917, described it as " an open and running sore that offers a ready weapon to every ill-wisher of our rule "; and Mr. Lloyd George, when Prime Minister, added his testimony to the unanimity of Indian opinion in demanding its abolition? Sir Basil Blackett himself, when he first came out to India three years ago, held out distinct hopes that it would be his privilege to right " this historic wrong," but he confesses now to seeing no prospect of doing so at present.

If it is in the All-India Legislative Assembly that by their discipline and their mastery of procedure and their vigour in debate the Swarajists may be said to have attained almost to the stature of a real Parliamentary party though for purposes not constructive but destructive, their wrecking tactics achieved more immediate results in the Provincial Councils which they decided also to enter at the second General Election in disregard of the Gandhi boycott. Dyarchy has been introduced into the Provincial Governments but not into the Government of India. Whilst they could browbeat the Government of India in the Legislative Assembly, they could not overturn it. In a Provincial Council they could throw the Provincial Government out of gear by using their power to paralyse its Indian wing. They were not everywhere equally successful at the polls, but in two provinces, Bengal and the Central Provinces, they had a sufficient majority to paralyse Dyarchy by refusing the supplies required for the transferred services, and even the grant for salaries to the Indian Ministers in charge of them, who naturally resigned. They might have escaped the reproach of being mere wreckers had they assumed the responsibilities which their action involved. In both Provinces the Governor gave them their chance by inviting them to take over the Indian portfolios, Lord Lytton in Bengal inviting Mr. C. R. Das himself to join the Provincial Government. But they refused in both Provinces, and the two Governors had to exercise the powers reserved to them under the Constitution and themselves take over the vacant portfolios, cutting down to the bone the expenditure of those departments for which the Council had refused supplies. The Swarajists boasted of their achievement as a splendid victory. But at what cost ? At the cost of starving the very departments which the people had been taught to regard as above all things " nation building." Such methods of destruction are close akin to revolution, and though the Swarajists may have kept their activities distinct and separate from the revolutionary activities in Bengal which Lord Lytton was driven to meet by a special Ordinance, they almost inevitably sometimes overlapped. The Swarajists virtually admitted as much when they declared that the Ordinance was in reality aimed at them. For a time they succeeded in raising something like the same outcry against it that Gandhi had raised three years previously against the Rowlatt Acts. There was a formal unanimity of protests against it from almost all political parties, but though Gandhi himself joined in them they lacked the religious fervour which he had breathed into the *Satyagraha* campaign in 1919.

The Swarajist movement began in fact to shed most if its glamour of idealism when it threw off Gandhi's leadership. All through 1924 there was still a considerable section of stubborn Non-Co-operators to whom Mr. Das's opportunism in entering the Councils was repugnant. They were called the " No-Changers," and though the " Council-entry " party had won the day from the moment it emerged triumphantly from the General Elections as the Swarajist party in the Assembly and Councils, it was not until the National Congress held its annual session at Belgaum at the end of 1924 that Gandhi finally abdicated his political leadership. He occupied the presidential chair, and his three-hours oration, which was a long and painful confession of failure, was listened to with all the deference still due to the Mahatma. The most painful moment of all to him, however, was doubtless not when the Congress acquiesced, however passively, in his abdication, but when it knocked the bottom out of the *Khaddar* movement as originally conceived and shaped by him. The visionary world of *Swaraj* that Gandhi dwelt in was a world not of reason, but of pure emotion. It was by a passionate appeal to emotion that Gandhi swept a great part of India with him. In its finer aspects his appeal was for self-sacrifice, for personal effort, translated for the multitude into the consecration of two hours' work every day at the domestic spinning-wheel as a symbol, nay, as the assured means of India's liberation from the incubus of Western materialism which had deliberately crushed her home industries in order the more surely to destroy her soul. The Congress substituted for the wholesome discipline of a daily task the facile option of an annual contribution of spun yarn, which anyone could purchase in the nearest market. For Gandhi the change meant a lamentable lapse from grace in which he acquiesced with a heavy heart

in order to save at least the outward appearances
of Congress unity. As for his dreams of Indian
fraternization, they were no less surely shattered
by the widespread recrudescence of communal
jealousies and suspicions which broke the spell of
Swaraj as the ending of all foreign domination and
the mending of all Indian discords.

CHAPTER XVII

THE FLIGHT FROM SWARAJ

IN the Legislative Assembly and the Provincial Councils dominated by the new Swarajist party little was heard of Gandhi's "soul-force." It was too abstract a term to lend itself to a definite policy—even though only a destructive policy—which relied for its success on what one of the Swarajist leaders called " the logic of facts." Its purpose was to demonstrate, by using against the constitution every weapon that it provided for ceaseless and relentless obstruction, that no constitution postulating the retention of the British Parliament's control, *i.e.*, the maintenance of the British *raj*, would ever be allowed to work, and that the only logical way out of such a deadlock must lie in a surrender to *Swaraj*. The facts did not altogether work out as they were logically expected to do. But a vigorous offensive served to keep *Swaraj* constantly to the fore, and Government's uncertain language as to the possibility of fresh constitutional changes before the date appointed by Parliament helped to create the impression that, however different were the circumstances, another Declaration of Policy might presently be wrung out of the British Government, more especially with a Labour Cabinet in office, as suddenly and effectively as that of 1917, which would carry India with another and bigger stride to full *Swaraj*, or something very near it. Even when, after many platonic assurances of sympathy from the Labour Party at home whilst it was still in opposition, Mr. Ramsay MacDonald quite frankly warned Indians that neither the British people nor any British Government would ever yield to an agitation that was backed by the menace of violence, Indians remembered Ireland and Egypt, and read into them the meaning they desired. The belief

persisted that England might yet grow weary and
pliable. *Swaraj* still continued to be at least in
the air.

But the Swarajist party had overshot the mark.
In proportion as their plan of campaign seemed to
bring *Swaraj* within the conceivable range of practical
politics, a change in an opposite direction went on
in the minds of many Indians. As they saw, or
thought they saw, the vision of *Swaraj*, which they
had chiefly pictured to themselves as a release from
an oppressive or at least vexatious foreign yoke,
growing less remote and shadowy, they began to
see also the other side of the picture, and one of
those rapid revulsions of feeling took place to which
people still politically immature are peculiarly liable.
Indians of different creeds and races took to figuring
out what *Swaraj* would actually mean for each
community, and in the process it was robbed of much
of its fascination. All the old communal antagonisms
and jealousies burst out afresh, and with increased
bitterness, and first and foremost between Mohammedans and Hindus. Gone was all the tumultuous
fraternization of the days when the great outburst
of racial hatred provoked by the Punjab tragedy
had enabled Gandhi to drive in double-harness as
parallel manifestations of religious fervour, the
Mohammedan Caliphate agitation and the *Satyagraha*
movement, which appealed more particularly to the
Hindu. It had waned fast after the horrors of the
Moplah rising brought to the Hindus a lurid reminder
of what the beginnings of Mohammedan domination
had meant to their forbears. When the Turk himself proceeded to abolish the sacred office of Caliph
many pious Mohammedans had their eyes opened to
the revolutionary aims of the Caliphate leaders who
had traded on their religious beliefs for the benefit of
Turkey. Such men as Mohammed and Shaukat Ali,
though, or because, they were gravely discredited,

and not least by the cloud of suspicion that had
gathered round the administration of the Caliphate
funds, still hung on to the skirts of Mahatma Gandhi.
But the All-India Moslem League, after several years
of suspended animation during which it had been
entirely overshadowed by the Caliphate Committee,
resumed its independent existence at the end of 1924,
and refusing the invitation of the National Congress
to hold at least a simultaneous session at Belgaum,
met in Bombay at a safe distance away from it as
well as from the Caliphate Conference whose resourcefulness did not go far beyond imputing to
British machinations the difficult situation created
for Indian Mohammedan pilgrims to Mecca by the
conflict between Ibn Saud's Wahabees and the
King of the Hedjaz. There was a marked change of
temperature in nearly the whole of the Mohammedan
community. It was no longer at fever-heat. The
Mohammedan University of Aligurh, which had
at one moment narrowly escaped capture by Gandhi
and the Ali brothers, accorded a respectful and even
warm welcome to Sir William Marris, the Governor
of the United Provinces, and its principal, Dr. Zia-
ud-Din, took the lead, with other responsible
Mohammedans who continued to profess fidelity to
the ideal of a great and united Indian Nation, in
emphasizing once more the claims of their community
and above all the retention of separate communal
representation as an indispensable condition of any
form of *Swaraj* that they could possibly accept. This
had always been a great bone of contention between
them and the Hindu Nationalists for whom communal representation was anathema as an insuperable obstacle to democratic progress, or perhaps more
accurately to the political predominance that should
accrue to them from their great numerical majority
in most parts of India. In the one Province where the
Mohammedans have a safe majority, they themselves

furnished a rather unwise object-lesson by using their communal majority in the Punjab Provincial Council as a powerful organization for the furtherance of Mohammedan interests, with little regard for the other two communities, Hindu and Sikh. Equally insistent became the Mohammedan demand for an assurance of a definite share of the loaves and fishes under a *Swaraj* dispensation. Mr. Das, anxious to retain Mohammedan support in the Assembly, went so far as to conclude a formal Pact, pledging the Hindus to reserve for the Mohammedans a proportion of public offices and appointments which, in view of the intellectual inferiority and educational backwardness of the Mohammedan community as a whole, was not ungenerous. It was far too generous to be acceptable to Hindu opinion, and when its terms were published, the Pact was so promptly and vehemently condemned that the Mohammedans were left with few illusions as to the chances of its ever being carried into effect under Hindu *Swaraj*.

The old tension between the lower orders of the two communities nearly reached the breaking-point. Even in the hey-day of Non-Co-operation joint demonstrations against a Satanic Government, begun in the Gandhi spirit of fraternization, were apt to end in free fights in which it was generally the Hindus who suffered most heavily, even when their Mohammedan " brothers " did not go to the length, as at Malegaon, of plundering the Hindu quarter and burning down Hindu temples and throwing into the flames an unfortunate Hindu policeman who was merely doing his duty in trying to protect his co-religionists. All through 1923 and 1924 a succession of Hindu-Mohammedan riots, commonly originating in the time-honoured forms of reciprocal provocation —cow killing by the Mohammedans and the playing of Hindu bands in proximity to Mohammedan places of worship—led to frequent violence and even bloodshed which showed how fierce was still the old religious hatred on both sides. These affrays occurred chiefly in the large cities of Upper India where the Mohammedan population is most considerable, and even at Delhi, the capital, there were on one occasion 20 killed and over 100 wounded. The more responsible members of the two communities, and the Swarajists themselves, who realized how damaging these feuds were to their own cause, made vain attempts to stem the growing evil, and after Gandhi had spent three weeks in penance to atone for his own responsibilities, a great " Unity " Conference was held in September, 1924, in Delhi, with the cordial co-operation of the Metropolitan of India and other Christian well-wishers besides Sikhs and Parsees. Mohammed Ali himself attended, though memories of the Moplah rising still clung about him. Many well-meant resolutions in favour of arbitration in all communal differences and for the creation of a permanent Central Conciliation Committee with local branches were passed with commendable unanimity. But they bore no visible fruits.

Far more significant has been the growth of militant organizations on both sides which vainly profess to be merely defensive whilst their aggressive purposes are writ large all over them. To the Mohammedan *Tanzim* movement for the better entrenchment of their communal position, the Hindus have opposed a parallel *Sangathan* movement promoted by Pundit Malavya, a pillar of the Hindu University of Benares, for encouraging physical drill and athletic exercises and sword-play amongst a rising generation that might some day have to defend Hindu *Swaraj* against the martial races of Mohammedan India ; and to the *Tabligh* movement for an intensive missionary campaign of conversion to Islam amongst the depressed castes of Hinduism, the Hindus have opposed, though not without searchings of orthodox hearts, the *Shuddi* movement for facilitating the return of Mohammedan converts to the Hindu fold. The imminence of *Swaraj*, or what Indians imagined for a time to be its imminence, had merely deepened the wide gulf between Hindus and Mohammedans. Nor could it well be otherwise as the more sanguine became the hopes of the leading Swarajists, for the most part Hindus, and the more freely they quoted Hindu philosophy as the basis of *Swaraj*, the greater the fears of pious Mohammedans that *Swaraj* would end in merely exalting the horn of Hinduism.

But the flight from *Swaraj* has not been confined to the Mohammedans. Its appeal to democratic principles and to self-determination was fundamentally repugnant to Hindu orthodoxy. For democracy postulates equality of birthright and equality of opportunity for all men, whereas the doctrine of *Karma* assigns to every Hindu the caste into which he is born and from which he cannot hope to emerge in his present life. Gandhi himself with all his saintliness is not a Brahman, and though he never condemned caste as an institution, he did condemn the lengths to which it is in practice carried and he frequently pleaded for the removal of the ban of " untouchability " from the depressed castes—never indeed more powerfully than in his quasi-valedictory address to the National Congress at Belgaum. On this issue he still carried the Congress with him. A few days later an orthodox Hindu Conference in Bombay actually threatened him with excommunication ! Nor was it the Mahatma alone who incurred the wrath of Brahmanical orthodoxy. From its ancient stronghold at Benares it warned the Congress itself to stick to politics and not to mix up religion with them. The warning may have been scarcely needed, as, except in its very earliest days, the Congress has seldom paid more than lip-worship to social reform which it has in fact consistently postponed to political agitation. A more serious menace to orthodoxy than the gesture at Belgaum, which could hardly be denied to Gandhi's moving appeal, is the growth of an organized movement amongst the depressed castes themselves to better their conditions and to secure some recognition of their right to live as self-respecting human beings. In spite of their heavy social handicap, education and economic changes have slowly but steadily produced amongst some of them a more or less conscious rebellion against the hardships inflicted upon them by ancient laws and customs which British rule has never recognized, though being pledged to non-interference in matters appertaining to religion it has in practice had to tolerate them as part of the religious and social system of Hinduism. They have now leaders of their own who have learnt, as others have, from the West the value of organization for the ventilation of their grievances, whilst they have obtained some measure of political representation under the new Indian constitution. At the same time as Gandhi was appealing to the National Congress at Belgaum, an " anti-untouchability " Conference was being held there at which a much more weighty, because closely-reasoned, speech was delivered by Sir Sankaran Nair, a former member of the Government of India and a determined opponent of Gandhi's Non-Co-operation movement, who had been a life-long champion of the depressed classes against Brahmanical intolerance. The movement, of which, as one of the few Indians who have caught the spirit of Western democracy in its best aspects, he has been from the beginning a vigorous protagonist, has gained no slight impetus from the crushing defeat inflicted upon the Brahmans by the non-Brahmans of the Madras Presidency at the elections to the Provincial Council under the Act of 1919.

Though with its capacity for subtle differentiation between what may be called the canonical and the secular status of castes, Hinduism may decline to see in that defeat any curtailment of Brahmanical supremacy in the hierarchy of caste, the Madras Brahmans have undeniably lost the monopoly of public appointments which they had hitherto retained under British rule. When Lord Willingdon, interpreting the Indian constitution in accordance with British Parliamentary practice, chose non-Brahmans alone to be his Ministers, the non-Brahman majority in the Provincial Council secured for its supporters the share of the spoils which communal feeling in India is apt to regard as due to the victors. The reply of Hindu orthodoxy to a challenge which is spreading from the Madras to the Bombay Presidency is to be seen in the renewed activity of the many caste associations which were a feature of the first reaction of the ancient forces of Hinduism against Western influence a quarter of a century ago, and in so far as *Swaraj* stands for a similar reaction it is drawn towards it. But on the other hand it relies on the principle of authority and it has its secular mainstay in the propertied classes of Hinduism which are essentially conservative. From this angle it cannot but distrust the democratic professions and revolutionary affinities of the Swarajist party, and amidst the confused ferment of hopes and fears which *Swaraj* has produced, it shows an increasing disposition to cling to the existing order of things rather than to take new and incalculable risks. The key-note of the many recent conferences held under rigidly orthodox auspices has been the urgency of organizing Hindu orthodoxy for self-defence against the dangers which on all sides beset it, and in such an organization the encouragement of caste steadfastness within each separate caste plays a very important part. It is another expression in terms of Hindu orthodoxy of the recrudescence of communal feeling of which the sharper edge cuts right athwart *Swaraj*.

More unexpected has been the tendency towards organization on separate but nationalist lines amongst educated Indian Christians. Those at least who belong to Protestant communities have felt for some time past that in the higher interests of Christianity they must be released from a subordination to ecclesiastical and missionary organizations in Europe which lays them open to the suspicion of subserviency to Western authorities, ignorant, if not careless, of India's peculiar needs. There must be Indian Christian Churches relieved of all ties that may hamper their freedom of organic growth. Christianity must not wear the appearance of being a foreign creed. The Indian Roman Catholics are taught to stand aloof from this movement, and it has so far taken most definite shape in the Anglican community which has already a large Indian clergy and considers the time to be ripe for the severance of all organic ties with the Church of England. Such a measure of disestablishment would place the Anglican Church in India on the same footing of independence as in the Dominions without impairing the unity of spiritual communion.

How self-centred Indian communal feeling can be has been shown, perhaps, most forcibly in the violent shape assumed by the Sikh *Akali* movement in the Punjab. Religious but not racial differences have set the Sikhs apart as a relatively small community confined mainly to the Punjab and some adjoining districts of the United Provinces and numbering altogether barely 3,500,000. Whilst the Non-Co-operation storm was sweeping over the rest of India a local storm broke out and raged still more fiercely amongst the Sikhs of the Punjab. Only a few years ago there was hardly any quarter in which trouble was less expected. The loyalty of the

Sikhs to British rule had never been in doubt since
the time when, only a few years after the destruction
of the old Sikh Confederacy and the annexation of
the Punjab, they rallied to the British cause during
the Mutiny and materially helped to save the
situation in Upper India. Their ancient customs
have nowhere been so faithfully cherished and
encouraged as in the Sikh regiments, generally
acknowledged to be amongst the very finest in the
Indian Army. Altogether 80,000 Sikhs served during
the great war—a larger proportion of fighting men
than from any other community in India—and their
record more than made up for the short-lived trouble
which broke out in the second year of the war with
the return of a few hundred Sikhs driven away from
Canada and bitterly estranged from British rule by
the anti-Asiatic immigration laws inexorably enforced against them in British Columbia. The
Akali movement was partly no doubt a product of
the general ferment into which India was plunged
by the aftermath of the great war, but it had a
distinct and separate character of its own. It
originated in a puritan reaction against the subtle
influence of Hinduism which threatened to under-
mine the work of Nanak and the great Sikh *Gurus*
who had rebelled against the social and religious
trammels of Hindu orthodoxy before they revolted
against Mohammedan domination. The downfall of
the Sikh Confederacy was followed by a period of
growing religious laxity, and the majority of the
Sikh shrines, many of them richly endowed, passed
into the hands of hereditary incumbents, or *Mahunts*,
of very doubtful orthodoxy and often of still more
doubtful character. The reformers began by
petitioning Government to dispossess the *Mahunts*
and make over the shrines to trustees for
the whole community. But the incumbents' titles
were good in law and Government could not

oust them in deference merely to the clamour of
one part of the community. The more ardent
reformers then banded themselves together to exert
popular pressure, almost indistinguishable from
coercion, upon the offending *Mahunts*. Whilst the
incumbent of the Golden Temple at Amritzar, most
sacred of all Sikh shrines, yielded and resigned his
office into the hands of the Reforms Committee, after
making a public confession of his wrong-doings, the
Mahunt of Nankanda Saheb, second only to Amritzar
in sanctity and wealth, prepared for resistance, and
a ghastly tragedy occurred on March 5, 1921, when
several thousand Akalis were gathering together to
bring mass-pressure to bear upon him. He admitted
a small party who claimed the right to worship at
the shrine and then closed the doors upon them and
had them butchered to the number of about a
hundred by a band of some fifty Pathan cutthroats
whom he had imported as a prætorian guard. He
had also imported a large stock of petrol in which
the corpses of his victims were so effectively soaked
and burned that they could scarcely be counted
except by the number of charred skulls when police
and troops were hurried to the scene. A thrill of
horror passed through the Punjab, and, with
Amritzar still casting its shadow over the Province
and the bitter memory of many inoffensive Sikhs
shot down in the crowd at Jalianwala *Bagh*, it was
easy for disaffected agitators to turn the wrath of
the Akalis upon the Provincial Government whose
weakness and dilatoriness were denounced as mainly
responsible for the tragedy. The *Akali* movement
caught the contagion of lawlessness which, under
Gandhi's misguided influence, was spreading all over
India. A militant plan of campaign brought large
bands of Akalis organized on a quasi-military basis
into frequent collision with the police and even with
the troops that had to be employed on various

occasions to quell serious disturbances. The Sikh State of Nabha whose Maharajah had a quarrel of his own with his neighbour, the Maharajah of Paliala, and through him with the Government of India, became a favourite base for turbulent demonstrations by bands of Akalis, sometimes several thousands strong, who professed to be merely marching to worship at the shrine of Jaito in Nabha territory. A state almost of civil war on a small scale arose, and whilst Gandhi took up the *Akali* cause just as he took up the Caliphate cause simply because he saw in it a great demonstration of religious faith, its increasing lawlessness was enough to commend it to his more violent followers. A Satanic Government was charged with an implacable hostility to the fine reforming impulses of the Sikh community and even the Maharajah was invested with a halo of martyrdom as a victim of British despotism when the cup of his evildoings, which had nothing to do with the *Akali* movement, was filled to the brim and the Government of India put an end to his persistent misrule by compelling him to abdicate. Yet Government had never lacked sympathy with the legitimate purposes of the reformers and was prepared to introduce legislation for the purpose of any lawful settlement which should satisfy the religious sentiment of the Sikh community. But the Akalis had worked themselves to such a pitch of religious frenzy that an extreme faction, known as *Babar* Akalis, practised murder as a legitimate means of propaganda on their weak-kneed brethren. The great majority were never prepared to go to such lengths, but they would yield neither to argument nor to force. They were ready to go to prison in thousands, and they would not listen even to the recommendations of a joint conciliation Committee, willing to hear all parties and factions, under the presidency of General Birdwood, probably the most popular officer of the Indian Army and nowhere more respected than in the Punjab. The Akalis insisted on the release of all who were then in jail for gross breaches of the law and would hear of no settlement except on the lines required by their own Committee. No agreement was possible on such terms and *Jathas*, as the disorderly marches to Jaito came to be called, continued in a more defiant spirit than ever.

The tide, however, turned at last in the Punjab as in other parts of India and largely for similar reasons. The Sikhs could hardly help realizing, in presence of the general revival of communal feeling, that so small a community as theirs could least afford to expend its slender forces in fruitless strife either amongst themselves or with the British *raj*, who had in fact always treated them rather as spoilt children. Sir Malcolm Hailey who was appointed to the Punjab in the spring of 1924 was quick to take advantage of the opportunities which usually present themselves more readily to a new Governor. His firmness won for him the support of influential Sikhs who, though in sympathy with all that was best in the *Akali* movement, were weary of the turmoil into which it had plunged the province at a time when it had every reason to look forward to great economic develop-ments. The trouble is not yet over, but a Bill introduced by a Sikh non-official member and passed by the Provincial Council with the full support of Government to settle the rights of ownership on a legal basis and to vest the control and management of the shrines in a representative board composed only of Sikhs promises to end a dispute which like so many others in India first arose out of a conflict between two rights.

If the flight from *Swaraj* is primarily due to searchings of heart as to the effect of *Swaraj* on the position of each community under a full *Swaraj* Government, recent happenings have driven Indians of all communities to ask themselves the further question whether *Swaraj* would be likely to maintain the same measure of security and justice to all communities alike for which experience has taught them to look to the British *raj*, alien though it be and as such repugnant to the natural pride of subject races. To that question there could only be one answer. In all the serious cases of intercommunal rioting which have occurred so frequently during the last few years in different parts of India, it is the intervention of British authority that has alone imposed peace, and often the appearance of British troops that has alone arrested pillage and bloodshed. Help has admittedly always been forthcoming impartially for whatever community stood in need of it. It might be argued that under *Swaraj* every community would be able to rely equally in similar circumstances upon the authority and forces of the State. But Indians are clearly not convinced that it would be so. For in disturbed areas both sides have been moved under the immediate pressure of a dangerous situation to apply for a British official to be specially appointed to take charge of the district, because they know that, whatever his faults may be, the Englishman is immune against the communal and sectarian prejudices or predilections by which Indian officials are naturally apt to be swayed and often must be, even unconsciously, and however anxious they may be to perform their duty. No Englishman is exposed to the temptations and the forms of pressure which beset an Indian surrounded by his fellow-caste-men or co-religionists whom long tradition has accustomed to claim his support almost as a matter of right. How strong that tradition is has also appeared of late, not only in connection with actual outbreaks of disorder, but, with much less excuse, in connection with the transaction of ordinary public business under the reforms which have placed the administration of provincial departments in the hands of Indian Ministers. One of the reasons for the reputed failure of Dyarchy is that an Indian Minister is disposed to regard it as his first duty as head of a department not so much to initiate a policy and supervise its execution as to fill as many posts in it as possible with his own caste-men or co-religionists. Indian Legislators themselves have quoted cases in which even personal bargains have been struck on the basis of alleged communal considerations. Nepotism is not unknown in the West and the system of party spoils still prevails largely in the United States. But nowhere can nepotism on the large scale which the constitution of Indian society and the fierce discords between creeds and communities invite be such a public danger as in India.

There has been dread too of another danger against which British rule has for more than a century protected India and still, as most Indians admit, can alone effectively protect her, and the dread has grown with the cumulative evidence which the condition of the whole world affords that the great war has failed of its promise to end war. It is the dread lest *Swaraj* should lead merely to the substitution of some other form of foreign rule for British rule, if India were to lose that protection before she had had time to substitute a national army, let alone a national fleet, for the armed forces of the British Empire which at present alone stand between her and foreign aggression. It does not come within the scope of this work to review the long course of British foreign policy in relation to India. But ever since the establishment of British dominion in India—which, it must be remembered occurred at the same time as Britain lost her ascendancy in North America with the successful revolt of the colonies that have grown up into the great United

States republic—the orientation of British foreign policy has been largely shifted to the East with the safety of India as one of the chief considerations that have guided it. In the Mediterranean and the Red Sea, in Egypt and Turkey and Persia, and even in the Far East, *i.e.*, in regions geographically far removed from her, India has been frequently called upon to contribute large contingents to British military expeditions on the ground that her own interests were equally at stake. All through the XIXth century British policy was constantly governed by the menace to the land frontiers of India arising out of Russian expansion across Central Asia, and to forestall Russian ambitions India waged three wars in Afghanistan and one in Southern Persia and sent an armed expedition into Tibet. An equal menace to India was held later on to arise out of the danger of German " world dominion " and German penetration through Asiatic Turkey down to the Persian Gulf. British policy in all these matters may not always have been wise, nor may it always have been inspired solely by an unselfish regard for Indian interests, and to-day it may be more difficult to descry any great war-cloud on the horizon as far as it can be surveyed through Indian eyes, though the policy of Bolshevist Russia tends to revert to the Tsarist type of aggressive expansion, with the new feature grafted on to it of a revolutionary propaganda specially addressed to India. But the part which India took in the great war has brought home to Indians how effectively the shrinkage of the whole world in terms of time and distance has destroyed her ancient isolation and brought her within reach of all the competitive ambitions from which British rule has hitherto shielded her. These may assume new forms, but she will continue to offer the same temptation to the strong, and an almost irresistible temptation when once that shield is withdrawn, and a *Swaraj* India has to shift for herself in a restless world.

If these are some of the heart-searchings that the contemplation of *Swaraj* has provoked in that part of the Indian Empire under direct British adminis-tration to which, let us say for argument's sake, Parliament might be willing to concede it, what must be the heart-searchings in that smaller but not incon-siderable part of the Indian Empire, viz., the Native States, to which no constitutional changes in British India can apply, so long as their Princes and Ruling Chiefs enjoy hereditary rights and in many cases almost complete autonomy under permanent treaties which Parliament is bound to respect? Those treaties were concluded a century and more ago in the days of the East India Company, but they were solemnly confirmed when the Crown assumed full and direct sovereignty after the Mutiny, and the Princes and Ruling Chiefs now generally pride themselves on standing in a sort of feudatory relationship to the British Crown of which they regard the Government of India and more especially the Viceroy as the appointed representative. A few of them have moved with the times and introduced into their States more enlightened forms of govern-ment and administration than those of their ancestors, but the majority still stand in the old ways of auto-cratic rulership. Even those who are best known in England have very little in common with the politically-minded class of Indians who form the majority in the new Legislative Assemblies at Delhi and profess principles which, in so far as they savour of democracy, are to them not only detestable in theory, but a menace to their established authority. They have their own methods to-day for dealing with any inconvenient manifestations of the new spirit of unrest which they see filtering into their

States from British India, and, as the Native
States are scattered all over India, their boundaries
are wide-open to such infiltration. How conscious
they are that it is taking place every day was
seen when a couple of years ago they moved the
Government of India to introduce a Bill for their
better protection against attacks in the Press of
British India, and, when it was rejected by the
Legislative Assembly, they prevailed upon the
Viceroy to override the Assembly and place the
provisions of the Bill upon the Statute Book by
straining in their favour the special emergency
powers reserved to him under the Act of 1919.
Imagine not merely the surrender of those powers,
but a *Swaraj* Government in full control of what is
now British India and prepared in dealing with
the Native States to regard all the restraints imposed
by ancient treaties as no less obsolete than the
British power that contracted them. There is no
need to press the point further. There are many
other and graver matters than newspaper diatribes
on which the Native States might and almost
certainly would sooner or later come into collision
with a *Swaraj* Government, and, if few of the
Princes' and Ruling Chiefs' States can claim, as
perhaps Mysore and Baroda and one or two others
may do, to have thrown themselves into the stream
of modern progress, the majority, counting amongst
their peoples some of the most martial races, still
live in the days when in India force was the first
rather than the last arbitrament of kings. At any
rate whatever may be the sympathies of some of
the Princes and Ruling Chiefs as Indians with the
national ideals of *Swaraj*, the Native States constitute, though we may be apt to forget it, a
distinct and separate India from British India, and
their interests and outlook not less than their rights
are often and largely different from those of the India

20

to which Parliament might be tempted or would have power to grant *Swaraj*.

Perhaps it was some of these signs of flight from *Swaraj* that induced Mr. C. R. Das, a man of fiercer emotions at times than Gandhi, but also at times a far more practical politician, to make, a few weeks before his premature death, a gesture of appeasement which many took to be an admission that the Swarajist plan of campaign had broken down. But the gesture was vague, and its meaning lies buried where the ashes of the Swarajist leader were consumed on the burning-ghat of Kalikat amidst the lamentations of the largest concourse of people that the great and modern city of Calcutta has ever known, and with Ghandi borne shoulder-high as chief mourner. A twofold portent ; for, if it showed the lasting hold upon the popular imagination of the cabalistic formula of *Swaraj*, hallowed by the Mahatma's inspiring personality, it heralded the disintegration of the only disciplined party, laboriously trained by the dead leader to bring *Swaraj* within the range of practical politics by pressing parliamentary institutions borrowed from the West into the service of his philosophic concept of an Indian revolt against Western civilization.

CHAPTER XVIII

BESIDES the conjuncture of singularly adverse circumstances with which Dyarchy has had to contend from the moment it came into being, it has had the misfortune of attracting a cross-fire both from Indians and from Englishmen in India, and still more at home, who are equally determined to convict it of failure, the former in order to press for the further curtailment of British control, the latter in order to discredit the whole reforms scheme of which it forms part. The firing is brisk on both sides, but it is heaviest on the Indian side. The Government of India were themselves moved to set up a Reforms Enquiry Committee in 1924, but under its terms of reference, it was restricted to the recommendation of changes, if any, within the scope of the new constitution as laid down in the Act of 1919, except in so far as amendments of the Act might appear necessary to rectify any administrative imperfections. The gist of the Majority Report signed by the three British and by two out of the six Indian members is that the reforms have worked on the whole well, and their recommendations for a variety of minor changes and amendments are within the terms of reference. The Minority Report is signed by the other four Indian members who travel far afield to support their finding, which is that no changes or amendments can be of any avail except such as must entirely transform the character of the new constitution by the abolition of provincial Dyarchy and the surrender—to what extent is not clearly indicated—of the control of Parliament over the Government of India. The views of Provincial Governments on the operation of the reforms, first in 1923 and then again in 1924, are annexed to the Commission's Report and serve amongst other things to illustrate the special difficulties imported into the working of the constitution by the activities of the new Swarajist party in 1924. The Minority Report represents a move towards full provincial autonomy as a stepping-stone to full *Swaraj* in the shape of Dominion Self-Government. But as its only immediate recommendation was for the appointment of a Royal Commission, it has been thrown into the shade by the action of a small and select group of former Moderates, now calling themselves the Indian Liberal Association, comprising Mr. Shrinivasa Shastri and Sir Tej Sapru, not long ago a member of the Government of India, and one of the Minority members of the Reforms Committee, with Mrs. Besant once more as their Egeria, who have drafted an elaborate " Commonwealth of India " Bill to be presented to Parliament as the latest expression of Indian self-determination. It would eliminate Dyarchy in the provinces, but it would introduce it, in a form still purposely no doubt elastic, in the Central Government.

That is the weak point in all the Indian attacks upon Dyarchy. It is turned out of one door, but it reappears at another. Let us assume that the dual form of government established in the provinces under the Act of 1919 with its division of executive and administrative responsibility for " reserved " and " transferred " subjects is abolished in favour of a unitary form of government, wholly or preponderatingly Indian and responsible to the provincial Legislative Council, also wholly or preponderatingly Indian, for the whole field of provincial administration. This means not merely a relaxation but the removal of the ultimate control over the Provincial Governments still reserved to Parliament through the Government of India and the Secretary of State under the Act of 1919. What will then be the relations between Provincial Governments released from that

control and the Central Government of India so
long as it remains entirely or even partially subject
to it ? As it is they are often enough severely
strained; but will not the strain be infinitely more
severe if the Central Government remains responsible
to Parliament and the Provincial Governments are
to be responsible only to their own Indian Legislatures ? The financial relations between them have
grown more difficult than ever under Dyarchy.
What prospect will there be of agreement between
them on the thorny question, let us say, of provincial contributions to the Central Government's
exchequer and of the distribution of the common
sources of revenue between the Central and Provincial Governments, when both parties will be tugging
at their own side of the blanket with no common
authority above them to keep their quarrels within
bounds ? Can the issue be confined even to their
financial relations ? As the former Secretary of
State for India in the Labour Government has
pointedly asked his Indian friends : " Do you
mean by provincial autonomy that every province
shall have its own customs duties, its own army, its
own marine if a coastal province, its own railway
system ? " And, he might have added, resume the
control of which the Central Government has just
deprived it, over its relations with the Native States
within its borders ? Provincial autonomy would
mean a dual government all over India, or Dyarchy
in excelsis and in the most dangerous form, without
any kind of liaison such as the Governor at least
now provides under the constitution for the two
wings of the Provincial Government. The Swarajists
are more logical who maintain that there is no half-
way house to full *Swaraj* and that only a *Swaraj*
India can settle the relations between the Central
Government and the Provincial Governments in
accordance with the interests of both on large

national lines, whereas provincial autonomy would queer the pitch for any such settlement by adding a fresh crop of inter-provincial differences and jealousies to the many other communal and racial and religious discords which, they admit, already offer serious impediments to the growth of a national spirit as the essential basis of *Swaraj*.

Englishmen of a reactionary type, perhaps, happily more common at home than in India, who see in Dyarchy the beginning of the end of the *raj* are really men of little faith, or they live in a past which is gone in India as in the rest of the world. It was not Dyarchy or any other part of the reforms scheme that produced the upheaval which followed the great war. The first great effort of the Non-Co-operation movement was to strangle the reforms before any of them were put into operation. The introduction of new Indian parts into the hitherto almost entirely British framework of Indian government and administration was bound to be in any case a delicate and difficult process, and the difficulties were aggravated quite as much by the coincidence of a period of acute economic depression for which the reforms were in no way responsible as by the *Swaraj* storm of revolt not against the reforms but against British rule itself. Yet the foundations of British rule remain unshaken. Even its elaborate machinery, though it was all the time going through a complicated process of readjustment to great constitutional changes, was never put out of action. The exalted helmsmen who dwell in their own Olympian atmosphere of rarefied isolation barely felt, or only indirectly, the breath of the storm which raged at their feet during the worst days of Non-Co-operation, except when it struck dangerously higher through the attempt to boycott the Prince of Wales's visit. The brunt was borne by the district officer and other agents of the Central and Provincial

whilst there is no such short cut to meet the former as Indians believe they have found for the latter in the adoption of fiscal protection. The future of Indian protected industries is not yet assured, as they present many peculiar problems which time alone can solve, *e.g.*, the effect, not yet sufficiently tested, of a tropical atmosphere on manufacturing processes that have approved themselves under very different climatic conditions. But the greater their future, the greater the danger that protection may tend to increase the poverty of rural India by increasing the cost of many necessaries of life, just as did the curtailment of imports during the war with alarming results in the spread of popular discontent ; whilst it will draw off into the industrial centres an increasing proportion of the most intelligent and progressive elements now on the land.

Long before the present *Swaraj* movement, clear-sighted and temperate Indian reformers saw that the social regeneration as well as the political advancement of India was bound up with the raising of rural India out of the slough of ignorance which is also that of poverty. It has been present to the minds of the greatest British rulers of India. It was present to the minds of the pioneers of Western education when they hoped with a too buoyant optimism that higher education would filter down of its own weight to the masses and moisten an arid soil in anticipation of the ultimate extension to them of more elementary forms of education. It was in Dalhousie's mind when he laid stress on the educative value of the great discoveries of applied science which it had been his privilege to introduce into India. It was present in Curzon's mind when he resorted to the creation of efficient organs of administration for what might be called the sphere of higher agricultural education. But the clearest vision and the plainest speech were Lord Mayo's, who said outright that " the progress

of India in wealth and in civilization must be directly
dependent on her progress in agriculture." That
was over fifty years ago, and the British *raj* has not
done more than touch the fringe of the problem with
which the progress of Indian agriculture is bound up.
The key to progress is education, and the task of
educating the rural masses must necessarily be a
long and costly and immensely difficult undertaking.
But no one has ever denied its urgency, and the only
argument which the Government of India has ever
been able to use to justify the long delay in starting
it has been that it was beyond its financial resources.

That is an argument which must lose much of its
force now that, in connection with fiscal policy, the
principle has for the first time been conceded that
Indian must prevail over British interests. For
implicit in that concession is an admission of the
Indian contention that in the allocation of Indian
revenue to the different branches of State expenditure England has constituted herself the sole judge
of what India can or cannot afford and has frequently
exercised her judgment to the benefit of British and
to the detriment of Indian interests. It is nevertheless an issue upon which British and Indian
opinions must be widely divided as it springs from
the twofold aspect which the possession of India
assumes in the British mind. For whilst Indians
hold England to her pledge that she has assumed
dominion over India as a trust committed to her for
the welfare and security of the peoples of India,
Englishmen, without being altogether unmindful of
this trust, have grown inclined to regard the possession of India as an Imperial asset to be administered
in accordance with the complex interests of an
expanding Empire and at a minimum charge upon
its heavily-taxed resources. Whether the Indian
case be a strong or a weak one, it must be understood and faced, for it will be pressed with all the

greater force after England's recognition of such a far-reaching principle as that involved in the fiscal freedom of India, and the introduction of constitutional changes which, though they may be carried no further, already afford Indians opportunities they never hitherto possessed of pressing it upon the Government of India.

The Indian case is chiefly and most effectively pressed against the military expenditure of the Government of India. As was shown in the previous chapter this has been one of the features of the Swarajist plan of campaign. Against England's financial stewardship in other respects the Indian case is not nearly so strong. Until the great war India was never saddled with any heavy dead-weight of public indebtedness. Indian loans had been raised for large amounts, chiefly on the London markets, but all had been devoted to reproductive purposes. For railway loans there was a great railway system to show which more than covered capital and interest, though Sir William Acworth's Commission disclosed after the war many grave shortcomings in general policy and methods of administration. The vast irrigation works which have been amongst the most beneficent works of British rule have yielded handsome revenues to the State. Even the hideous but utilitarian buildings erected by the Public Works Department represent their market value in bricks and mortar, and if British rule were suddenly to cease it would leave behind almost enough material assets to cover all the expenditure for which it has pledged Indian credit. Including the financial contributions made by India to the Imperial Exchequer during the war, her total debt does not amount to 1,000 crores of rupees (£650,000,000) and how little of it can be properly called unproductive is shown by the fact that debt services other than the interest on railway loans

which is covered by railway revenue, figure in the
Budget estimate for 1924–5 at only 1,815 lakhs, or
less than £13,000,000 out of a total expenditure set
down approximately at nearly £87,000,000. Indian
capital has begun now to come forward more freely
for investment in Indian loans, but until recently
India has been almost entirely dependent upon
British capital, which but for confidence in the
stability of British rule would not have been forthcoming. Indians can show good cause for complaining
that India has incurred enormous losses by the
currency and exchange policy, which has, they
believe, been imposed upon the Government of
India from Whitehall, and they may be excused
for suspecting that the reserves which have to be
maintained by it in London are excessive and
enure mainly to the benefit of British capitalists
at home. It was the only Indian member of the
last Currency Commission who alone dissented from
its recommendations and foretold their disastrous
consequences. There is less foundation for Indian
complaints that the civil administration of the country
is unduly costly, for in no country is so much work
thrown on to the State in so many fields of activity
which are elsewhere left to individual or municipal
enterprise. The real Indian grievance, and the one
which strikes at the control hitherto exercised by
the British Government over the financial policy of
the Government of India, lies in the proportion of
military to civil expenditure. That military expenditure has at all times clogged the wheels of Indian
finance is beyond all dispute. It has constantly tied
the hands of the Finance Member who is driven to
subordinate to the more pressing necessity of
balancing his Budget larger schemes of public utility
of which the benefit cannot be expected to mature
in his day. To-day it is not only the Western-
educated but much wider classes reaching down

into the stratum of the silent masses that clamour for more liberal expenditure on what they have learned to call the " nation building " departments. They realize the need, not only for railways, roads, irrigation canals and, if only dimly for sanitation, for the fight against malaria, and above all, for primary education.   The reforms, it was hoped, would enable more money to be spent on them in each Province according to its special requirements by Indian Ministers in immediate contact with local opinion.   But once again the military expenditure imposed upon the Central Government blocked the way by delaying the remission of the heavy provincial contributions which each province has now to make to the All-India exchequer, and Indian ministers have not been slow to plead this explanation for their failure to fulfil popular expectations of expansion and progress just where Indian opinion most keenly and legitimately looked for them.

Fiscal independence is regarded as a first step towards India's emancipation from the rigid control hitherto exercised, it is alleged, with an eye to British rather than to Indian interests over the allocation of revenues which she alone provides.   The well-wishers of the *raj* hold very strongly that the next step will be a recognition of India's right to a larger allocation of revenue to agricultural development, even if it involves a redistribution of military expenditure so that, where the latter is shown to be required for Imperial rather than Indian purposes, it should not fall exclusively on the Indian tax-payers' overburdened shoulders, or should be counter-balanced by a generous policy of capital expenditure, financed as in other parts of the Empire by pledging British credit. Such an association of India with the Empire would in the eyes of almost all Indians be more fruitful than a seat at Imperial Conferences or at Geneva.   It would be an earnest, too, of a

determination to consider the interests of agriculture
from another point of view than that of the
production of revenue with which land has been until
recently almost as closely associated, in the mind
of Government, as it had been in the days of the
Moghul Empire. The same member of the Viceroy's
Executive Council used to be in charge of " Revenue
and Agriculture " and the order in which the two
subjects were placed in the designation of his department betrayed the relative importance officially
assigned to them. Only within the last twenty years,
since Lord Curzon created a special Board of Agriculture, has there been a wider recognition of the
supremely important part which agriculture plays
in the economic life of India. Though much useful
spade-work has been done since then by research
and experiment to introduce improved methods and
crops, and by the opening of agricultural colleges and
model farms to provide higher training and practical
demonstrations of its value for the Indian farmer,
land revenue is still a constant reminder of the claim
which the State makes as tax-collector upon agriculture, and Gandhi showed his understanding of
rural India when he projected to make the non-
payment of land-tax the next stage after Non-
Co-operation in the great forward march to *Swaraj*.

It is not without significance that the land revenue
has already ceased to be the principal source of
revenue in British India and that its place has been
taken by Customs revenue. Some regard it as
evidence that the whole land revenue system
which is largely an inheritance from Moghul times
is obsolete and stands in need of complete revision.
It is, at any rate, a clear indication that new life
must be put into rural India, and rural India is
occupying to-day the minds of many educated
Indians, often, unfortunately, as an undeveloped field
of political agitation, but also, and more usefully, as

an undeveloped field of national prosperity. Some
of the keenest amongst the Western-educated classes
are studying agricultural questions or getting into
still closer touch with them on the land itself. Old-
fashioned landlords are waking up. New manufacturing interests are pressing for improvement of the
raw materials which they require from the soil.
Increasing interest is shown in model farms and
agricultural schools and the work of the agricultural
departments in which not a few Englishmen have
recovered the same spirit of enthusiastic service
that animated the pioneers of Western education a
hundred years ago. Experiments have been made
on a sufficient scale to show that the careful selection
of seeds and scientific hybridization, the use of
special fertilizers, the systematic destruction of
parasitic pests, etc., increase the yield of the land
four and fivefold within a very few years. The
Co-operative Societies have shown that the Indian
peasant can be taught the elements of agricultural
organization. The consolidation of small and
scattered holdings has produced amazing results.
New implements and new methods are slowly
gaining acceptance. But all these new efforts require
to be co-ordinated, and that can only be done, in
India's present stage of development, by the State.
In other directions there is much leeway to be made
up. The need for improved means of transportation
is enormous. The immemorial bullock-cart is too
cumbersome and in the long run too costly when
India has to compete in the markets of an up-to-date
world, and yet there are large neglected areas in
which it still has no competitor. The cost of
building and running strategic railways on the desert
fringe of the North-West Frontier has to be made good
elsewhere. Only since the Acworth Commission has
the railway administration been to some extent
released from the leading strings of the Finance

department and allowed to take longer views of economic policy. The forest wealth of India is still undeveloped ; for though an admirable forestry service has been trained in the most experienced schools of continental forestry, Government has constantly shrunk from a capital outlay necessarily yielding very slow returns, and during the war, when every ton of shipping was invaluable, fine timber had to be imported by sea from the Western slope of the Pacific. Irrigation works on a splendid scale have been amongst the finest and most remunerative achievements of British rule, but, though they have transformed some of the great waste spaces of India, they can bring prosperity only to some selected regions. In less favoured regions a backward peasantry has yet to be taught and helped to develop and husband such scanty supplies of water as nature has grudgingly placed within its reach. Government has only slowly begun to move, but the holding of a " grand inquest " into the condition of Indian agriculture is being freely discussed to-day. India is too vast a country for the same principles and same methods to be applicable everywhere. Agriculture is now one of the departments " transferred " to Provincial Governments, and provinces larger and more populous than England sometimes differ widely as to soil and climate, but there is still room for a central authority to give them a co-operative lead and check a short-sighted tendency towards wastefully competitive production.

But if much can be done to improve the technique of agriculture and to bring many practical improvements within the reach of the *ryot*, the breath of a new life for which rural India has been kept too long waiting will not come until a broad system of education suited to the needs of an agricultural population breaks down the wall of ignorance behind which are entrenched all the prejudices and superstitions and all the mingled fatalism and improvidence that have for countless generations bred and perpetuated poverty. Such a system of education must be the simplest that can possibly be devised. For its purpose should be solely to give the *ryot* a better understanding of the land to which he is wedded by inclination as much as by necessity, and not to divorce him from it. Even within these modest limits it will call for an immense effort which in the present condition of India must come mainly from the State. It will need also every ounce of Indian co-operation, but it is in this direction that lies the best hope of regaining Indian confidence. It was in this direction that Gandhi himself pointed in one of the speeches in which, even at the height of the Non-Co-operation movement, he occasionally showed signs of returning to his old faith in British rule. "Much of my opposition to Government would," he said, "abate if I found that it was truly solicitous for India's economic and moral welfare."

"There is a tide in the affairs of men which taken at the flood leads on to fortune"—or the reverse. There are many Indians as well as Englishmen who see very clearly to-day that India must be overwhelmed by the economic tide which is beating in upon her from the outside world unless her rulers are prepared to meet it with all the great reserves of strength still waiting to be roused to life in her own soil and in the countless millions whose immemorial devotion to it, as deep as that of any peasantry in the world, still awaits release from the twofold incubus of ignorance and poverty. Otherwise ignorance and poverty may easily be captured, as the Non-Co-operation movement for the time captured them, by those who believe or profess to believe that from the days of the East India Company England has compassed India's economic ruin in her own selfish interests; and we should then

21

witness in the more slowly-moving minds of the silent masses a revolution, different in kind, but even more disastrous than that which has estranged the educated classes from the West. The loss of their goodwill has left British rule dangerously top-heavy. The moral and material redemption of rural India would place it on a broader base with more secure foundations than ever before.

CHAPTER XIX

A NEW STAGE IN THE GREAT EXPERIMENT

IT does not fall within the writer's province to speculate as to the future or to propound solutions of one of the most formidable complex problems with which British statesmanship can be confronted. His purpose—and one that he is conscious of having only very inadequately achieved—has been to trace the growth and the reactions of the great forces, spiritual and material, ancient and modern, which have made India what she is to-day—a nation whose title to rank amongst the nations of the modern world has been formally recognized since her name appeared as one of the signatories of the Treaty of Versailles and an original member of the League of Nations—but a nation still in many ways unformed, and with a vision rather than the reality of common nationhood, towards which she is groping her way out of a welter of different races and creeds and languages, and with only one symbol of national unity, and that symbol a foreign one—the British Crown. Even in regard to the exercise of British sovereignty, paramount as it is over the whole Indian Empire, a sharp distinction has to be drawn between British India which is alone subject to British administration, and the Native States of India where hereditary rulers enjoy large rights of autonomy under the overlordship of King George, Emperor of India. But if the political unity of India is altogether more real and more stable to-day under British rule and has lasted already longer than at any earlier period known to history, she still shows all her old lines of religious and social cleavage, sometimes attenuated and sometimes deepened by new lines of cleavage crossing and recrossing the old ones, produced by British rule and Western education and increasing contact with the outer world, and last but not least, the cosmic earthquake of the great war.

When once British rule was firmly established it tended rather to preserve than to disturb India's isolation from the rest of the outer world. The struggle between Western nations for the possession of India was over, and British rule was accepted as a saving release from the great internal anarchy of the XVIIIth century. It gave her peace and security, and she continued, throughout the greater part of the XIXth century to live a sheltered life almost inaccessible to any other Western influences than those which reached her from this country. All this has been changed during the first quarter of the XXth century. Within the British Empire itself Indians have been rudely brought up against the colour-bar by which the white man now seeks to emphasize his claim to racial supremacy, and a new sense of solidarity has grown up between them and the other coloured races of the East. Whilst the failure of the Imperial Government to secure the redress of Indian wrongs in South Africa shook India's faith in the British sense of justice, the Japanese victories over Russia, the great European Power which the British Empire then still regarded as its most dangerous rival, filled Indians with a new pride and hope, and the lesson they drew from them was that the nations of Asia could and must learn to assert, as Japan has done, their right to equality of treatment whatever the pigmentation of their skin. But with the Morley-Minto Reforms, though they only partially satisfied the political aspirations of the Western-educated classes, the first great wave of Indian unrest subsided, and, when the great war broke out, the heart of India warmed again towards the British power that had given her more than a century of peace and security; and she forgot all her racial grievances when she saw an Indian Army fighting gallantly side by side with British troops on the battlefields of Europe itself. The war, however, brought other less welcome experiences and raised too many hopes and expectations that were never fulfilled. It has been well said that President Wilson's "self-determination" exploded like a shell loaded with dynamite, and the noise of it reverberated nowhere more loudly than amongst Eastern nations. With the disastrous aftermath of the war many dark shadows besides that of the Punjab lengthened over the face of India. A still more bitter cry came from the Indians of Kenya than from those of South Africa where fresh anti-Asiatic legislation followed the close of a war in which Indians had never been denied equality on the day of battle. The ruin into which four years of devastating warfare plunged the white nations of Europe, victors and vanquished, shook the faith which many Indians still preserved in the superiority of Western civilization, and intensified the hatred which others had conceived for it. It was not only Mohammedan India that responded to the Caliphate agitation which exalted Turkey to the stature of an invincible protagonist of Asia against the West. From Morocco to China there runs a live wire of hatred through all the peoples of the East, and it is to that common hatred of the West that Bolshevism appeals in India as in other parts of Asia with its loud-mouthed promise of liberation for all the downtrodden peoples of the East, whilst the sinister shadow which it projects over Europe stretches still more menacing across Central Asia to the gates of India.

In other ways also the pressure of the outside world has closed in upon India as it had scarcely begun to do before the XXth century. We can realize to-day more fully than before the catastrophe of 1914 that behind Germany's overweening pretensions

the mentality of the people than has hitherto been reached by the importation of Western ideas and theories only imperfectly translated into practice. Englishmen as well as Indians are following with genuine interest and sympathy the remarkable experiment which is being conducted by Sir Rabindranath Tagore in his school at Bolpur where he has sought to revive not only the spirit of ancient Hindu education but many of its processes of intellectual and physical training, and similar essays are being made by many other Indian educational workers whose names are less widely known. At the same time as Western science is finding enthusiastic disciples both in the most advanced forms of research-work and in the application of scientific knowledge to practical purposes of material progress, Indian art, whether in music or in painting, is seeking a renewal of life not in the slavish acceptance of Western canons, but in its old sources of Indian inspiration. In another field, too, Indians are beginning to bring to the study of Indian history and of Indian social and economic problems the critical methods and the spirit of honest research for truth of which they could hardly have had more convincing examples than in the great Orientalists of Europe who, during the last century, have revealed to India herself as well as to the Western world so many of the treasures of her ancient literature and so much of the significance they lend to her ancient civilization.

Against all these signs of progress towards a better understanding and towards closer association in many departments of life, there must be set off the evidence of an estrangement, not only political but racial, which has rapidly assumed the appearance of an angry temper of revolt against the substance of British rule and the spirit of Western civilization. It has been engendered partly by a renewal of India's faith in her ancient creeds and in her own type of civilization, and partly by the impact of modern ideas of democratic self-government and national independence. India is not the only country in what we were pleased to call " the unchanging East," in which has sprung up a stubborn temper of revolt against Western ascendancy. But nowhere else is there such a large and well-equipped class ready to oppose to Western ascendancy as much even of passive resistance as has been deliberately set up in India. For nowhere else has the leaven of Western education, slight as it may still seem to be in India in proportion to the huge mass which it has still left untouched, been so potent as in India, or stimulated by the many other educative influences which British rule has brought in its train, over and above a highly if not altogether wisely organized educational system. The classes not inaptly described in the Montagu-Chelmsford Report as the "politically-minded classes " are the offspring of British rule, and it is in order to satisfy, not without long hesitation and delay, their aspirations to a larger share in the government and administration of their country that India has been endowed now with political institutions for which they had, perhaps, too long been denied any real effective training. That they should have chosen the moment when far greater political recognition has been extended to them than ever before under British rule to challenge the civilization for which British rule stands is something more than a mere coincidence; and the revolt has a deeper meaning than the mere resentment of the political restraints still placed on India's professed ambition to govern herself with the same measure of freedom as the great Dominions. Full partnership in the British Empire is not the ambition of Indians who justify *Swaraj* out of the ancient philosophy of Hinduism as the revolt of a more spiritually-minded India against the materialism of the West. All they have seen in the reforms has been an opportunity for conveying in a political formula something of the bitterness of soul laid bare in Mr. C. R. Das's death-bed message to his people : " I feel the handcuffs on my wrists and the weight of iron chains on my body. It is the agony of bondage ; the whole of India is a vast prison. . . . What matters it whether I am dead or alive ? "

The psychology of India is not that of the West, and if the revolt of the politically-minded classes is a psychological rather than a political phenomenon, its gravity is all the greater. It is useless, then, to try to make light of it and comfort ourselves with the reflection that they are extremely few in numbers, and that so long as we have the silent masses with us we have nothing to fear. Few as they may be, and as the intellectual caste always was in ancient India, they include the most active brains of the new India that has grown up under British rule and they have entered into possession of all the modern fields of activity which British rule opened up to them. Nor can their influence over the masses be measured by the mere counting of heads, for if there is anything that can be demonstrated by the experience of the last five-and-twenty years it is that nowhere do the uneducated masses follow more blindly the lead of the few than in Oriental countries where there would seem to be the widest gulf between the illiterate multitudes and the small educated classes, but where the same mentality makes them akin. There the power of the orator over illiterate crowds is enormous, and incalculably further still carries the power of the printed word, the power of the vernacular Press, broadcasted over a whole country-side by the one or two lettered men of the villages. It was an Indian, Western-educated and called to the London Bar, who first preached as the goal of *Swaraj* not merely India's political freedom, but the liberation of her soul from the trammels of the alien civilization which British rule has brought with it—a civilization which might be best for the Western nations who evolved it for the West, but was wholly evil for India who long ages ago evolved her own, and for herself infinitely superior, civilization. That was Gandhi's message to India, and never in our time have the silent masses, whose apathy British statesmen had not long before deplored, thrilled as they did to his apocalyptic denunciation of the Satanic West. Western-educated, too, are most of the leaders of the Swarajist party who have translated Gandhi's message into new terms of Parliamentary obstruction in the new representative assemblies, created to secure Indian co-operation, but which they have entered for the avowed purpose of wrecking them.

The more passionate their convictions, the stronger their hold upon the bulk of the politically-minded classes, let alone the masses, the further India must drift from the constitutional goal set before her for the first time by the Declaration of Policy of 1917 and the Act of 1919. To measure how far she has already drifted away from it, and in how short a time, many Indians, and perhaps Englishmen too, have been slow to realize. In 1919, little more than five years ago, Parliament framed a new Constitution for India in the belief that it would meet the aspirations of a new generation of Indians who, professing to be inspired by the ideals which the study of British history and British institutions and of the political evolution of the British people had placed before them, claimed on behalf of the peoples of India the right to tread under the ægis of Britain the same path which we had ourselves trodden towards responsible government based on democratic principles of popular representation. Even if they professed also to represent a new sense of Indian nationhood impatient of foreign domination in the autocratic form of which British rule had still hardly begun to divest itself, Indian Nationalism claimed at least to derive directly from the great Nationalist movements of the West in the XIXth century and more especially from the Italian *risorgimento* which heralded the national unification and freedom of Italy. Indians had studied Mill *On Liberty* as well as the fervid orations of Burke, the works of Herbert Spencer as well as the poetry of Milton and Wordsworth, and as Nationalists they worshipped at the shrine of Garibaldi and Mazzini. At none of these things could Englishmen properly cavil. We had, ourselves, sown the seeds, the soil had been fertile, and the harvest was only what we ought to have expected and even welcomed. So long, therefore, as there were grounds for hoping that in spite of the many difficulties peculiar to Indian social conditions the political evolution of the peoples of India would proceed on the same lines as that of the British people, it was not unreasonable to believe that through carefully-appointed stages of increasing powers and responsibilities they would acquire the practice of self-government, and India would ultimately qualify to take her place as a self-governing Dominion in the commonwealth of free nations that has been built up within the British Empire.

Swaraj, in the form in which it has been preached by Gandhi and the Swarajist party, has darkened that prospect. For the grant of Dominion Self-Government to an India instinct with hostility to Western civilization, ceases to have any analogy with the grant of self-government to our great overseas colonies. In the first place, they were colonies, and India never has been a colony. They were created by people of our own stock, with the same creed, the same traditions, the same language ; and even if they now include non-British peoples such as the French in Canada and the Dutch in South Africa, all are heirs to the same Western civilization. We could safely grant them full rights of self-government because we had in their long experience and steady progress along those lines a sufficient assurance that they would govern themselves according to standards of national conduct which they share with us and believe in as firmly as we do. The relations at present existing between Britain and the self-governing Dominions are based not merely upon a general community of interests, but upon a fundamental community of national ideals which makes them and us proud to call ourselves sister nations in the great federation of which we and they are part, the Commonwealth of British Nations. The ties which unite us, whether of national ideals or of material interest, were strong enough to stand the severe test of the great war, and that tremendous ordeal with its memories of heavy sacrifices borne in common has only served to strengthen them. It is admittedly conceivable that at some future time, which seems as yet remote, the form which those ties has so far assumed may grow irksome and be severed, but what is inconceivable is that compulsion should in that event be employed to prevent the dissolution of a partnership which would lose all its value if it ceased to be on both sides voluntary. The Mother Country realizes that the Dominions have grown to the full stature of nationhood and that should the demand ever come from any of them for complete independence it will be the demand of a nation united in formulating it and qualified to face all the responsibilities of independence, whilst the survival of a great common inheritance which the dissolution of partnership would leave intact would afford a substantial guarantee for the preservation of close friendship under new and not necessarily unfavourable conditions. Can any of these things be predicated in the case of India when at the very first stage at which she has had an opportunity of expressing herself under the new constitution, the most powerful party representing the Indian electorate as constituted by the Act of 1919 demands *Swaraj* in the shape, it may be, only of Dominion Self-Government, but in a spirit that must loosen, if not destroy all the ties which, from the nature of things much weaker in the case of India than of the other Dominions, make for the maintenance of that enduring community of sentiment and of interests without which there can be no British Commonwealth of Nations ?

But India is a country of tropical storms which, fiercely as they rage, subside and pass away after clearing the atmosphere and restoring fertility to the sun-scorched soil. It may be so with the Swarajist movement if *Swaraj* is a fierce storm of emotion rather than a policy. In so far as it is a policy to be judged in the spirit of the Charter of 1919, it cannot be held to have found convincing expression in the wrecking tactics of a party which does not represent even a majority of a small electorate, many of whom at present still decline to exercise their electoral rights. However strongly Indians may feel, they have clearly not yet learnt the use of the ballot-box, and some other mode than the direct vote may have to be found for them to express themselves. It may well be that a reforms scheme worked out in this country at a time of extreme war pressure did not take sufficient account of the Indian mentality which is as yet only very imperfectly attuned to democracy, and that many of the assumptions on which it was based were premature and over-sanguine. Some of the older forms of Indian self-expression may have to be called in aid, as Lord Ronaldshay saw them put into very effective operation less than ten years ago in Calcutta. But in any case the clock can no more be put back as some Englishmen would have it than put forward at the furious rate which many, but certainly not all, Indians desire. There will have to be much clear thinking done both in India and in England before it is taken to pieces again.

If we look behind the politics and beyond the philosophy of *Swaraj* for a more simple explanation of the emotional cloudburst of which *Swaraj* has, perhaps, been the occasion rather than the cause, it may be sought equally in an accumulation of popular discontents, arising out of economic conditions of which the ancient hardships were suddenly aggravated by the acute depression that followed the war. From that point of view the Swarajist movement conveys a lesson which has been, perhaps, too long neglected under British rule, and is all the more urgent to-day when India and the whole world are confronted with a battle of economic forces more intensive and more highly organized than ever. Is India equipped to hold her own in it ? One step has been taken in continuing since the war the great endeavour made under the spur of war necessities to speed-up Indian industries—the first great endeavour of the kind ever made under British rule. But there is no Indian industry comparable with agriculture to which four-fifths of a population of over 300,000,000 look for their very existence. Few can deny that the condition of rural India, where appalling poverty has its roots in equally appalling ignorance, is still a reproach to British rule, which has mitigated many hardships, but has shrunk from the magnitude of the effort required for a resolute frontal attack upon the twin evils of poverty and ignorance. That such an effort must be one of the main features of the new stage upon which the great experiment of British rule is entering, some Indians as well as Englishmen already quite clearly perceive. It is the most urgent of India's needs. It is not less urgent in the interests of the whole Empire, if India is to be a source of strength to it in the economic struggle to which it is committed for the maintenance of its high place in the world. It is equally imperative for the discharge of England's duty as trustee for the welfare of India, and in the fulfilment of that trust still lies, as it has ever since Burke propounded and Pitt enacted the principle of British trusteeship, the great moral justification for British rule in India.

Will the young democracy of these islands rise to the understanding of so complex a problem as the governance of India now presents—an India as painfully in travail as is the rest of the world, Western and Eastern alike, and, with her own peculiar individuality, holding a still uncertain place half-way between the Eastern and the Western world ? Much new wine has been rapidly poured into old bottles in India, but has not almost as much new wine been poured into old bottles in these islands ? Political power is passing rapidly into the hands of a democracy which claims to have at least as large a share of idealism as the old governing classes under whose dispensation the unique fabric of British rule in India has grown up with all the responsibilities which this nation has, perhaps, more than any other learnt to associate with the possession of great power. The future of British rule in India may be obscure, but if it has been no more free from reproach than other human institutions, even the best, its long history shows very little that a British democracy which prides itself on new and higher standards of national conduct, has any cause to disown. British dominion in India was never established by the sword alone. Not all the methods by which it was founded and extended may commend themselves to modern conceptions of freedom, but

it has always owed its real strength to the willing
assent, explicit or implicit, of the peoples of India,
many of whom welcomed and even invited the consolidation of British power as their one salvation
from greater evils, and for similar reasons still dread
the thought of its withdrawal. To-day, at any rate,
it would be folly for us to talk of force as a solution
of our Indian difficulties. It is not by force, as all
but the extreme factions admit, that India can hope
to throw off British rule, and, after the disillusion-
ment which has followed the great war, the British
people are more than ever, and rightly, determined
to discountenance the use of force except in the most
extreme necessity for self-defence. British rule has
many other reserves of strength. It has a fine
administrative record. It has created great public
services to whose integrity, ability and sense of justice
all but their blindest Indian critics bear testimony.
It commands the reasoned loyalty of the Native
States who can rely on their Treaty rights being
faithfully respected so long as it endures, but only
so long; for, should it cease, one of the most
difficult problems it would leave behind it would be
the adjustment of the Native States to a new order
of things in the India that has been directly shaped
by British methods of administration. It commands
equally the reasoned confidence of large conservative classes whether wedded as of old to the land or
committed to modern forms of industrial and
financial enterprise, but all inclined to prefer the
security of British rule to the hazards of a revolution.
If it has fallen short of the higher purpose set before
it one hundred years ago by one of the great makers
of British India as " the training of Indians to govern
and protect themselves," it has given them good
government on British lines and it has been a bulwark
to them against foreign aggression. If the *Swaraj*
movement has revealed unsuspected depths of racial

22

antagonism and of hostility to the Western civilization which British rule has imported into India, it
has had a very different result in leading many
Indians to ask themselves whether British rule is
not, after all, the *raj* which divides them least. It
would be criminal to exploit these discords for
selfish ends, but their recrudescence, for which we
bear no blame, may well bid us pause before we
jeopardize the maintenance of the *pax Britannica*
which is the supreme boon that British rule has
brought to a multitude of peoples crowded together
in circumstances that made for constant strife before
its advent and would make almost as surely for a
renewal of strife if British rule were to cease.

That it should ever cease may seem almost
inconceivable ; for it has endured so long and has
ploughed so many fruitful furrows in the ancient
soil of India that we have come to assume its per-
manency almost as a matter of course. But from
its very nature the dominion of the British people,
whose centre of stability lies thousands of miles
away on the western fringe of the European
continent, over an Asiatic sub-continent containing
nearly a fifth of the human race, can scarcely be
more than a great and wonderful incident in the
world's history, just as was once the dominion of
Rome or that of still more ancient empires whose
higher civilization gave them for a time undisputed
supremacy over many alien peoples and distant
countries, relatively as remote in those days from
their own seat of power as India is to-day from the
British Isles. From the very beginning British rule
in India has been a gigantic experiment, unique on
such a scale and unique, too, in the success which it
has so far achieved. But it has never ceased to be an
experiment passing almost insensibly from one stage
into another as each one has in turn produced new
problems which we have successively tried to solve

in accordance with the genius of our race, by the combination of broad principles of policy, inspired on the whole by a fine idealism, with a cautious use of empiric methods in their practical application to changing conditions. In the different stages through which British rule has already passed it has been subjected to many new strains and tests, and it has stood them all. It is entering now upon a fresh stage in which it will be and is already being subjected to fresh strains and tests more severe, probably, than ever before; and to withstand them will require the same courage, the same tenacity, the same righteousness of purpose that has inspired the best of the long line of Englishmen who have gone out to India to serve her as well as their own country, and the same gift of prudent compromise and rational adaptability to changing circumstances with which British statesmanship has hitherto been justly credited; but on a still higher plane of endeavour, because the discharge of our trusteeship will be tested by new forces not only in India and in this country, but in a great and fast-moving world, knit together, more closely than ever before, by the modern conquests of time and distance, but also more than ever in bondage to the competitive instincts of self-preservation.

A hungry materialism threatens to live down the finer idealism which seemed at first to have wrung out of the horror of a world war the atoning promise of a better future to mankind. Least of all can idealism be allowed to die out of our strange relationship with India. No charge is more frequently levelled at British rule than that of importing the selfish materialism of the West into her more spiritual life. It is a charge which fewer Indians would have ventured to bring a century or so ago when a great generation of British rulers acted under a deep sense of the moral responsibility devolved upon the

British people by the assumption of British dominion over India. They were themselves endued with a strong religious faith, and they looked upon England's mission in India as one specially conferred upon her by Providence. It was one of the most fruitful periods of British rule, when it reflected the great liberal movements at home that derived much of their strength from spiritual forces, then amongst the most deep and dynamic in our national life. That period was, perhaps, inevitably fated to pass away in India when those forces receded in our own country before an unparalleled inrush of material prosperity which was prone to express itself in the overweening pride of wealth and power. The change made itself felt when, as the century wore on and Disraeli founded the latter-day school of Victorian Imperialism, Englishmen in India came to think more of Empire, and of India as a great Imperial asset, and less of England's responsibilities as a trustee. They began to talk more of the white man's burden and less of his duty. British efficiency, hardening into a shibboleth, served as an excuse for postponing indefinitely the fulfilment in practice of solemn promises into which Indians had read an unreserved acknowledgment of their rights to equal treatment. Simultaneously there came with the growth of white racialism within the Empire a corresponding growth of Indian racialism.

It was a fine renewal of idealism engendered by a five years' partnership of sacrifice and endurance in war that produced the Government of India Act of 1919 in which the British Parliament offered India the opportunity of proving her title to the same full partnership of peace within the British Commonwealth as the self-governing Dominions have achieved by their wise use of progressive freedom. The vision was worthy of fulfilment. It has been at least temporarily obscured by Indians who claim to rely solely on the ancient " soul-force " of India. How far *Swaraj* is a mere temporary gust of emotion from a past which is more legendary than real, and an ideal which, however powerfully it may appeal to their imagination, belongs to the world of illusions portrayed in one of their greatest schools of philosophy, the future alone can show. A mere revision of the constitution whether within or beyond the framework of the Act of 1919 can be of no avail so long as the spirit in which Indians press for it is one that baffles all efforts at appeasement on any well-ordered lines of constitutional evolution. In this connection Englishmen and Indians may be reasonably reminded of the warning uttered by Bacon, who was a philosopher as well as a statesman, for it is a warning applicable to all peoples and all ages : " Beware that it be the reformation that waiteth on the change and not the desire for change that precedeth the reformation." British patience, if coupled with greater singleness and clarity of purpose than British Ministers or the responsible exponents of British policy in India have been wont of late to exhibit, can afford to wait for India's recovery of a balanced judgment, no less violently disturbed, perhaps, by shell-shock from the war than even by the obsession of *Swaraj* itself.

Of good omen, just as these pages are going to Press, is the appointment as Viceroy of a great English gentleman who stands for all that is best in British public life. Unsullied by the faintest breath of political intrigue, Mr. Edward Wood is by general consent credited with the qualities of character to which Indians are most responsive and which should enable him to restore the confidence of Indians and of Englishmen in India in the sincerity and steadfastness of British statesmanship. He takes out with him not only a good record of administrative work in the sphere of education and of agriculture—both at the present moment of supreme importance in India—but also memorable title-deeds inherited from his grand-father, Sir Charles Wood, afterwards Lord Halifax, whose great Educational Dispatch of 1854 still stands out as an auspicious landmark of British rule.

There is still much work for England to do in India, and as in this volume more stress has, of set purpose, been laid on England's duty than on the rights she may be held to have acquired through the work she has already done in India, the writer must be allowed to conclude with an expression of his faith in the undiminished value of British rule in India as a great agency of permanent progress if England is ready to fulfil with the same courage as in the past the duty which she owes not only to India and to herself but to the whole world, just now in a state of more than ever unstable equilibrium between new forces of attraction and repulsion, of appeasement and of conflict. For it is in India, if anywhere, that, unless our own civilization is to be brought to shame, a synthesis must be found—and can hardly be found unless British rule endures—between the East and the West, if an irrevocable clash is to be averted in which neither could escape disaster.

INDEX

343

Gupta, Birendranath, 123.
Gwalior, Native State of, 69.

H

Hailey, Sir Malcolm, Governor of
Punjab, 300.
Hardinge, Lady, 157, 159.
Hardinge, Lady, Medical School at
Delhi, 152.
Hardinge of Penshurst, Lord, Viceroy, 125, 160, 161, 177.
Hastings, Warren, Governor-
General, 63, 64, 72.
Hinduism :—Great antiquity of, 2,
6, 11 ; its fluidity as a religious
system, 12 ; origin and evolution
of caste, 14–19 ; supremacy of
the Brahman, 16, 22, 25–9 ;
marriage laws, 20, 21 ; " untouchability," 18–20, 293, 294 ;
doctrine of *Karma*, 23, 24, 99,
172 ; *Dharma*, the law of righteousness, 23, 25 ; early marriages,
24, 170 ; continuity of Hindu
family, 24, 25 ; tenacity of caste
traditions, 26–9 ; failure to
build up an Indian nation, 29–
34 ; vitality under Mohammedan
domination, 40–3 ; influence of
Western education, 72 ; social
and religious reform movements
under British rule, 73–7, 102 ;
orthodox reaction, 98–9 ; revi-
valist movements, 106 ; basis of
Swaraj movement (*see Swaraj*
and Gandhi) ; wave of fraternization with Mohammedans (*see*
Mohammedans) ; revival of sectarian antagonism, 291–6 ; *Sangathan* and *Shuddi* anti-Moham-
medan organizations, 292 ; *Swaraj*
conflict with Western civilization,
329–34.
Holland, Sir Thomas, Chairman of
Industrial Commission, 192.
" Home Rule League " launched by
Mrs. Besant, 161, 162.
Hume, Mr. A. O., and Indian
National Congress, 89.
Hyderabad, Nizam of, 66, 69, 175,
223.

I

Ilbert Bill, 87, 88, 110.
Imperial War Councils, 68.

Inchcape, Lord, Retrenchment Com-
mittee, 249, 279.
Industrialization of India (*see* Indian
Labour and Fiscal autonomy).
Industries and Labour, Department of, 245.
Indian Army (*see* Army).
Indian " Labour " :—importation of
Western industrialism, 189, 191 ;
growth of a new industrial population, 193 ; congestion in new
manufacturing centres, 194 ;
Labour legislation, 195, 254 ;
female and child labour, 195, 196 ;
Trades Union Movement, 196–7 ;
Gandhi's influence, 197 ; Labour
troubles and strikes, 215 ; Department of Industries and Labour
created, 245 ; a field for Bolshevist propaganda (*see* Bolshevism).
Indian Legislatures :—Earlier Legislative Councils, 102 ; Councils
under Morley-Minto Reforms,
155, 156, 227, 232 ; Reformed
Legislatures under Act of 1919,
227 ; Council of State, 230, 249 ;
All-India Legislative Assembly,
229–56, 244–55, 259, 273–4 (*see
also Swaraj*) ; Provincial Councils, 228–33, 255, 257, 284, 285 ;
constituencies and franchise, 233,
235.
Indian National Congress :—Foundation of, 86–9 ; first profession
of faith, 90, 91 ; indifference to
social reforms, 102 ; political
grievances, 103 ; growth of hostility toward government and
official distrust, 104, 105 ; demand
for Dominion Self-Government,
120 ; violence at Surat session,
156 ; revival of extremism during
the Great War, 161, 163 ; accession of Mohammedan extremists,
220 (*see also* Non-Co-operation
and *Swaraj*).
Indian Press, 85, 99, 103, 111, 119,
120, 161, 248, 270, 330.
Indian Public Services : — under
East India Company, 60, 63 ;
Parliament and the admission
of Indians, 81 ; after the transfer
to the Crown, 83, 84 ; Lord
Lytton on British promises, 85,
86 ; Indian demands for larger
share, 87 ; Public Services Commission, 1886–7, 102, 131, 132 ;

Ripon, Marquess of, Viceroy, 128, 131.
Roe, Sir Thomas, Embassy to Delhi, 44.
Ronaldshay, Earl of, Governor of Bengal, 27, 28, 111.
Rowlatt Acts :—agitation against (*see* Gandhi and *Satyagraha*) ; repeal of, 248, 270.
Rowlatt, Mr. Justice, 204.
Rural population :—general characteristics, 4 ; immense preponderance over urban population, 168 ; poverty and ignorance, 168 ; rapid growth under British rule, 170 ; fragmentation of land, 171 ; conditions of life, 171, 172 ; indebtedness, 173–7 ; Co-operative Societies, 177, 178 ; religious obstacles to progress, 180 ; sufferings from famines, 47–50, 106, 182 ; bubonic plague, 101, 109, 183 ; great influenza epidemic, 183 ; Montagu-Chelmsford Report, 167, 182, 183 ; effects of the Great War, 185 ; recruitment for urban industries, 193 ; Gandhi's magnetic influence, 213, 214 ; " civil disobedience," 216 ; agrarian movements, 175, 216 ; misery under Moghul rule, 46–50 ; wave of disaffection in the Deccan, 100, 101 ; and in Bengal (*see* Partition of Bengal), 117–21 ; land revenue, 39, 161, 176 ; systems of land tenure, 175 ; attitude towards British *raj*, 180–6, 312–14, 321, 322, 335.
Russia :—Russian Nihilists and Indian extremists, 114 ; Tsarist ambitions in Asia, 266, 303 ; defeated by Japan, 112, 113, 186 ; Bolshevist propaganda (*see* Bolshevism).

S

Sadler, Sir Thomas, 125, 127 (*see* Education).
Sakai, Gopinath, 269.
Salisbury, Marquess of, and Turkey, 218.
Sapru, Sir Tej, 308.
Salt Tax, 249, 252, 284.
Sati, self-immolation of Hindu widows, 21, 38, 77.
Savarkar, Vinayak, 122.

Serampore College, 72.
Sèvres, Treaty of, 222.
Shah Alam, Moghul Emperor, surrenders the *Diwanee* to East India Company, 60.
Shah Jehan, the Emperor, 39, 40, 47 (*see* Moghul Empire).
Shankara, philosophy of, 32.
Shastri, Mr. Shrinivasa, 262, 263, 265, 266.
Shiva, cult of, 12, 31.
Sikh regiments in Indian Army, 297.
Sikhs :—racial and religious characteristics of, 296, 297 ; loyalty during the Mutiny and the Great War, 297 ; religious reform movement, 297 ; Sikh shrines, 298 ; *Akali* violence, 299 ; communal feeling, 300.
Sinha (afterwards Lord), 162.
Slavery, under Hindu and Mohammedan law, 46, 47.
Social Reform movements :—the flowing tide, 73, 74 ; the reaction, 98, 101 ; National Social Conference, 101.
" Society of India," the, 107.
Somnath, Hindu temple of, 36.
South African War :—effect on Indian opinion, 110 ; Gandhi's services, 201.
Sudra caste, 15.
Swadeshi :—boycott of British-made goods in the Deccan and in Bengal, 118 ; revival with the Non-Co-operation movement, 213, 283 ; translated into demand for protection, 198, 283, 284.
Swaraj :—two millenniums of ancient Hindu *Swaraj*, 29–34 ; Congress demand for *Swaraj* as Dominion Self-Government, 120 ; " Home Rule League " started during the Great War, 162 ; Gandhi's conception of *Swaraj*, 212, 215 ; Non-Co-operation campaign, 211–16, 261 ; Caliphate movement and Mohammedan fraternization, 216–17 ; abstention of *Swaraj* party from first general elections, 211, 225, 253 ; the King-Emperor's promise of *Swaraj* within the Empire, 225 ; failure of Gandhi's political leadership, 250, 260, 293 ; formation of new *Swaraj* party inside the Councils, 260, 272, 273, 288 ; spirit of